SHARKS
Nature's Perfect Hunter

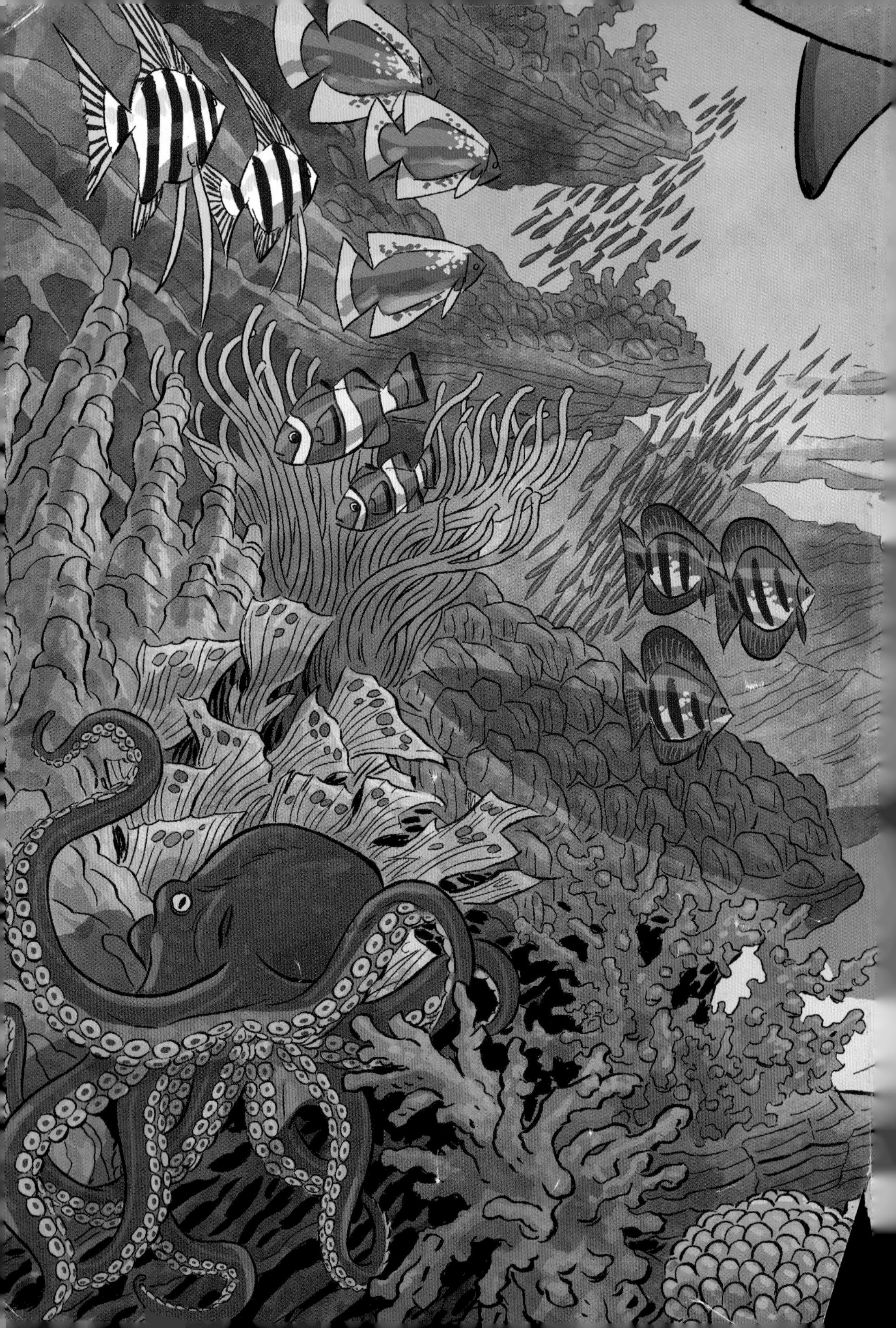

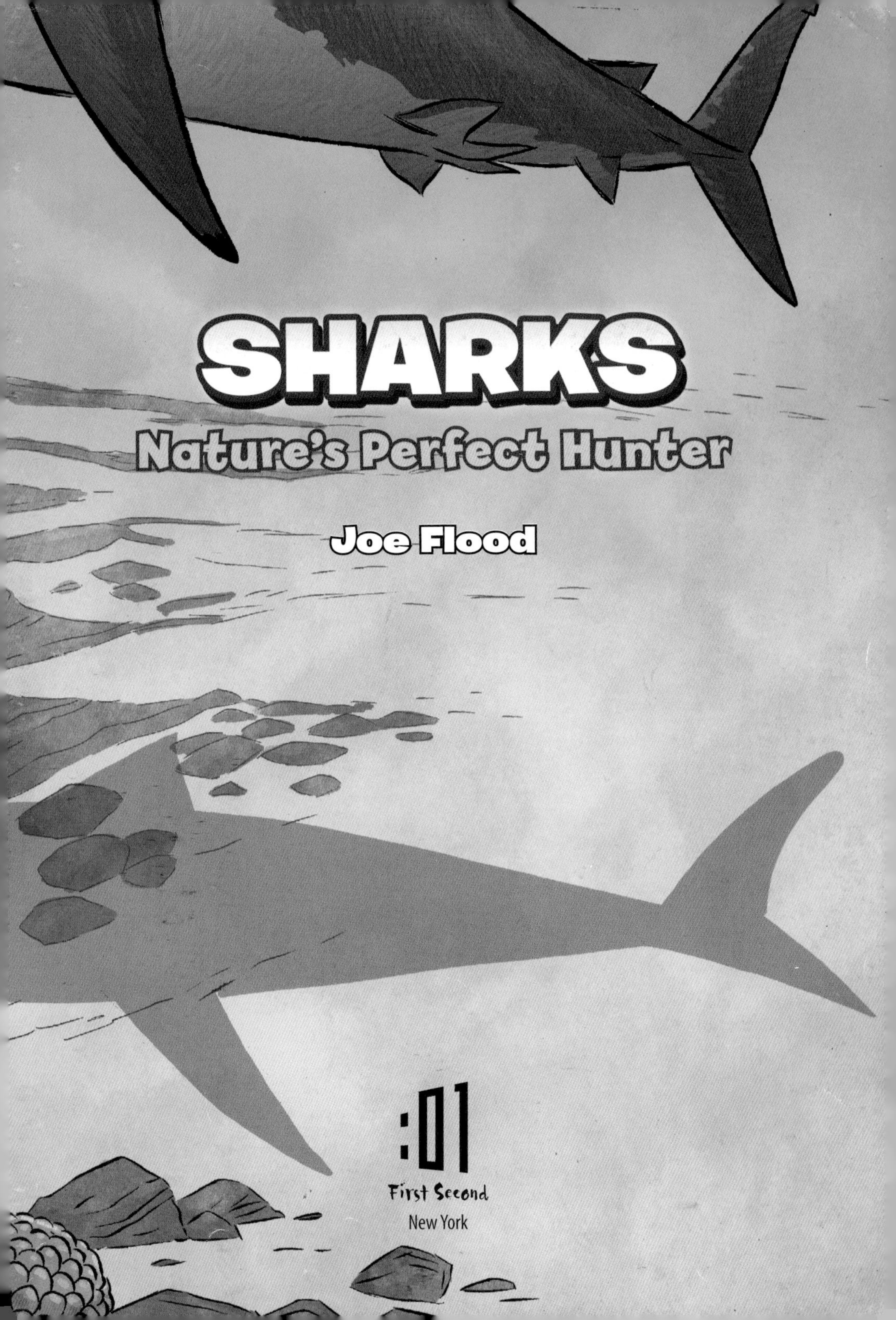

SHARKS

Nature's Perfect Hunter

Joe Flood

:01 First Second
New York

Dedicated to the staff at First Second,
whose hard work and commitment inspire me daily.
—Joe

First Second

Created using Strathmore 500 Series Vellum Bristol with Pilot Color Eno blue lead in an Alvin Draft-Matic 0.7 mm mechanical pencil, inked with Dr. Ph. Martin's Bombay India ink using a Raphaël Kolinsky sable watercolor brush size 1 and a Nikko Maru pen nib. Colored with a combination of hand-painted watercolor and digital colors using Adobe Photoshop. Lettered with Comicrazy font by Comicraft.

Published by First Second
First Second is an imprint of Roaring Brook Press,
a division of Holtzbrinck Publishing Holdings Limited Partnership
175 Fifth Avenue, New York, NY 10010
All rights reserved

Library of Congress Congress Control Number: 2017941169

Paperback ISBN: 978-1-62672-788-5
Hardcover ISBN: 978-1-62672-787-8

Our books may be purchased in bulk for promotional, educational, or business use. Please contact your local bookseller or the Macmillan Corporate and Premium Sales Department at (800) 221-7945 ext. 5442 or by e-mail at MacmillanSpecialMarkets@macmillan.com.

First edition, 2018
Edited by Dave Roman
Book design by John Green

Printed in China by Toppan Leefung Printing Ltd., Dongguan City, Guangdong Province
Paperback: 10 9 8 7 6 5 4 3 2 1
Hardcover: 10 9 8 7 6 5 4 3 2 1

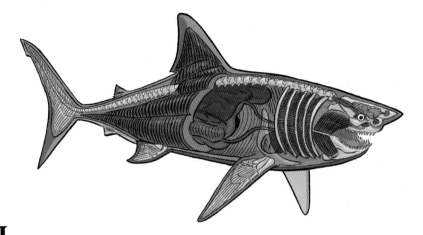

Lots of kids, including many of you who are reading this book, go through an "I love sharks" phase. Sharks are powerful and beautiful animals, and these traits, combined with a hint of danger, make it easy to understand why people are so fascinated by them. I know this phase well because I had one too. In fact, I never grew out of mine! I've loved sharks as long as my family can remember, and I was able to turn my childhood love of sharks into a career as a marine conservation biologist.

I get to spend lots of time on the water catching, measuring, tagging, and sampling sharks, and despite the smell of sweat, bait, and sunscreen, it's everything that I always dreamed it would be! Every time I get to feel a shark's strong muscles rippling under their tough skin, I get a powerful reminder of where we fit into the food chain. Even though I've now seen thousands of sharks all over the world, I still get just as excited as I did the first time I saw a shark at the Pittsburgh Zoo when I was a kid. When all the fun fieldwork is done, though, there's still a lot of other work to do!

As a marine conservation biologist, my goal is to generate scientific data that can be used by the government to help protect threatened species. To do that, we need to process our scientific samples, analyze our data, and write reports to be shared with fellow experts. When all of the analysis is done, scientists get to experience the thrill of being some of the first people to know something new about the world!

One of the most important things that shark scientists have learned is that sharks are in trouble—and they need your help! Sharks are not only some of the most misunderstood animals on Earth, they're some of the most threatened. Almost ¼ of all known species of sharks and their relatives are in danger of extinction, with some populations having decreased by 90% within your parents' lifetimes, because of humans. As a science educator, I truly believe that this happens not because no one cares but because few know about it. That makes books like this one so important!

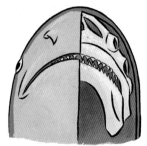

As you read, you'll take a journey through the world's oceans, meeting some incredible shark species and learning all about them. You'll learn about shark biology, shark biodiversity, and shark behavior. You'll learn all about what makes a shark a shark and how they evolved. You'll learn why, despite some scary media coverage, you really don't need to be afraid of sharks when you go to the beach. You'll learn about threats facing sharks and how you can help protect them.

The future of these amazing animals depends on people like you learning more about them and caring enough to protect them. So as a marine conservation biologist who has loved sharks since I was a kid, I thank you for reading this book, and I hope you enjoy it as much as I did.

—David Shiffman, Ph.D.
Marine Conservation Biologist and Science Blogger

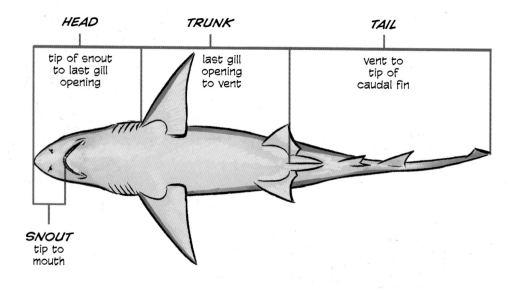

HEAD
tip of snout
to last gill
opening

TRUNK
last gill
opening
to vent

TAIL
vent to
tip of
caudal fin

SNOUT
tip to
mouth

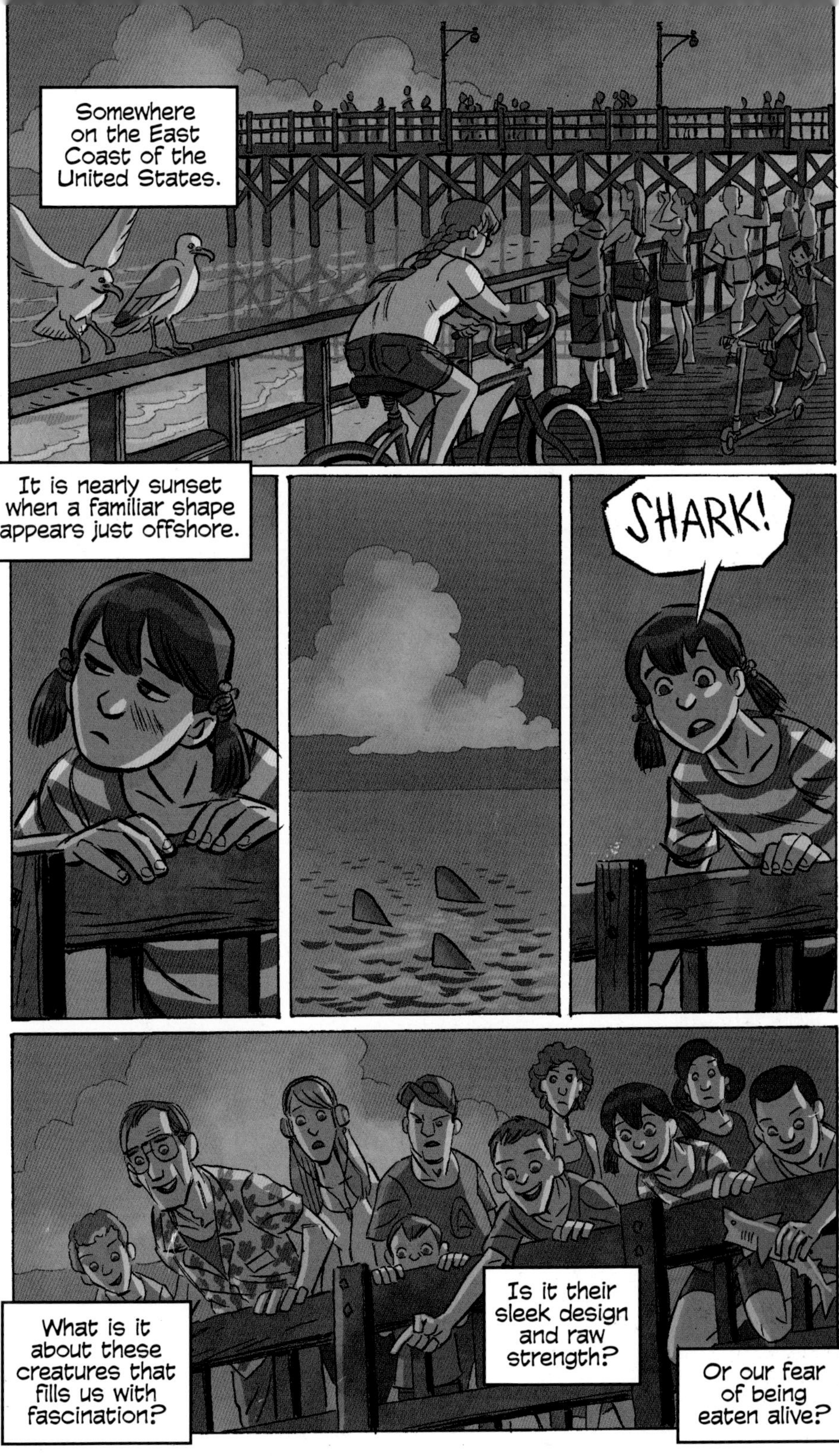
Somewhere on the East Coast of the United States.
It is nearly sunset when a familiar shape appears just offshore.
SHARK!
What is it about these creatures that fills us with fascination?
Is it their sleek design and raw strength?
Or our fear of being eaten alive?

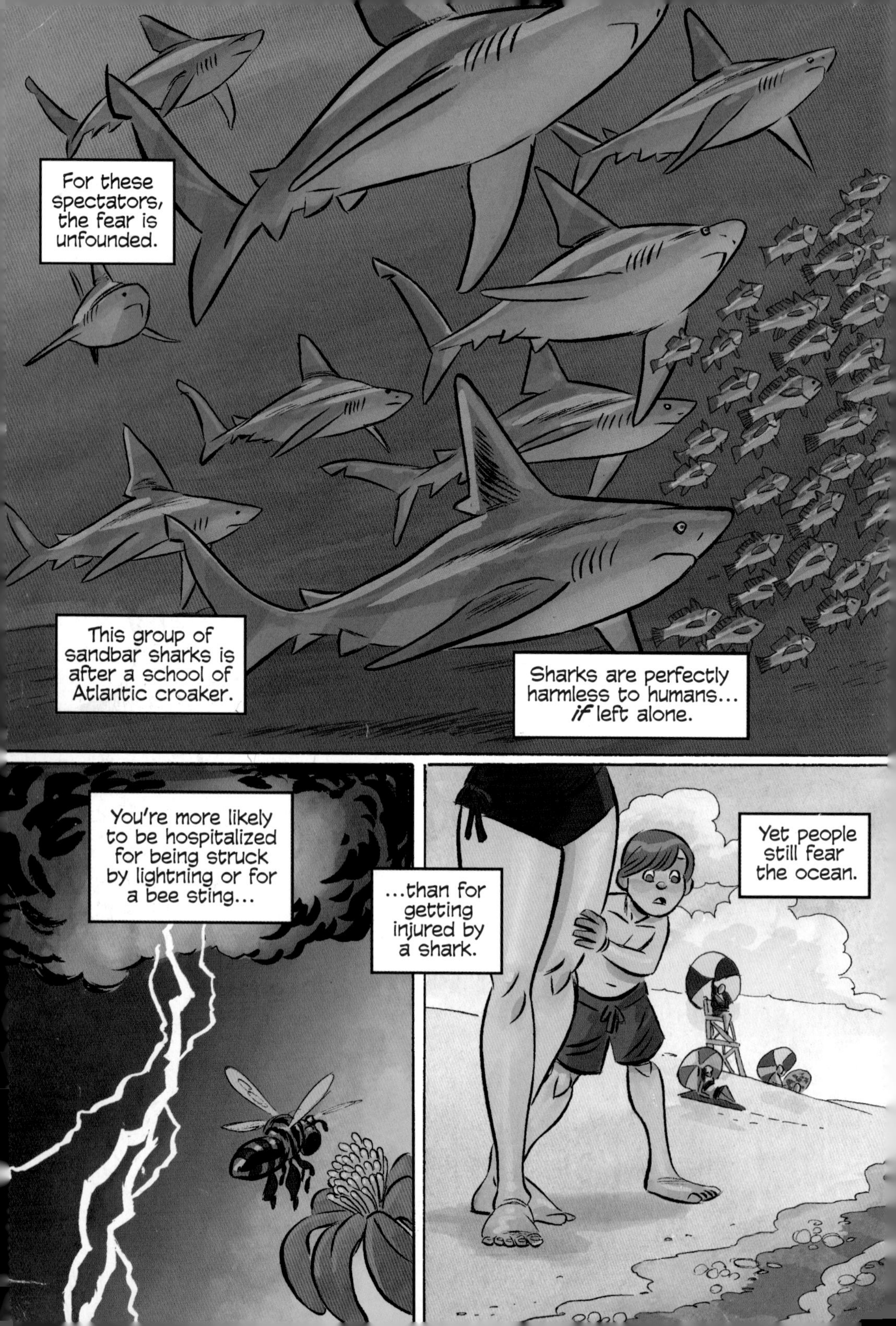
For these spectators, the fear is unfounded.
This group of sandbar sharks is after a school of Atlantic croaker.
Sharks are perfectly harmless to humans... *if* left alone.
You're more likely to be hospitalized for being struck by lightning or for a bee sting...
...than for getting injured by a shark.
Yet people still fear the ocean.

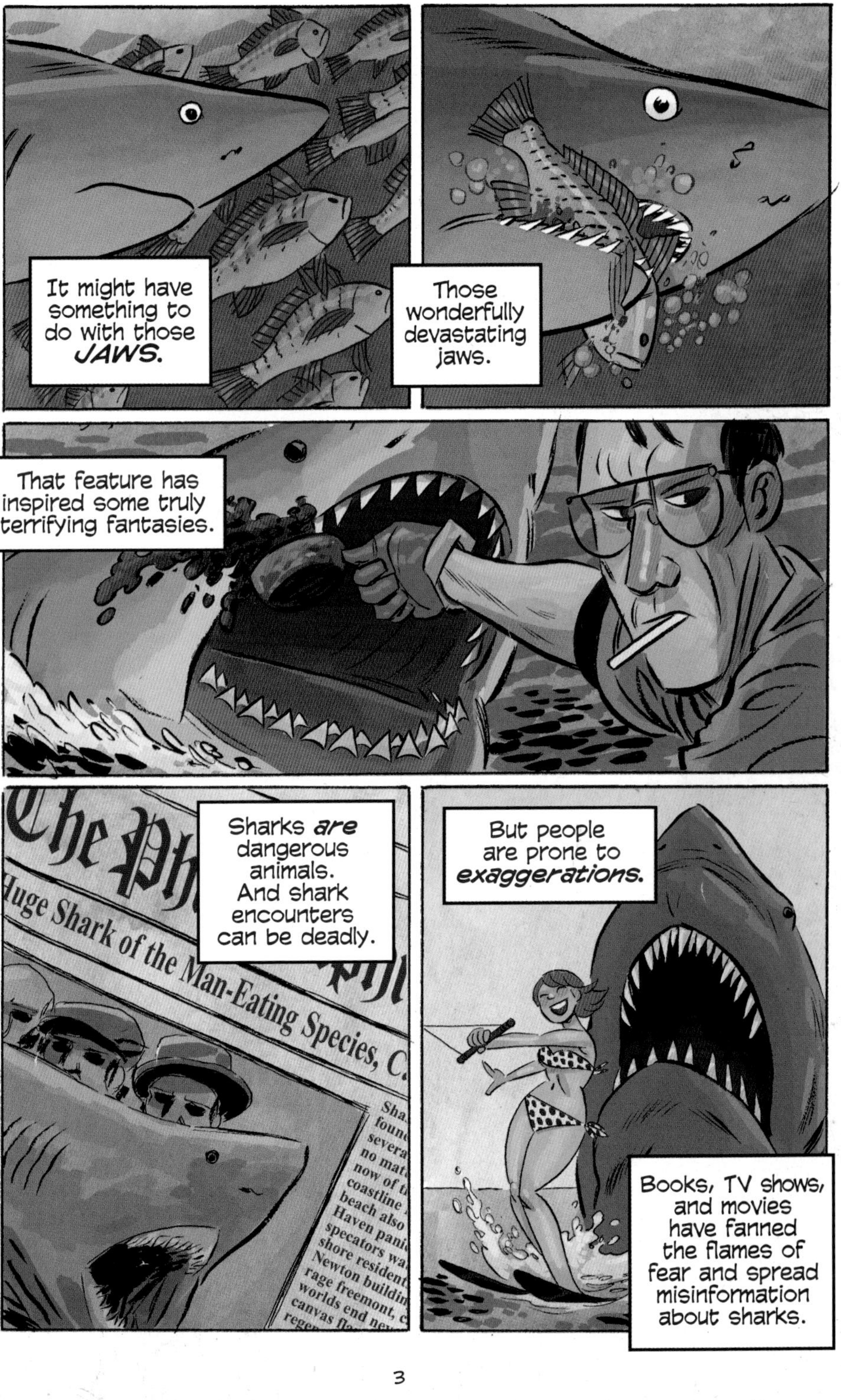
It might have something to do with those *JAWS.*
Those wonderfully devastating jaws.
That feature has inspired some truly terrifying fantasies.
Sharks *are* dangerous animals. And shark encounters can be deadly.
Huge Shark of the Man-Eating Species,
But people are prone to *exaggerations.*
Books, TV shows, and movies have fanned the flames of fear and spread misinformation about sharks.

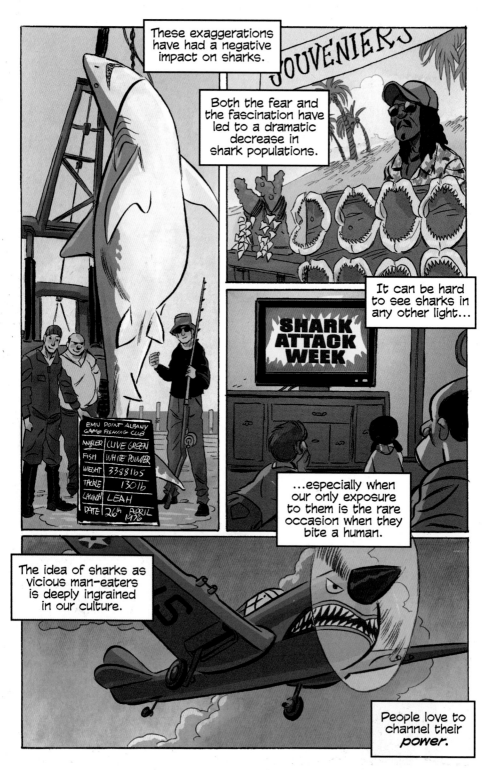

These exaggerations have had a negative impact on sharks.

Both the fear and the fascination have led to a dramatic decrease in shark populations.

It can be hard to see sharks in any other light...

...especially when our only exposure to them is the rare occasion when they bite a human.

The idea of sharks as vicious man-eaters is deeply ingrained in our culture.

People love to channel their *power.*

SOUVENIERS

SHARK ATTACK WEEK

EMU POINT ALBANY
GAME FISHING CLUB
ANGLER | CLIVE GREEN
FISH | WHITE POINTER
WEIGHT | 333 8 lbs
TACKLE | 130 lb
LAUNCH | LEAH
DATE | 26th APRIL 1976

4

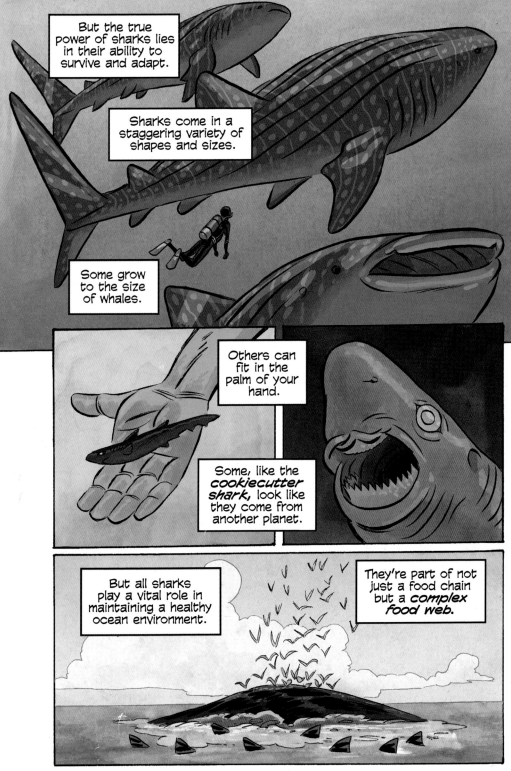

But the true power of sharks lies in their ability to survive and adapt.

Sharks come in a staggering variety of shapes and sizes.

Some grow to the size of whales.

Others can fit in the palm of your hand.

Some, like the *cookiecutter shark,* look like they come from another planet.

But all sharks play a vital role in maintaining a healthy ocean environment.

They're part of not just a food chain but a *complex food web.*

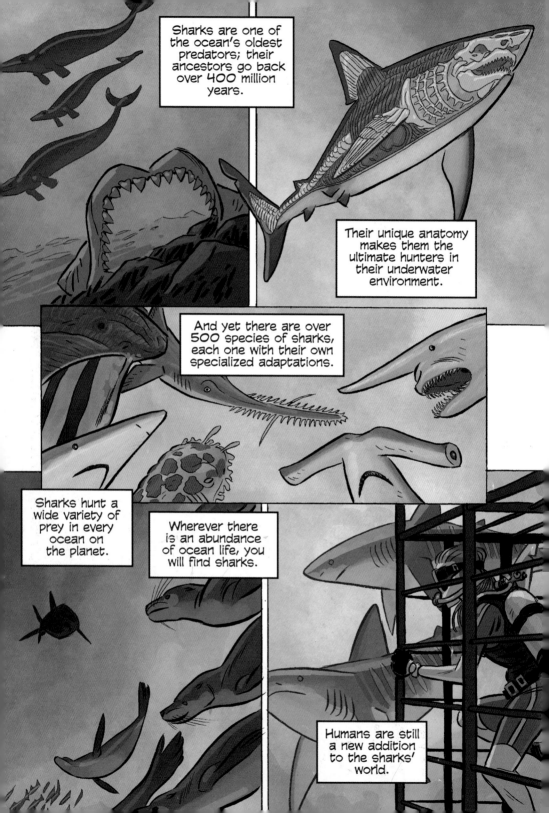

Sharks are one of the ocean's oldest predators; their ancestors go back over 400 million years.

Their unique anatomy makes them the ultimate hunters in their underwater environment.

And yet there are over 500 species of sharks, each one with their own specialized adaptations.

Sharks hunt a wide variety of prey in every ocean on the planet.

Wherever there is an abundance of ocean life, you will find sharks.

Humans are still a new addition to the sharks' world.

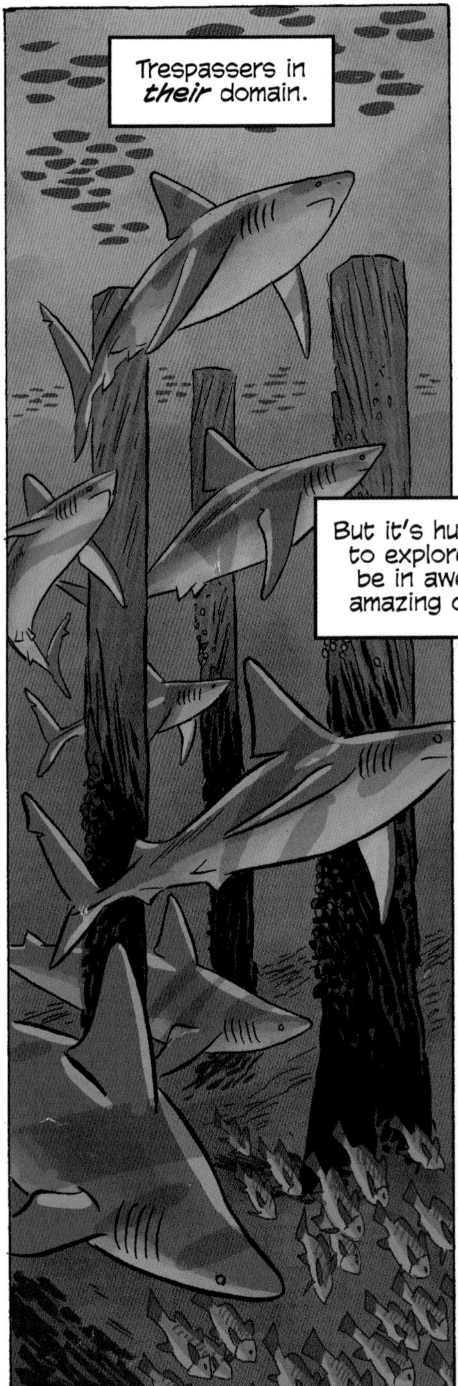
Trespassers in *their* domain.
But it's human nature to explore...and to be in awe of such amazing creatures.
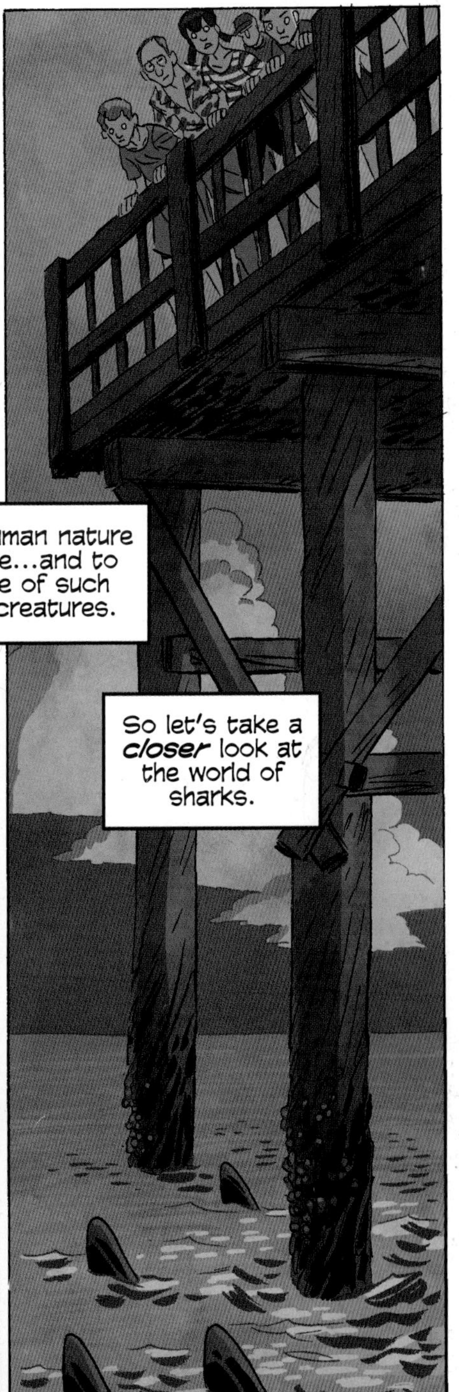
So let's take a *closer* look at the world of sharks.

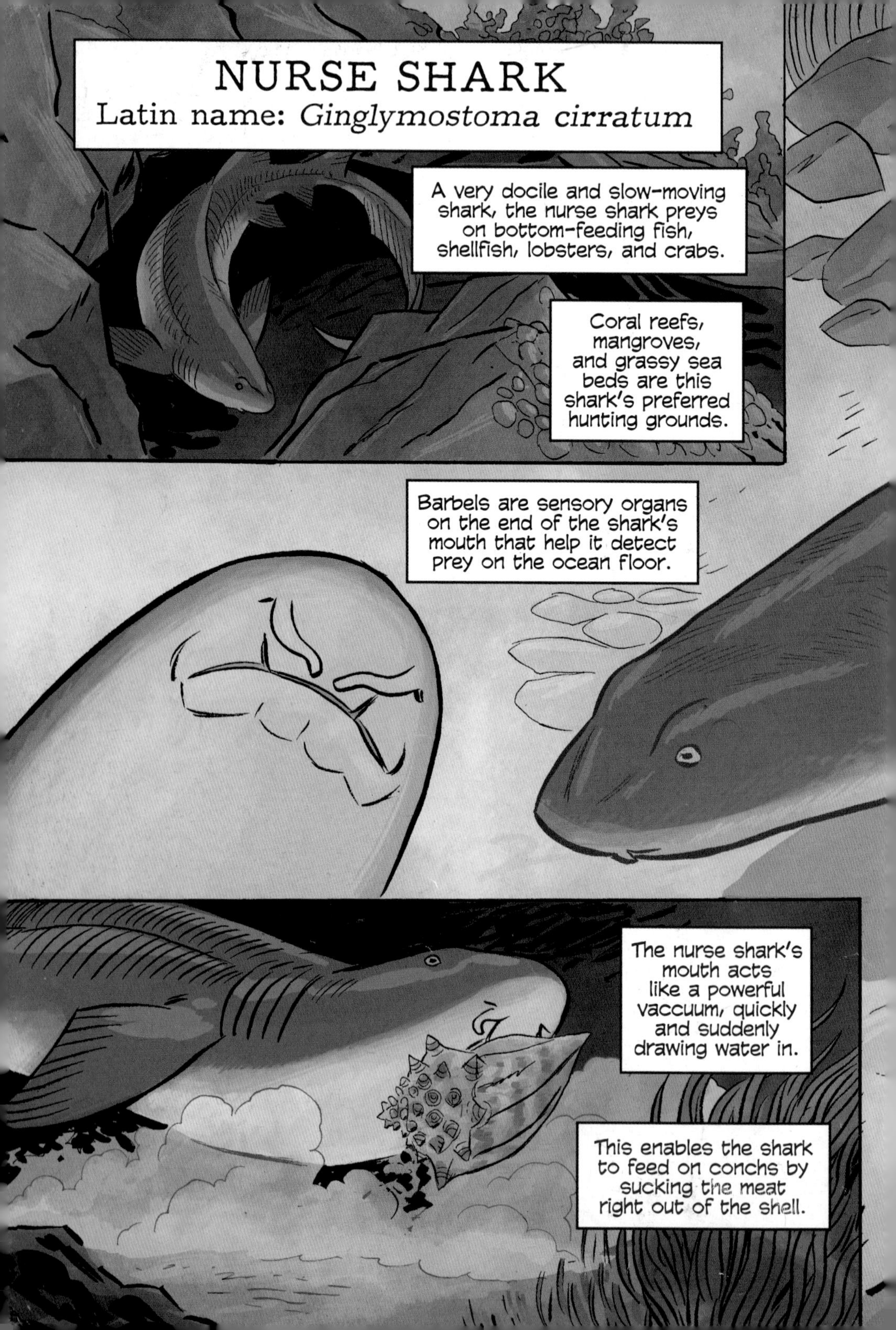
NURSE SHARK
Latin name: *Ginglymostoma cirratum*
A very docile and slow-moving shark, the nurse shark preys on bottom-feeding fish, shellfish, lobsters, and crabs.
Coral reefs, mangroves, and grassy sea beds are this shark's preferred hunting grounds.
Barbels are sensory organs on the end of the shark's mouth that help it detect prey on the ocean floor.
The nurse shark's mouth acts like a powerful vaccuum, quickly and suddenly drawing water in.
This enables the shark to feed on conchs by sucking the meat right out of the shell.

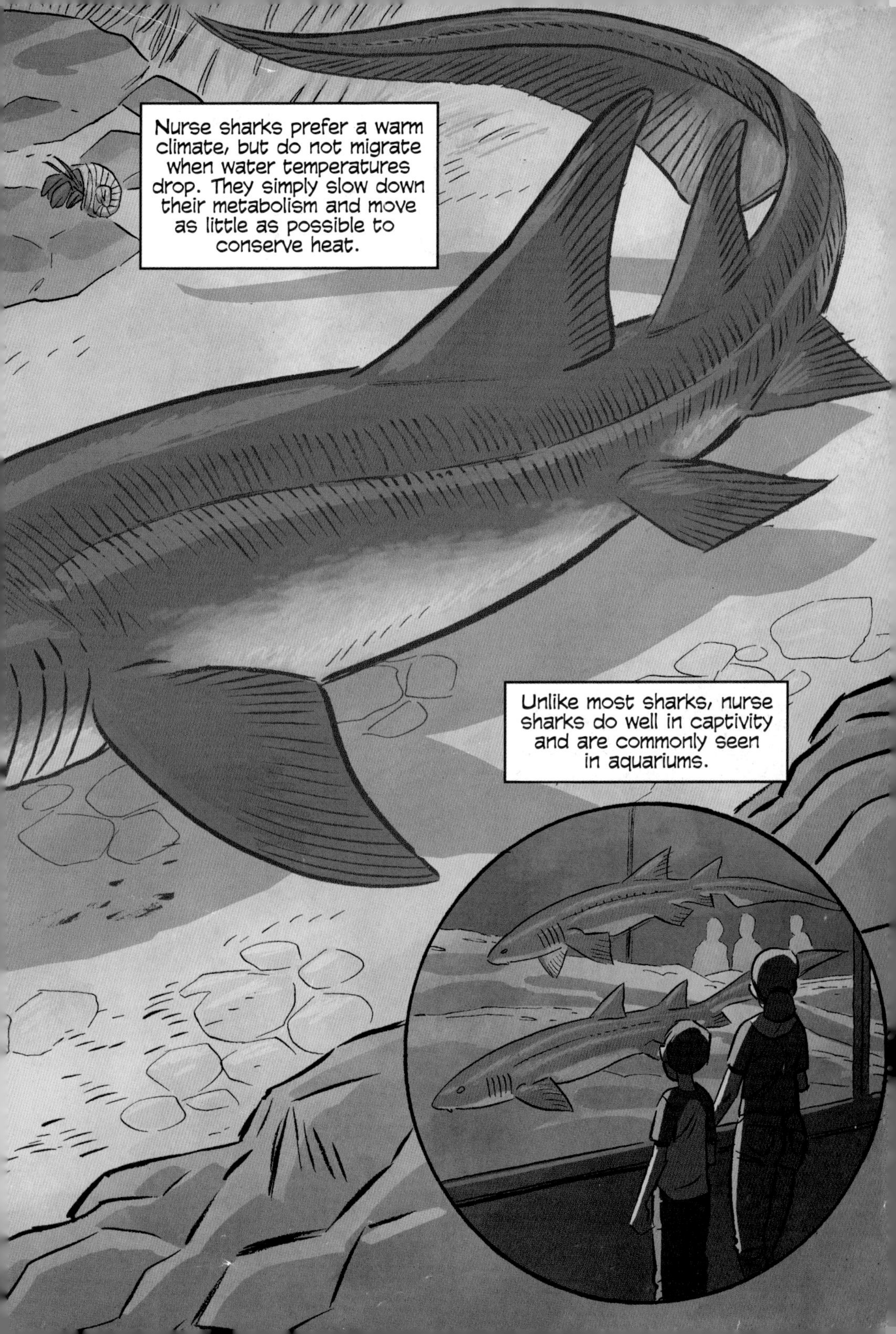
Nurse sharks prefer a warm climate, but do not migrate when water temperatures drop. They simply slow down their metabolism and move as little as possible to conserve heat.
Unlike most sharks, nurse sharks do well in captivity and are commonly seen in aquariums.

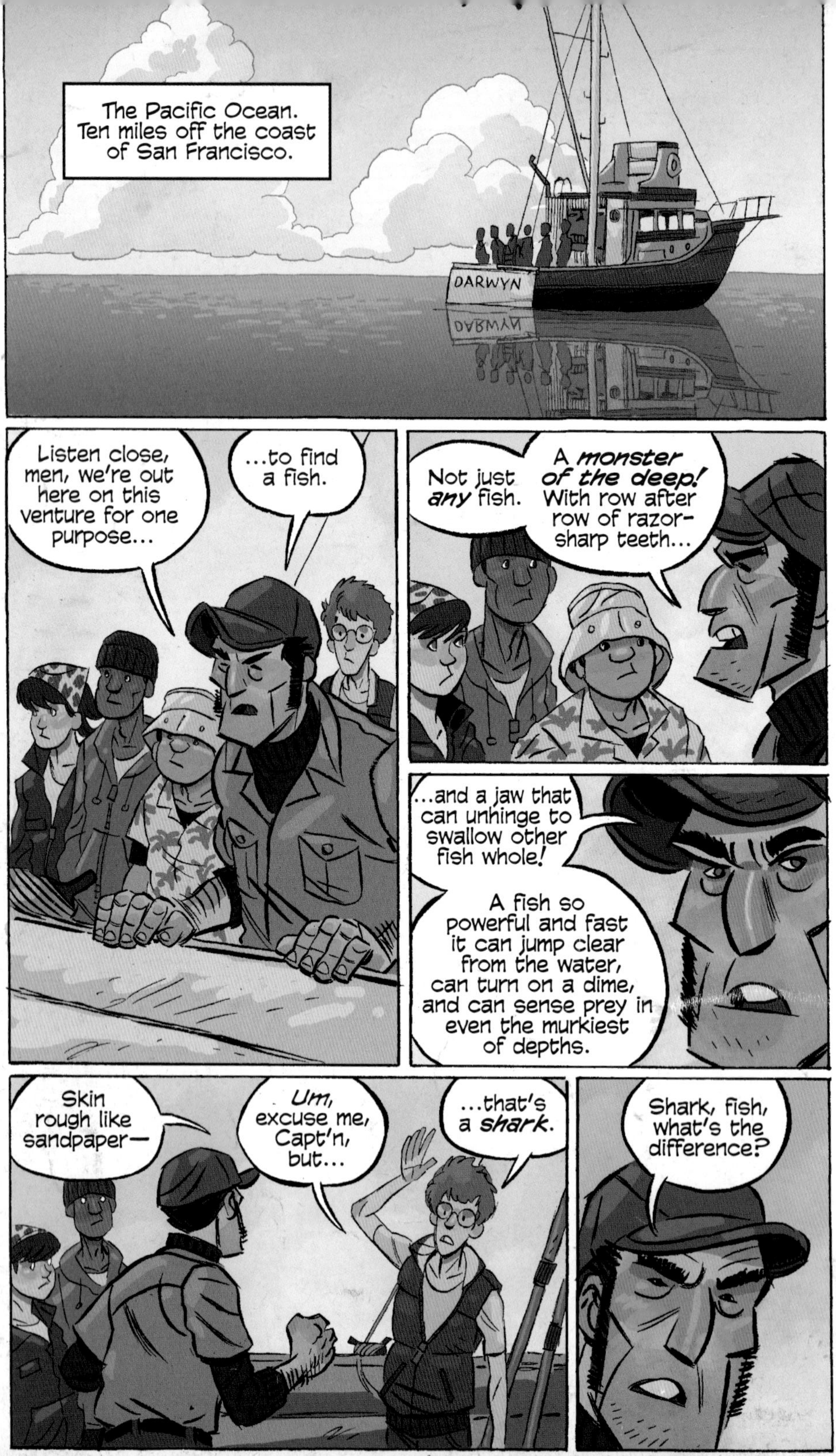
The Pacific Ocean. Ten miles off the coast of San Francisco.
DARWYN
Listen close, men, we're out here on this venture for one purpose...
...to find a fish.
Not just *any* fish.
A ***monster of the deep!*** With row after row of razor-sharp teeth...
...and a jaw that can unhinge to swallow other fish whole!
A fish so powerful and fast it can jump clear from the water, can turn on a dime, and can sense prey in even the murkiest of depths.
Skin rough like sandpaper—
Um, excuse me, Capt'n, but...
...that's a ***shark***.
Shark, fish, what's the difference?

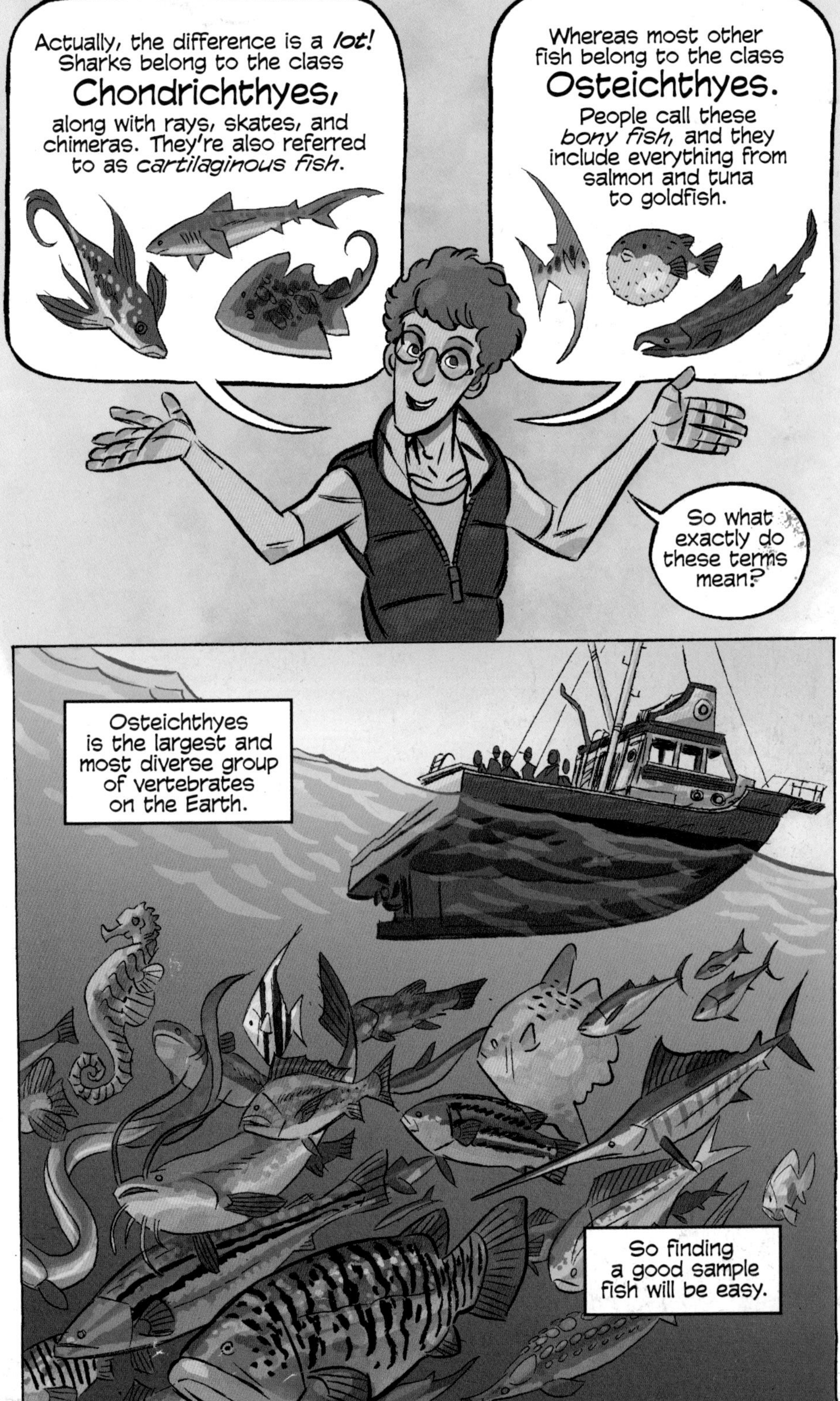

Actually, the difference is a *lot!* Sharks belong to the class
Chondrichthyes,
along with rays, skates, and chimeras. They're also referred to as *cartilaginous fish*.
Whereas most other fish belong to the class
Osteichthyes.
People call these *bony fish*, and they include everything from salmon and tuna to goldfish.
So what exactly do these terms mean?
Osteichthyes is the largest and most diverse group of vertebrates on the Earth.
So finding a good sample fish will be easy.

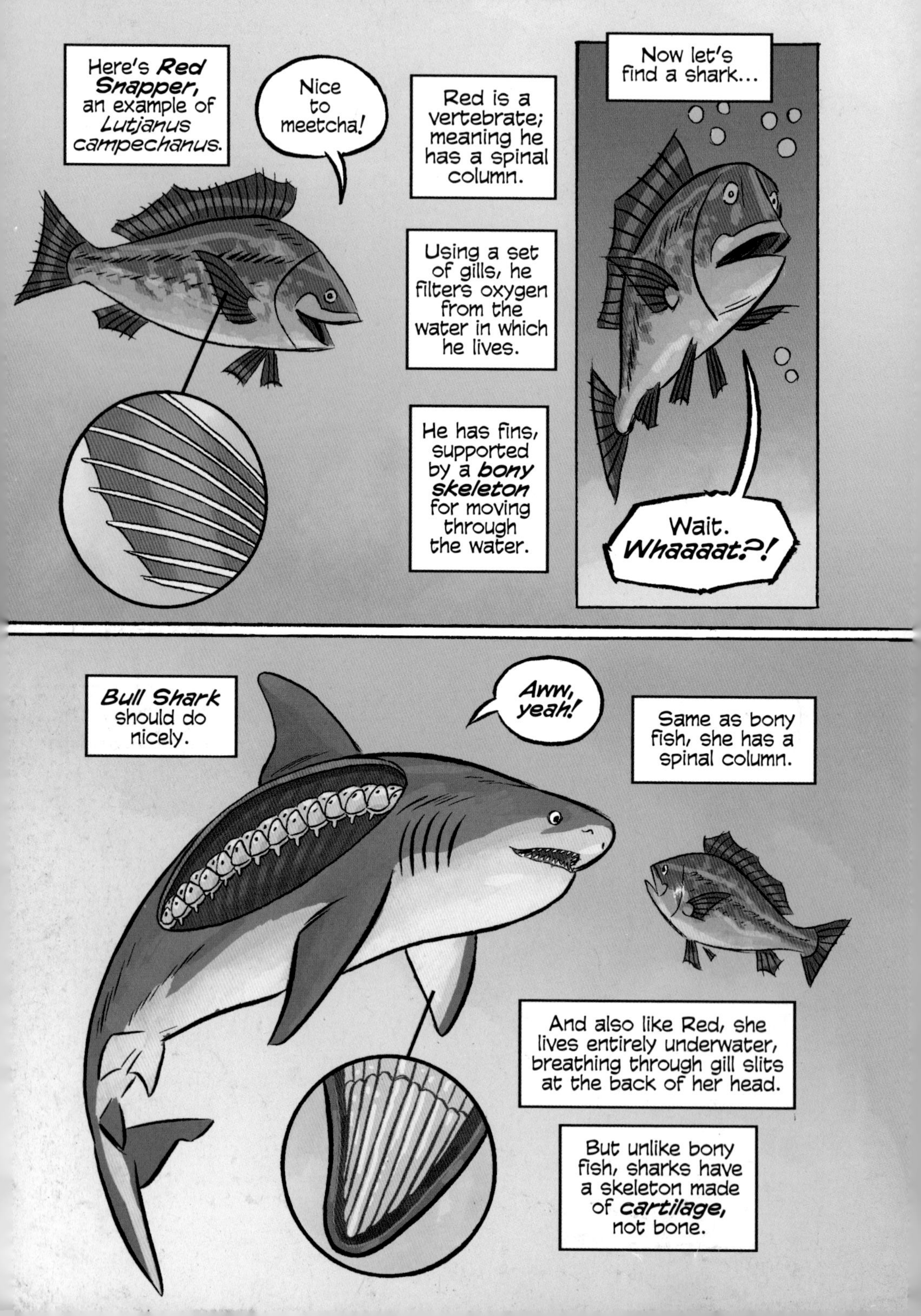
Here's *Red Snapper,* an example of *Lutjanus campechanus.*
Nice to meetcha!
Red is a vertebrate; meaning he has a spinal column.
Using a set of gills, he filters oxygen from the water in which he lives.
He has fins, supported by a *bony skeleton* for moving through the water.
Now let's find a shark...
Wait. *Whaaaat?!*
Bull Shark should do nicely.
Aww, yeah!
Same as bony fish, she has a spinal column.
And also like Red, she lives entirely underwater, breathing through gill slits at the back of her head.
But unlike bony fish, sharks have a skeleton made of *cartilage,* not bone.

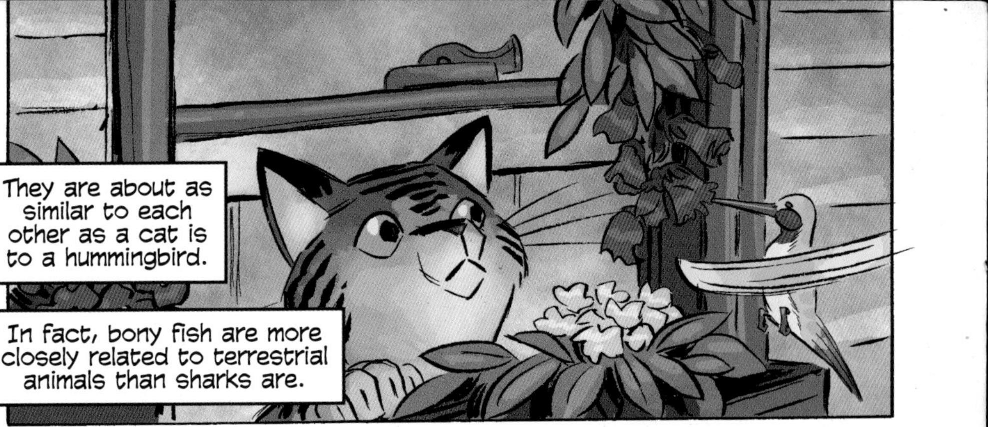
They are about as similar to each other as a cat is to a hummingbird.
In fact, bony fish are more closely related to terrestrial animals than sharks are.

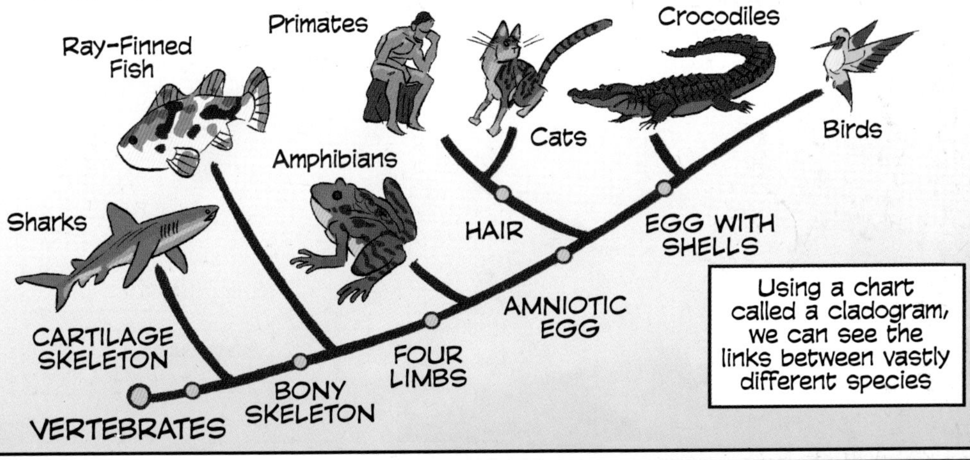
Primates
Crocodiles
Ray-Finned Fish
Cats
Birds
Amphibians
Sharks
HAIR
EGG WITH SHELLS
AMNIOTIC EGG
CARTILAGE SKELETON
FOUR LIMBS
BONY SKELETON
VERTEBRATES
Using a chart called a cladogram, we can see the links between vastly different species

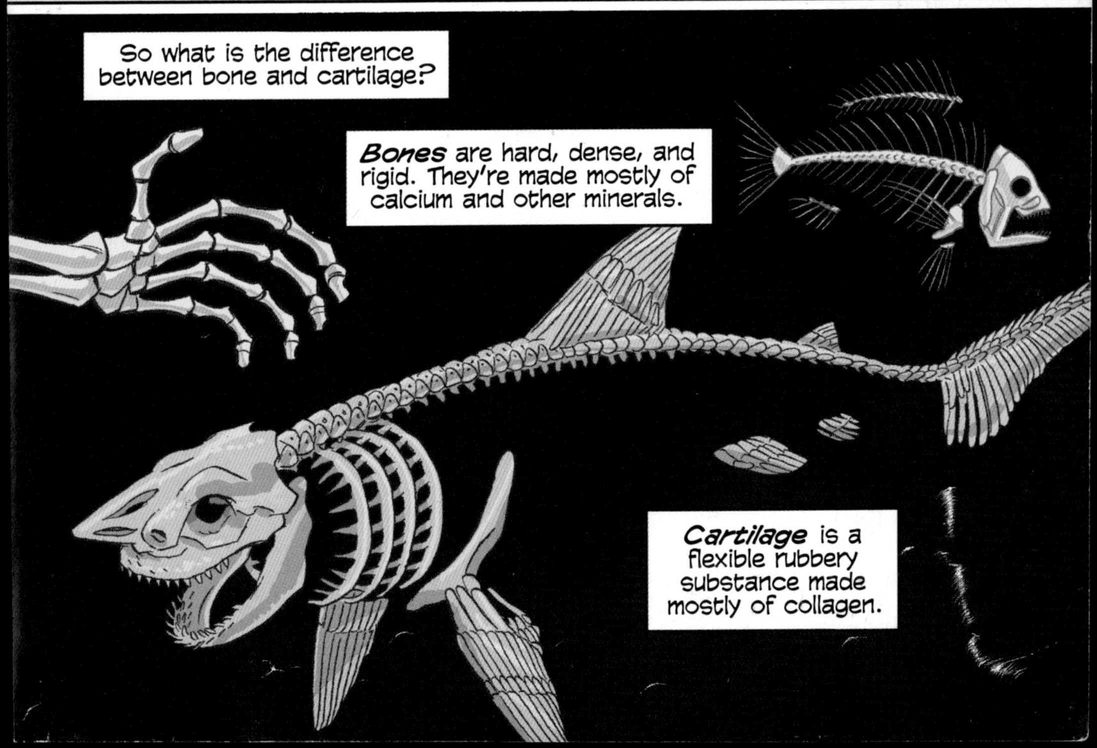
So what is the difference between bone and cartilage?
Bones are hard, dense, and rigid. They're made mostly of calcium and other minerals.
Cartilage is a flexible rubbery substance made mostly of collagen.

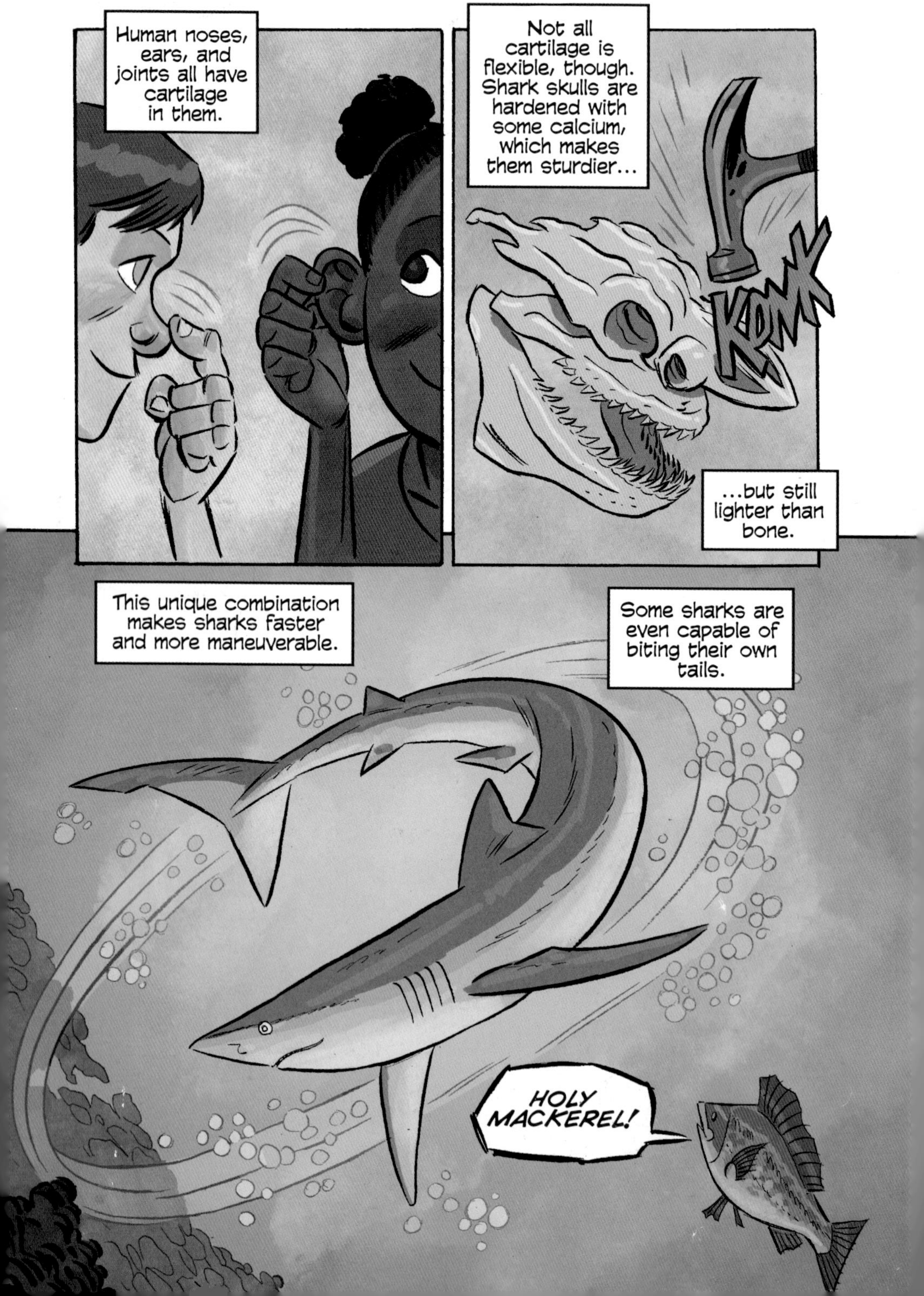
Human noses, ears, and joints all have cartilage in them.
Not all cartilage is flexible, though. Shark skulls are hardened with some calcium, which makes them sturdier...
KONK
...but still lighter than bone.
This unique combination makes sharks faster and more maneuverable.
Some sharks are even capable of biting their own tails.
HOLY MACKEREL!

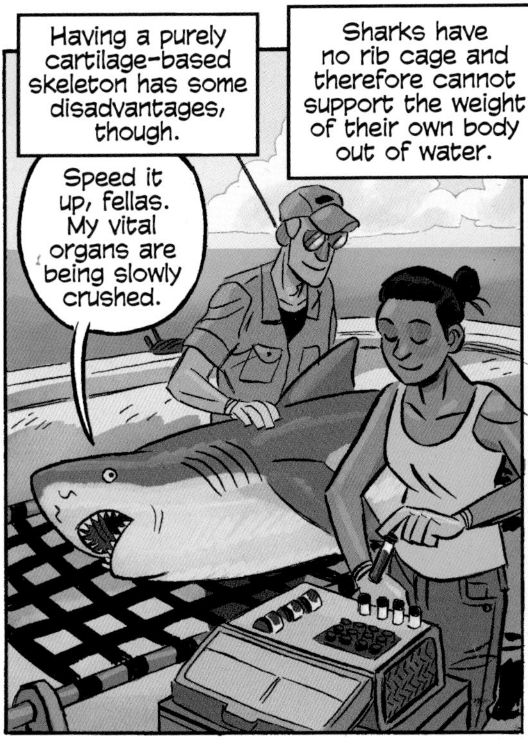
Having a purely cartilage-based skeleton has some disadvantages, though.
Sharks have no rib cage and therefore cannot support the weight of their own body out of water.
Speed it up, fellas. My vital organs are being slowly crushed.

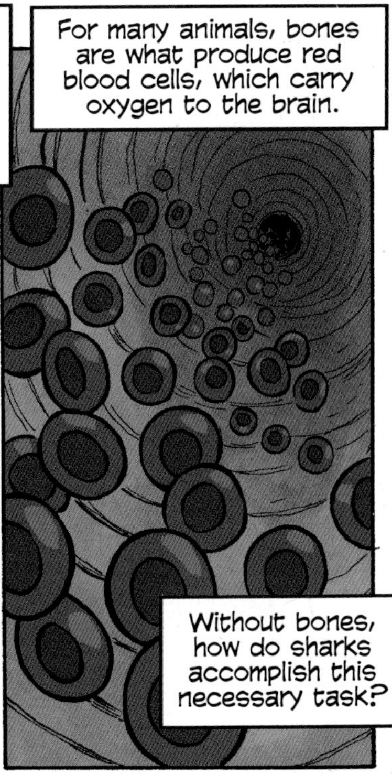
For many animals, bones are what produce red blood cells, which carry oxygen to the brain.
Without bones, how do sharks accomplish this necessary task?

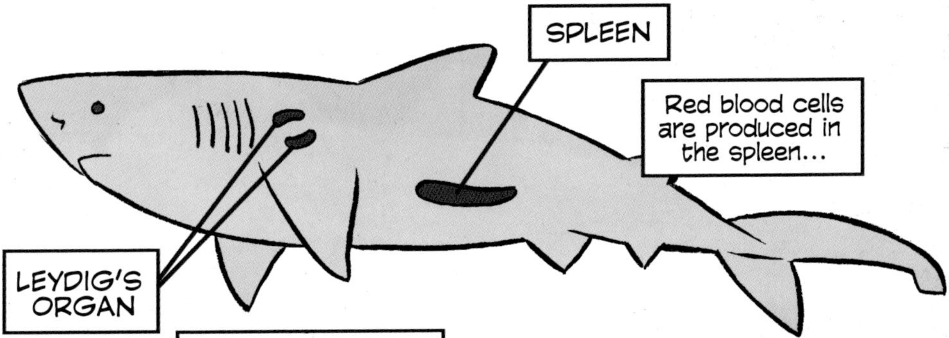
SPLEEN
Red blood cells are produced in the spleen...
LEYDIG'S ORGAN

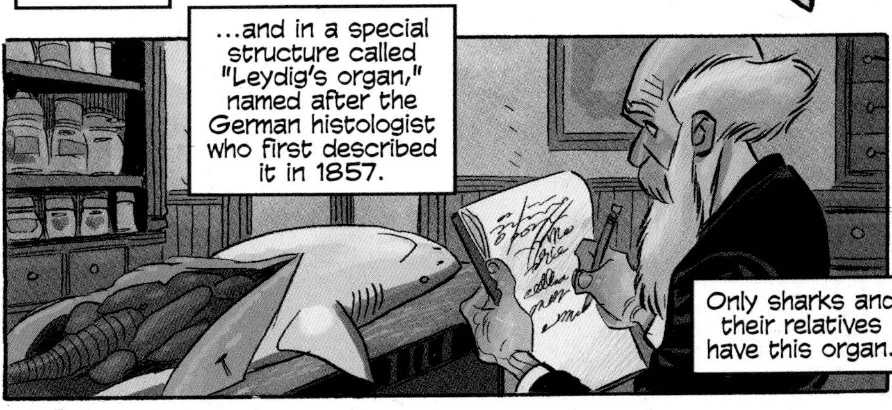
...and in a special structure called "Leydig's organ," named after the German histologist who first described it in 1857.
Only sharks and their relatives have this organ.

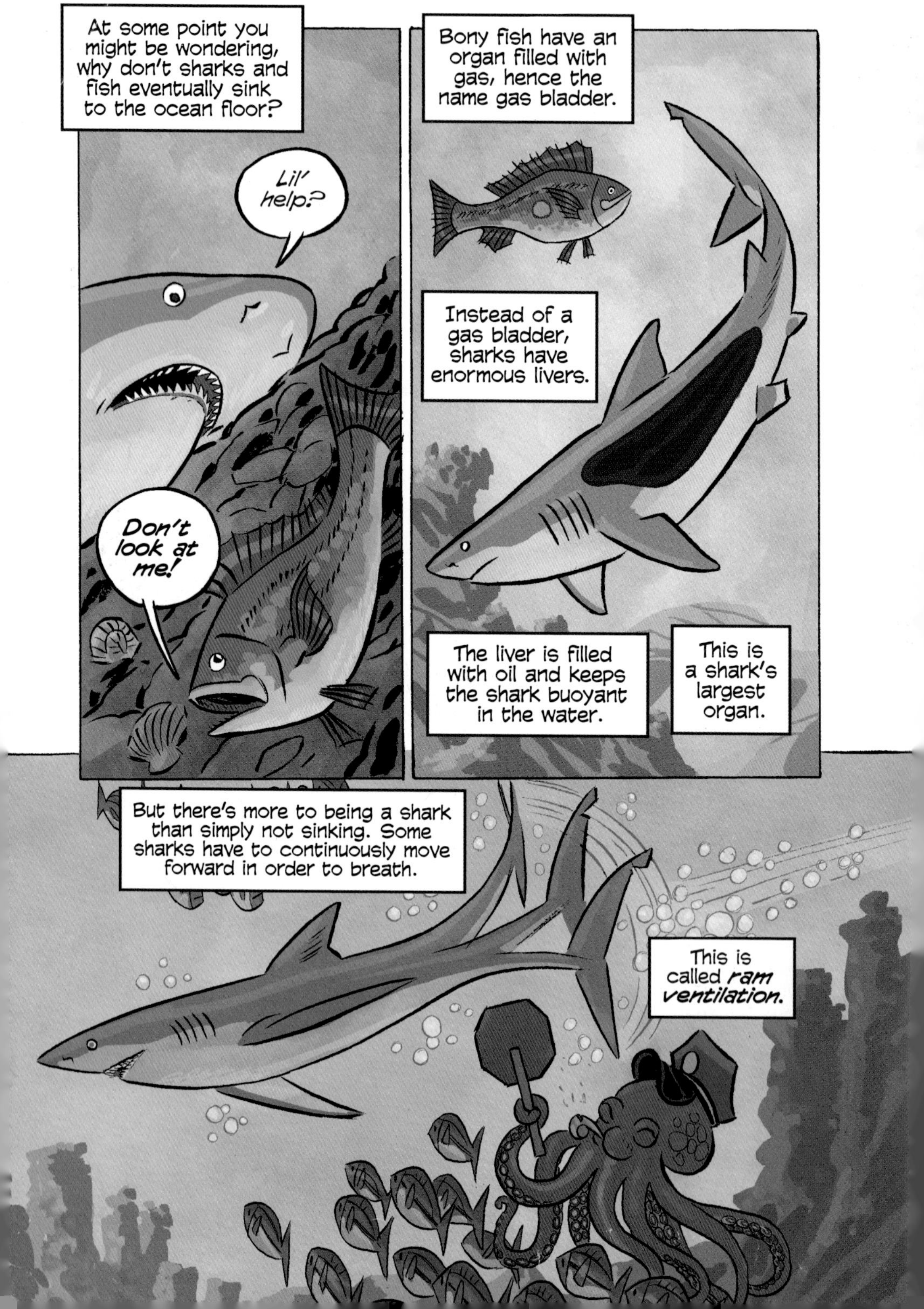
At some point you might be wondering, why don't sharks and fish eventually sink to the ocean floor?
Lil' help?
Don't look at me!
Bony fish have an organ filled with gas, hence the name gas bladder.
Instead of a gas bladder, sharks have enormous livers.
The liver is filled with oil and keeps the shark buoyant in the water.
This is a shark's largest organ.
But there's more to being a shark than simply not sinking. Some sharks have to continuously move forward in order to breath.
This is called *ram ventilation*.

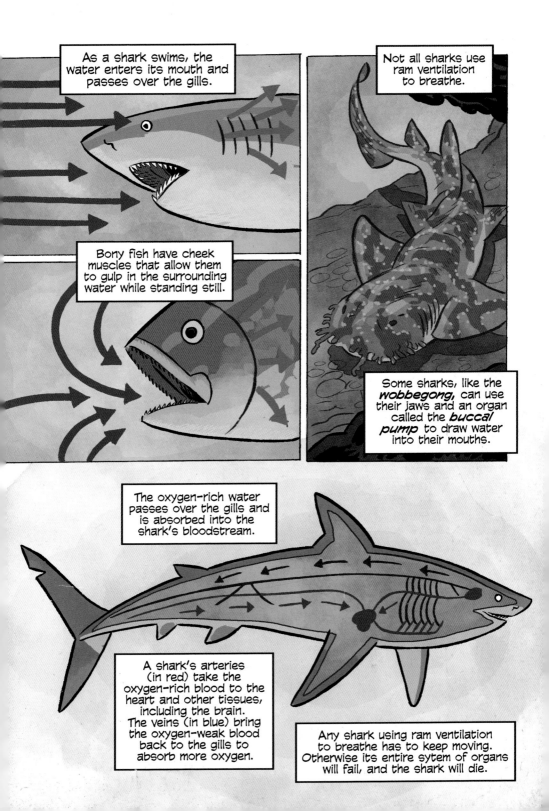

As a shark swims, the water enters its mouth and passes over the gills.

Not all sharks use ram ventilation to breathe.

Bony fish have cheek muscles that allow them to gulp in the surrounding water while standing still.

Some sharks, like the *wobbegong,* can use their jaws and an organ called the *buccal pump* to draw water into their mouths.

The oxygen-rich water passes over the gills and is absorbed into the shark's bloodstream.

A shark's arteries (in red) take the oxygen-rich blood to the heart and other tissues, including the brain. The veins (in blue) bring the oxygen-weak blood back to the gills to absorb more oxygen.

Any shark using ram ventilation to breathe has to keep moving. Otherwise its entire sytem of organs will fail, and the shark will die.

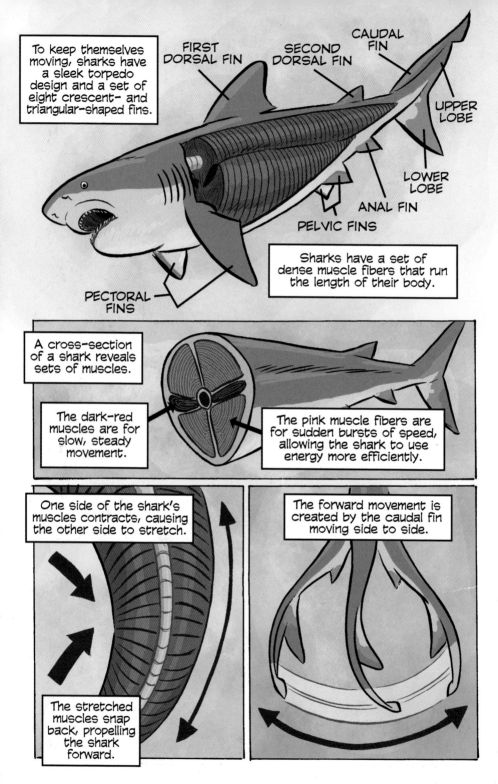

To keep themselves moving, sharks have a sleek torpedo design and a set of eight crescent- and triangular-shaped fins.

FIRST DORSAL FIN

SECOND DORSAL FIN

CAUDAL FIN

UPPER LOBE

LOWER LOBE

ANAL FIN

PELVIC FINS

PECTORAL FINS

Sharks have a set of dense muscle fibers that run the length of their body.

A cross-section of a shark reveals sets of muscles.

The dark-red muscles are for slow, steady movement.

The pink muscle fibers are for sudden bursts of speed, allowing the shark to use energy more efficiently.

One side of the shark's muscles contracts, causing the other side to stretch.

The stretched muscles snap back, propelling the shark forward.

The forward movement is created by the caudal fin moving side to side.

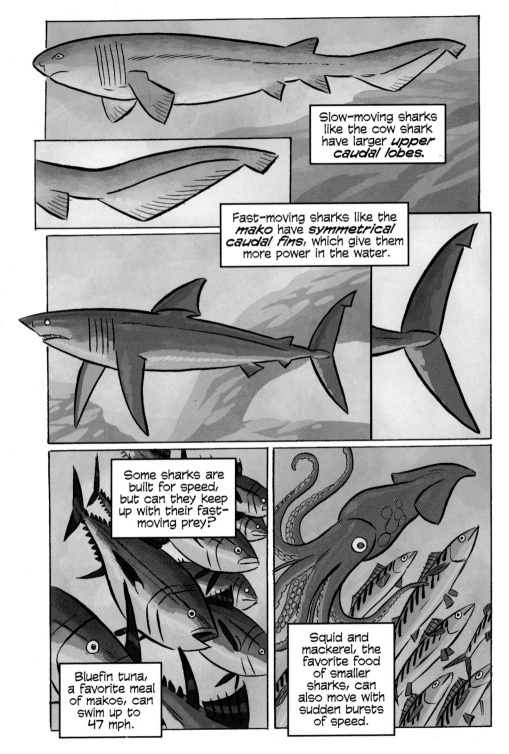

Slow-moving sharks like the cow shark have larger *upper caudal lobes.*

Fast-moving sharks like the *mako* have *symmetrical caudal fins,* which give them more power in the water.

Some sharks are built for speed, but can they keep up with their fast-moving prey?

Bluefin tuna, a favorite meal of makos, can swim up to 47 mph.

Squid and mackerel, the favorite food of smaller sharks, can also move with sudden bursts of speed.

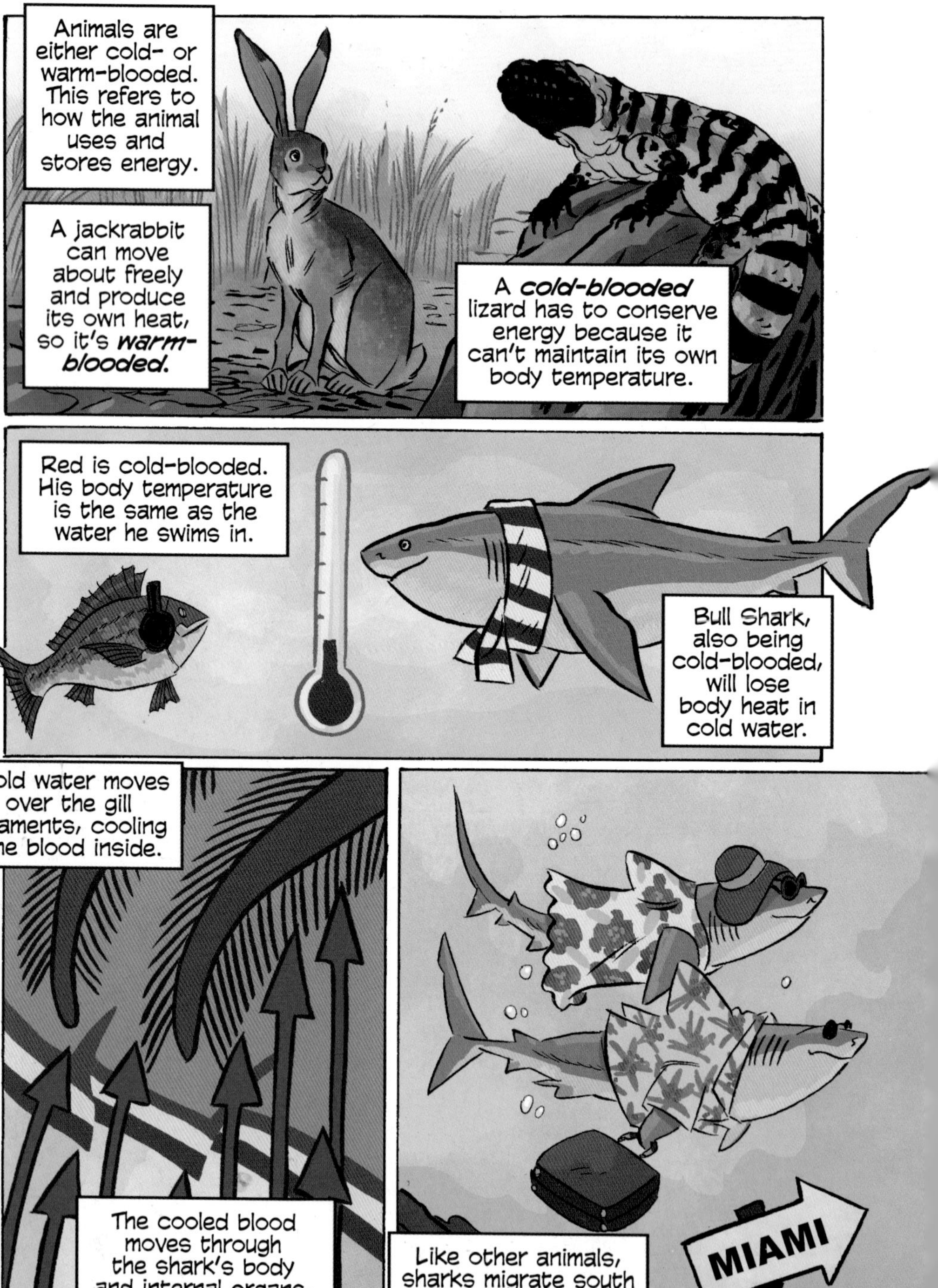
Animals are either cold- or warm-blooded. This refers to how the animal uses and stores energy.
A jackrabbit can move about freely and produce its own heat, so it's *warm-blooded.*
A *cold-blooded* lizard has to conserve energy because it can't maintain its own body temperature.
Red is cold-blooded. His body temperature is the same as the water he swims in.
Bull Shark, also being cold-blooded, will lose body heat in cold water.
Cold water moves over the gill filaments, cooling the blood inside.
The cooled blood moves through the shark's body and internal organs, causing the shark's temperature to drop.
Like other animals, sharks migrate south to warmer waters when winter comes.
MIAMI

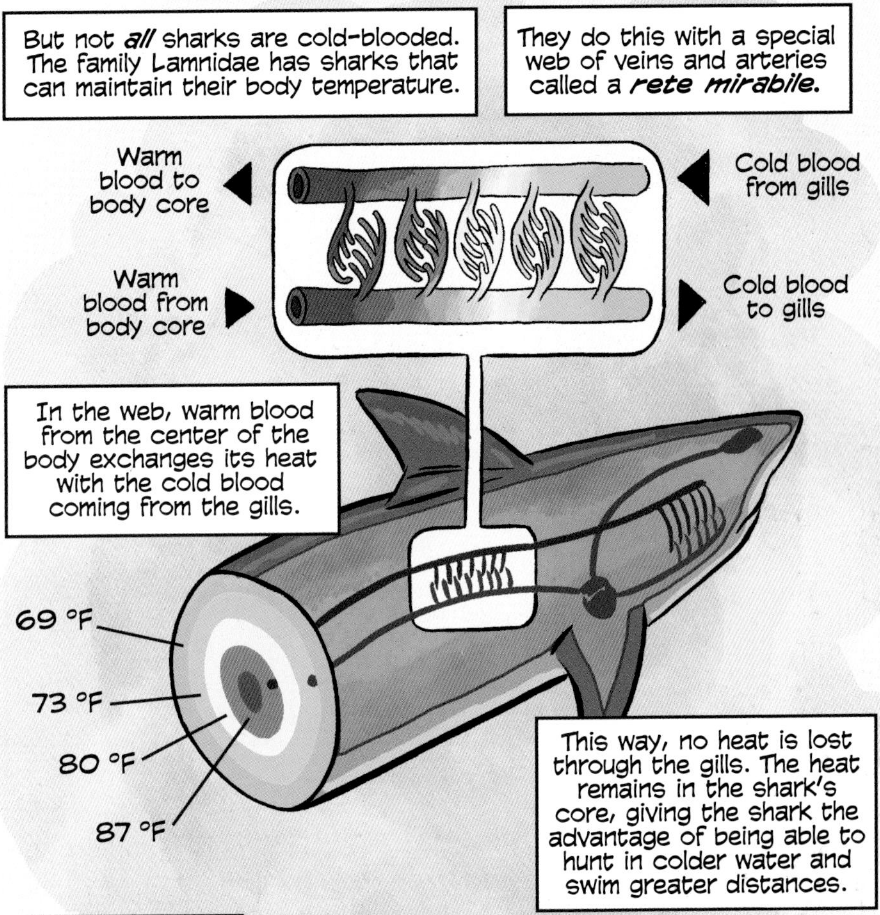

But not *all* sharks are cold-blooded. The family Lamnidae has sharks that can maintain their body temperature.
They do this with a special web of veins and arteries called a ***rete mirabile.***
Warm blood to body core
Cold blood from gills
Warm blood from body core
Cold blood to gills
In the web, warm blood from the center of the body exchanges its heat with the cold blood coming from the gills.
69 °F
73 °F
80 °F
87 °F
This way, no heat is lost through the gills. The heat remains in the shark's core, giving the shark the advantage of being able to hunt in colder water and swim greater distances.

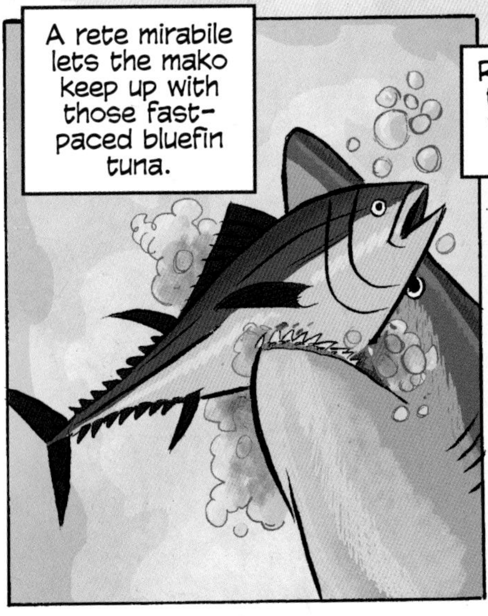

A rete mirabile lets the mako keep up with those fast-paced bluefin tuna.

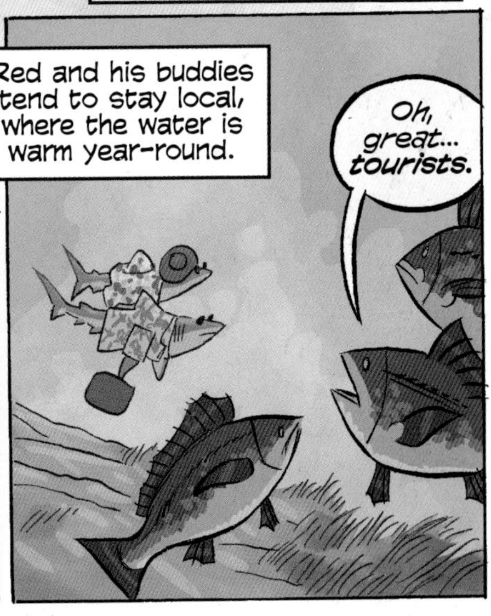

Red and his buddies tend to stay local, where the water is warm year-round.
*Oh, great... **tourists.***

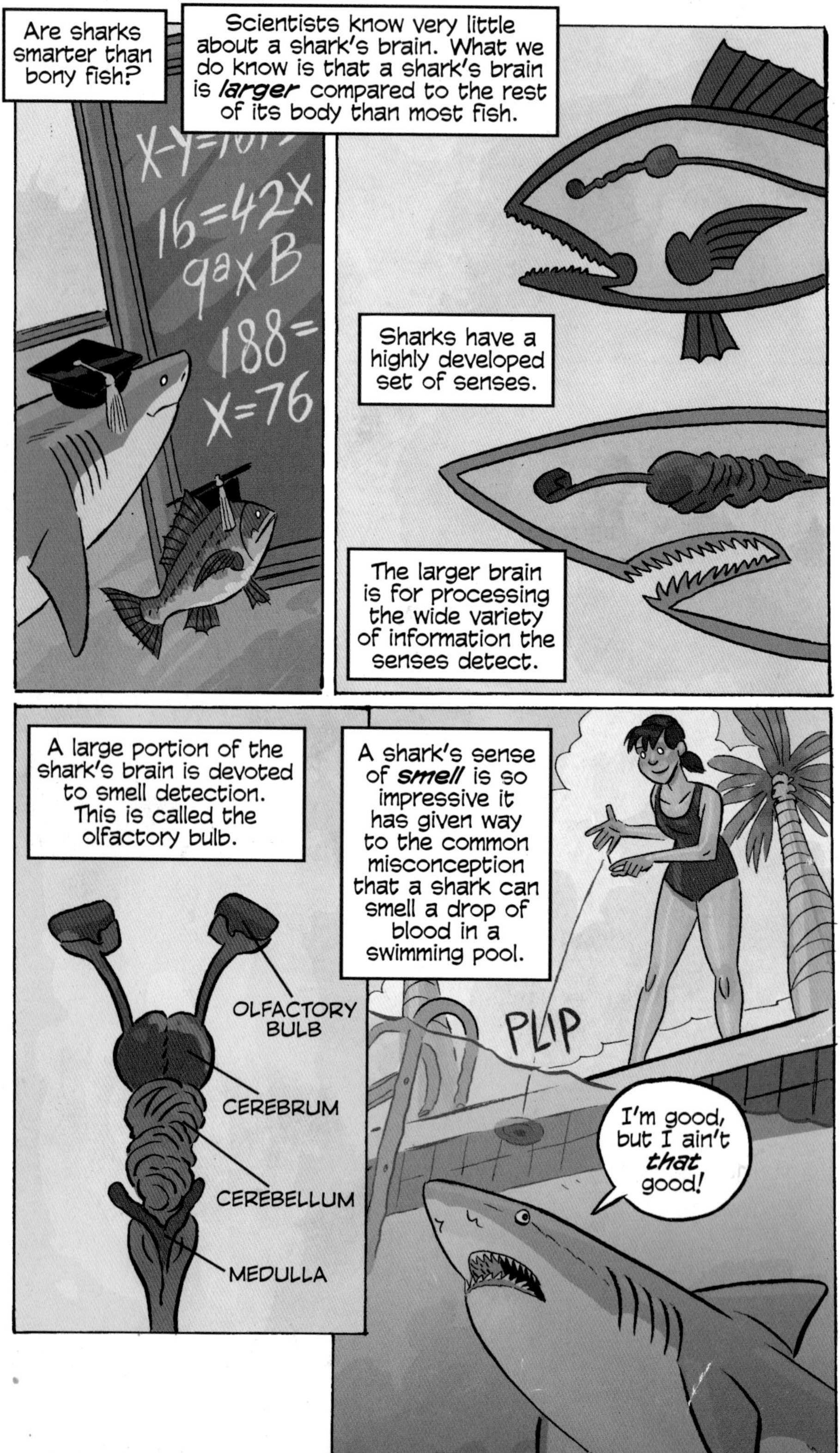
Are sharks smarter than bony fish?
Scientists know very little about a shark's brain. What we do know is that a shark's brain is *larger* compared to the rest of its body than most fish.
X-Y=
16=42x
9ªxB
188=
X=76
Sharks have a highly developed set of senses.
The larger brain is for processing the wide variety of information the senses detect.
A large portion of the shark's brain is devoted to smell detection. This is called the olfactory bulb.
OLFACTORY BULB
CEREBRUM
CEREBELLUM
MEDULLA
A shark's sense of *smell* is so impressive it has given way to the common misconception that a shark can smell a drop of blood in a swimming pool.
PLIP
I'm good, but I ain't *that* good!

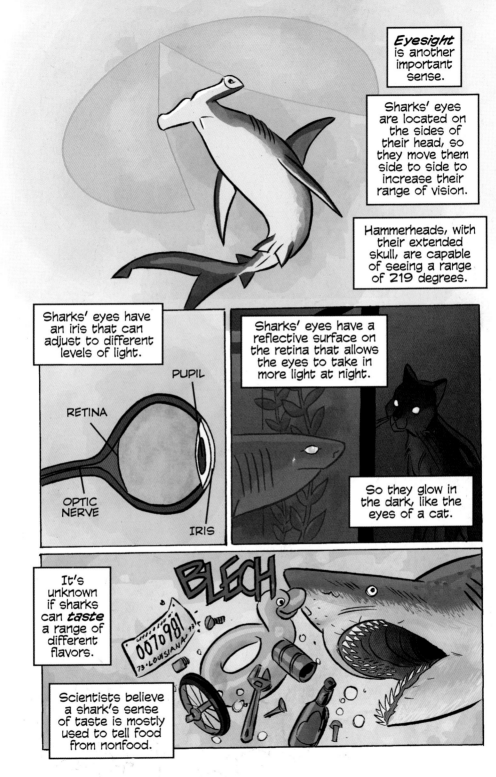

Eyesight is another important sense.

Sharks' eyes are located on the sides of their head, so they move them side to side to increase their range of vision.

Hammerheads, with their extended skull, are capable of seeing a range of 219 degrees.

Sharks' eyes have an iris that can adjust to different levels of light.

PUPIL

RETINA

OPTIC NERVE

IRIS

Sharks' eyes have a reflective surface on the retina that allows the eyes to take in more light at night.

So they glow in the dark, like the eyes of a cat.

It's unknown if sharks can *taste* a range of different flavors.

BLECH

0070981
73·LOUISIANA·73

Scientists believe a shark's sense of taste is mostly used to tell food from nonfood.

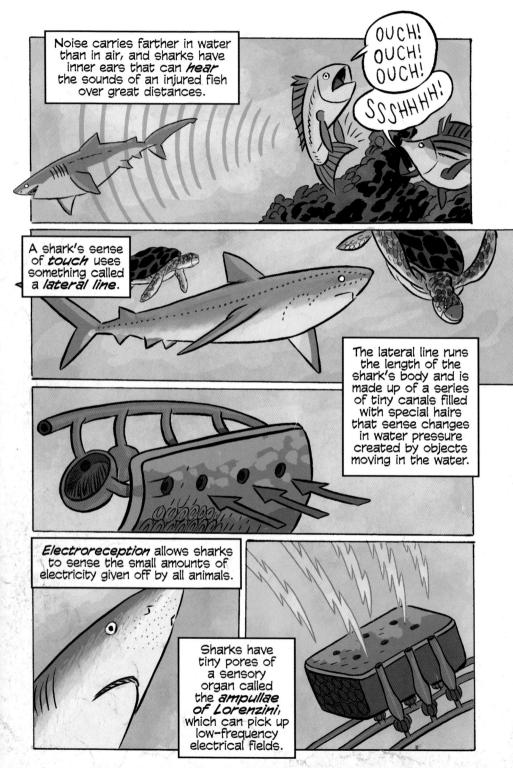

Noise carries farther in water than in air, and sharks have inner ears that can *hear* the sounds of an injured fish over great distances.

OUCH! OUCH! OUCH!

SSSHHHH!

A shark's sense of *touch* uses something called a *lateral line*.

The lateral line runs the length of the shark's body and is made up of a series of tiny canals filled with special hairs that sense changes in water pressure created by objects moving in the water.

Electroreception allows sharks to sense the small amounts of electricity given off by all animals.

Sharks have tiny pores of a sensory organ called the *ampullae of Lorenzini,* which can pick up low-frequency electrical fields.

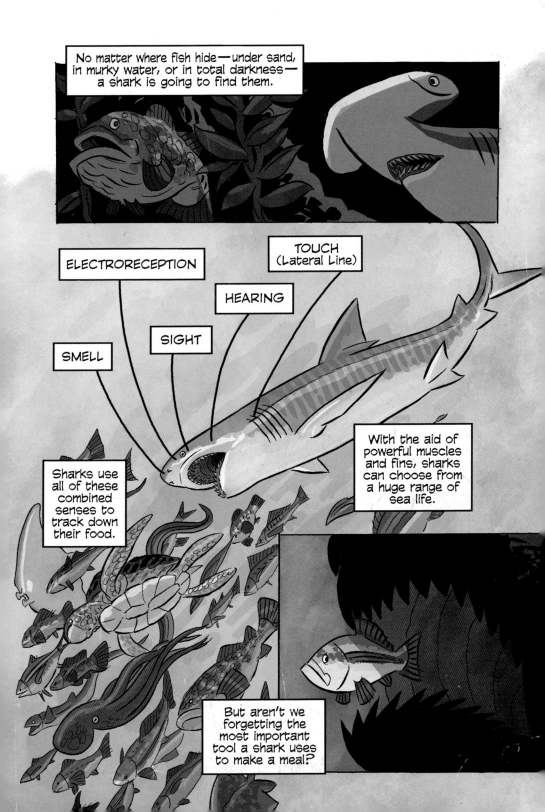

No matter where fish hide—under sand, in murky water, or in total darkness—a shark is going to find them.

ELECTRORECEPTION

TOUCH
(Lateral Line)

HEARING

SIGHT

SMELL

Sharks use all of these combined senses to track down their food.

With the aid of powerful muscles and fins, sharks can choose from a huge range of sea life.

But aren't we forgetting the most important tool a shark uses to make a meal?

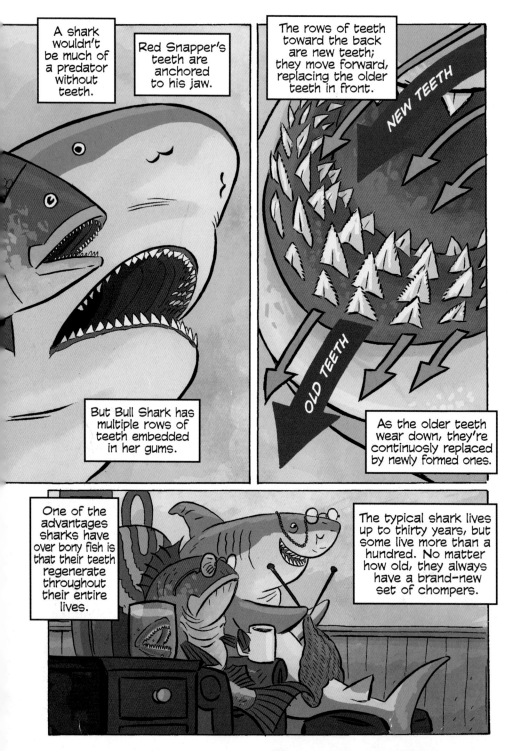

A shark wouldn't be much of a predator without teeth.

Red Snapper's teeth are anchored to his jaw.

The rows of teeth toward the back are new teeth; they move forward, replacing the older teeth in front.

NEW TEETH

OLD TEETH

But Bull Shark has multiple rows of teeth embedded in her gums.

As the older teeth wear down, they're continuosly replaced by newly formed ones.

One of the advantages sharks have over bony fish is that their teeth regenerate throughout their entire lives.

The typical shark lives up to thirty years, but some live more than a hundred. No matter how old, they always have a brand-new set of chompers.

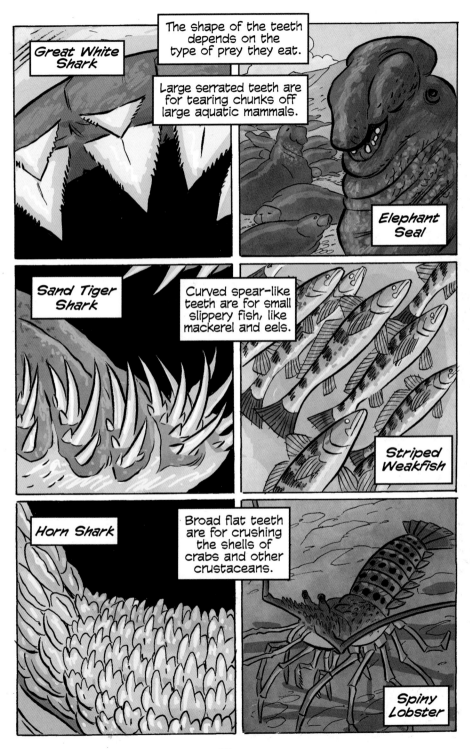

The shape of the teeth depends on the type of prey they eat.

Great White Shark

Large serrated teeth are for tearing chunks off large aquatic mammals.

Elephant Seal

Sand Tiger Shark

Curved spear-like teeth are for small slippery fish, like mackerel and eels.

Striped Weakfish

Horn Shark

Broad flat teeth are for crushing the shells of crabs and other crustaceans.

Spiny Lobster

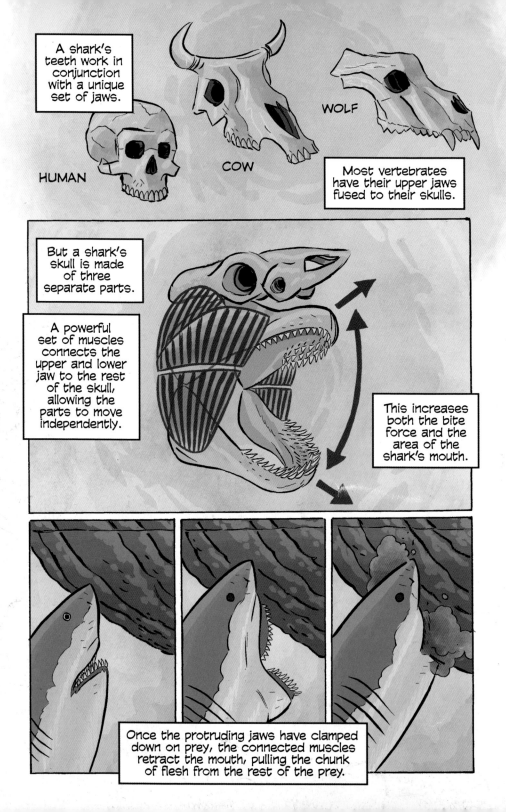

A shark's teeth work in conjunction with a unique set of jaws.

WOLF

HUMAN

COW

Most vertebrates have their upper jaws fused to their skulls.

But a shark's skull is made of three separate parts.

A powerful set of muscles connects the upper and lower jaw to the rest of the skull, allowing the parts to move independently.

This increases both the bite force and the area of the shark's mouth.

Once the protruding jaws have clamped down on prey, the connected muscles retract the mouth, pulling the chunk of flesh from the rest of the prey.

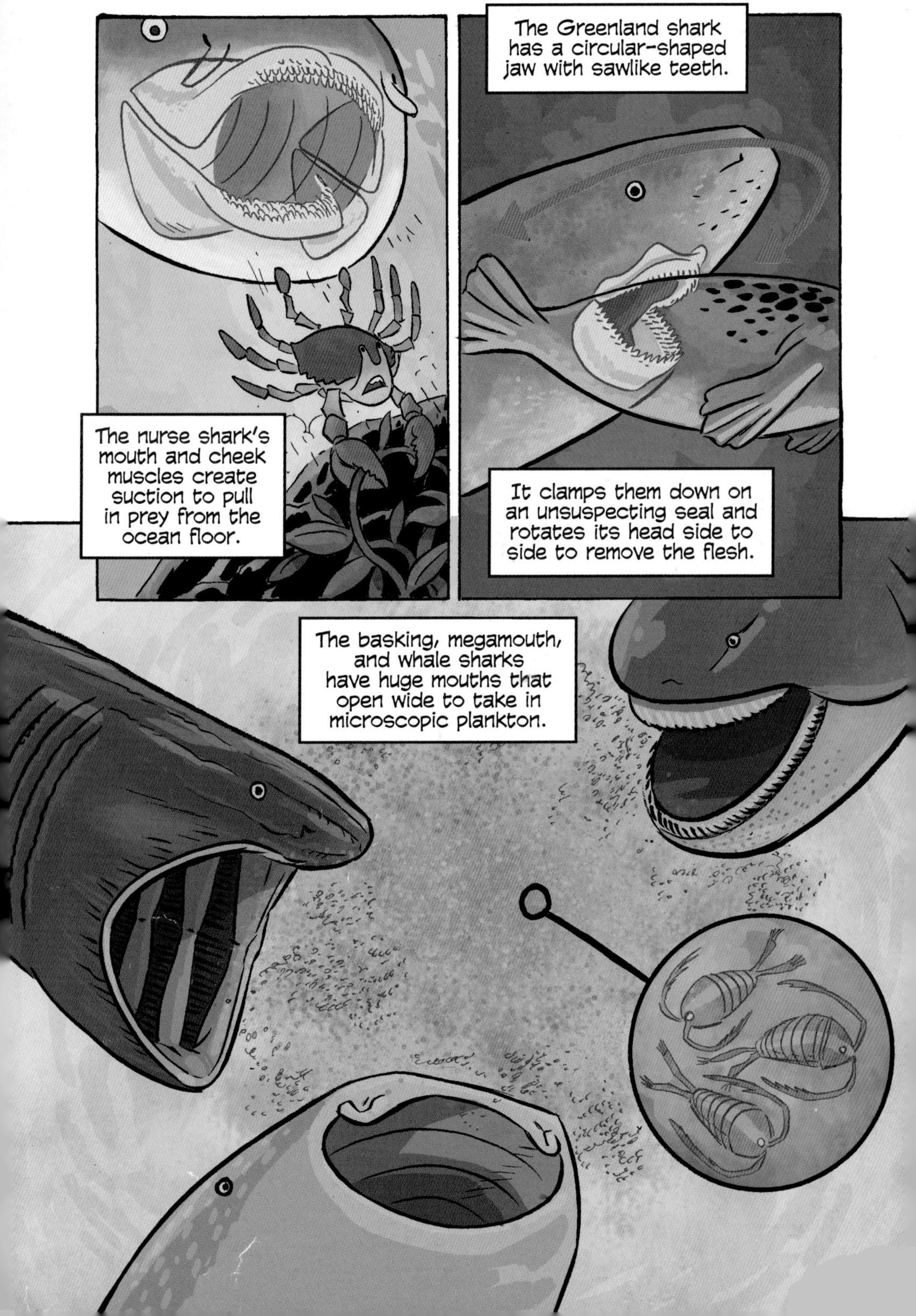
The nurse shark's mouth and cheek muscles create suction to pull in prey from the ocean floor.
The Greenland shark has a circular-shaped jaw with sawlike teeth.
It clamps them down on an unsuspecting seal and rotates its head side to side to remove the flesh.
The basking, megamouth, and whale sharks have huge mouths that open wide to take in microscopic plankton.

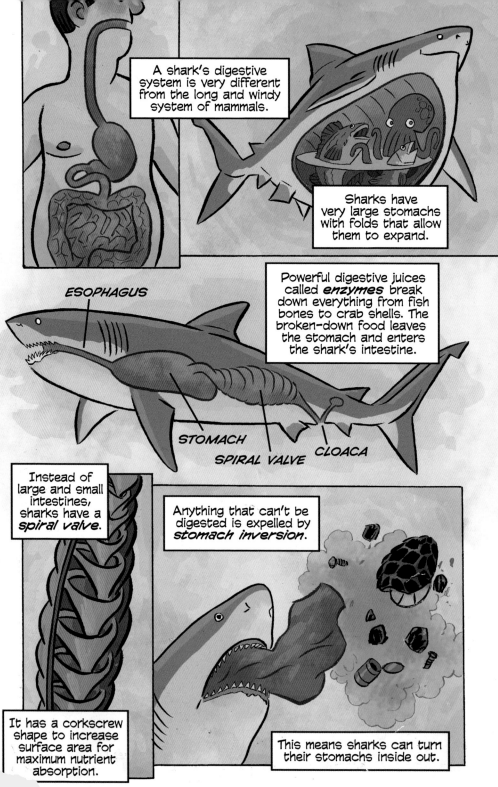

A shark's digestive system is very different from the long and windy system of mammals.

Sharks have very large stomachs with folds that allow them to expand.

Powerful digestive juices called *enzymes* break down everything from fish bones to crab shells. The broken-down food leaves the stomach and enters the shark's intestine.

ESOPHAGUS

STOMACH

SPIRAL VALVE

CLOACA

Instead of large and small intestines, sharks have a *spiral valve*.

Anything that can't be digested is expelled by *stomach inversion*.

It has a corkscrew shape to increase surface area for maximum nutrient absorption.

This means sharks can turn their stomachs inside out.

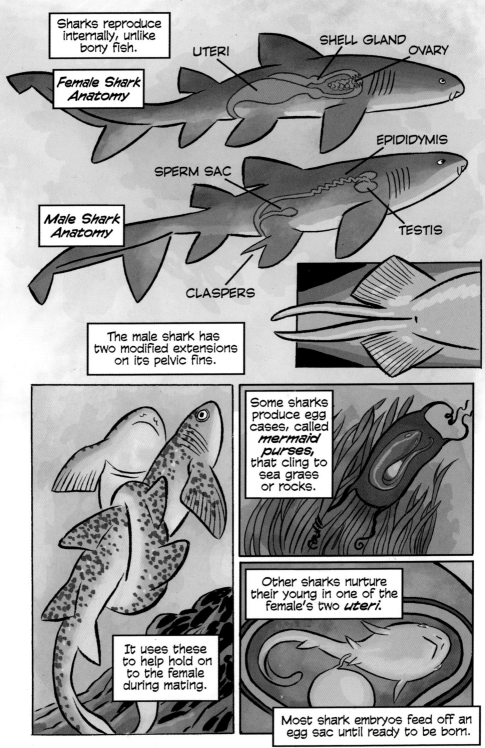

Sharks reproduce internally, unlike bony fish.

Female Shark Anatomy

UTERI

SHELL GLAND

OVARY

EPIDIDYMIS

SPERM SAC

TESTIS

Male Shark Anatomy

CLASPERS

The male shark has two modified extensions on its pelvic fins.

Some sharks produce egg cases, called *mermaid purses*, that cling to sea grass or rocks.

It uses these to help hold on to the female during mating.

Other sharks nurture their young in one of the female's two *uteri*.

Most shark embryos feed off an egg sac until ready to be born.

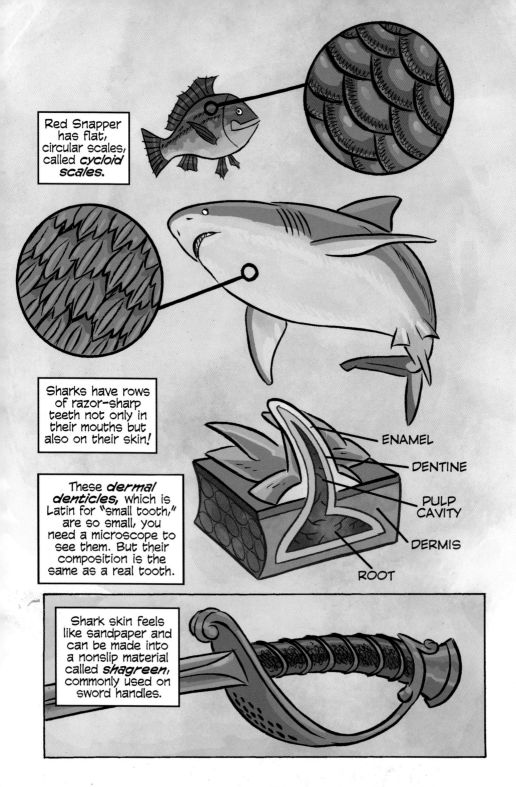

Red Snapper has flat, circular scales, called *cycloid scales.*

Sharks have rows of razor-sharp teeth not only in their mouths but also on their skin!

These *dermal denticles,* which is Latin for "small tooth," are so small, you need a microscope to see them. But their composition is the same as a real tooth.

ENAMEL

DENTINE

PULP CAVITY

DERMIS

ROOT

Shark skin feels like sandpaper and can be made into a nonslip material called *shagreen,* commonly used on sword handles.

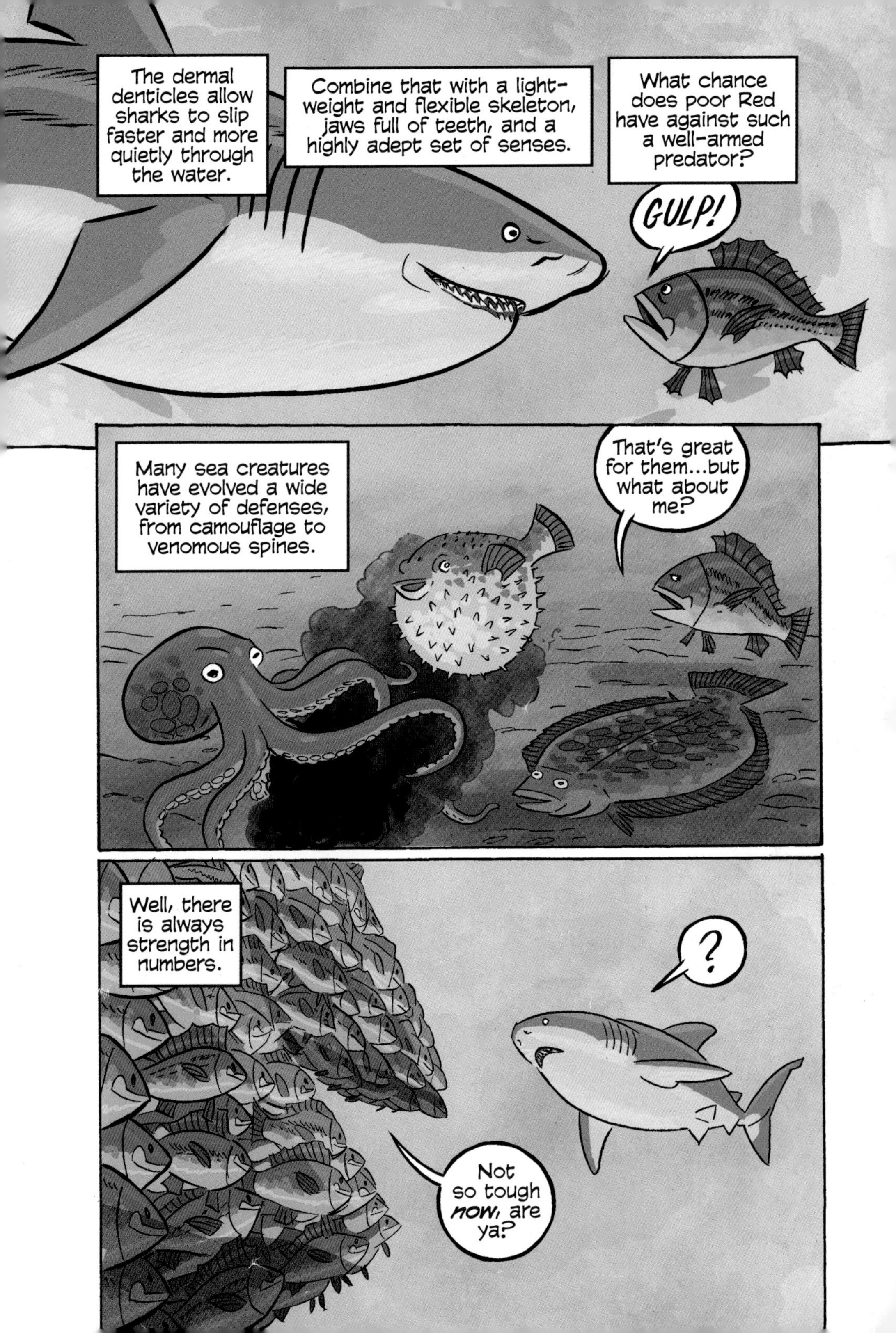
The dermal denticles allow sharks to slip faster and more quietly through the water.
Combine that with a light-weight and flexible skeleton, jaws full of teeth, and a highly adept set of senses.
What chance does poor Red have against such a well-armed predator?
GULP!
Many sea creatures have evolved a wide variety of defenses, from camouflage to venomous spines.
That's great for them...but what about me?
Well, there is always strength in numbers.
?
Not so tough *now*, are ya?

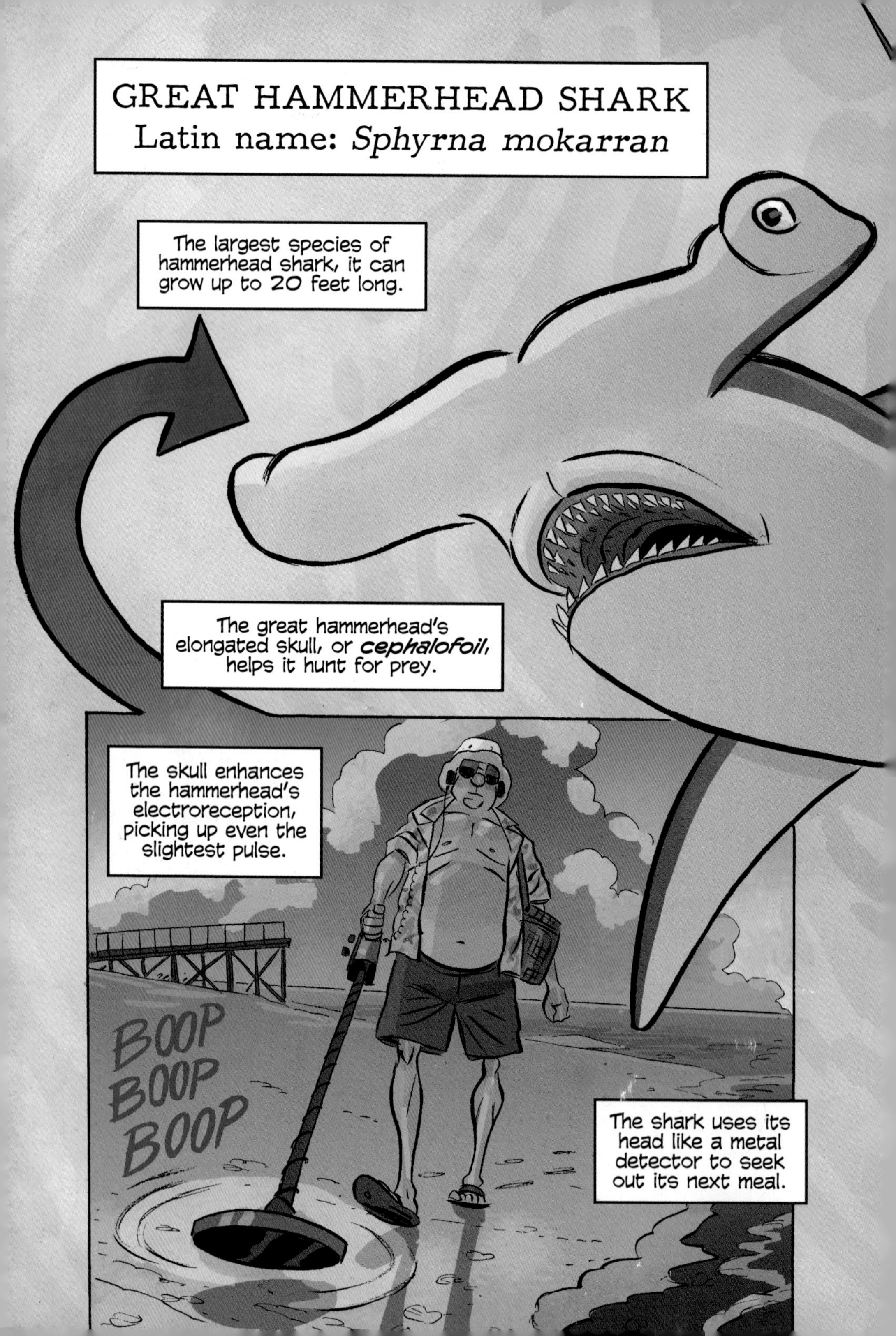
GREAT HAMMERHEAD SHARK
Latin name: Sphyrna mokarran
The largest species of hammerhead shark, it can grow up to 20 feet long.
The great hammerhead's elongated skull, or cephalofoil, helps it hunt for prey.
The skull enhances the hammerhead's electroreception, picking up even the slightest pulse.
BOOP BOOP BOOP
The shark uses its head like a metal detector to seek out its next meal.

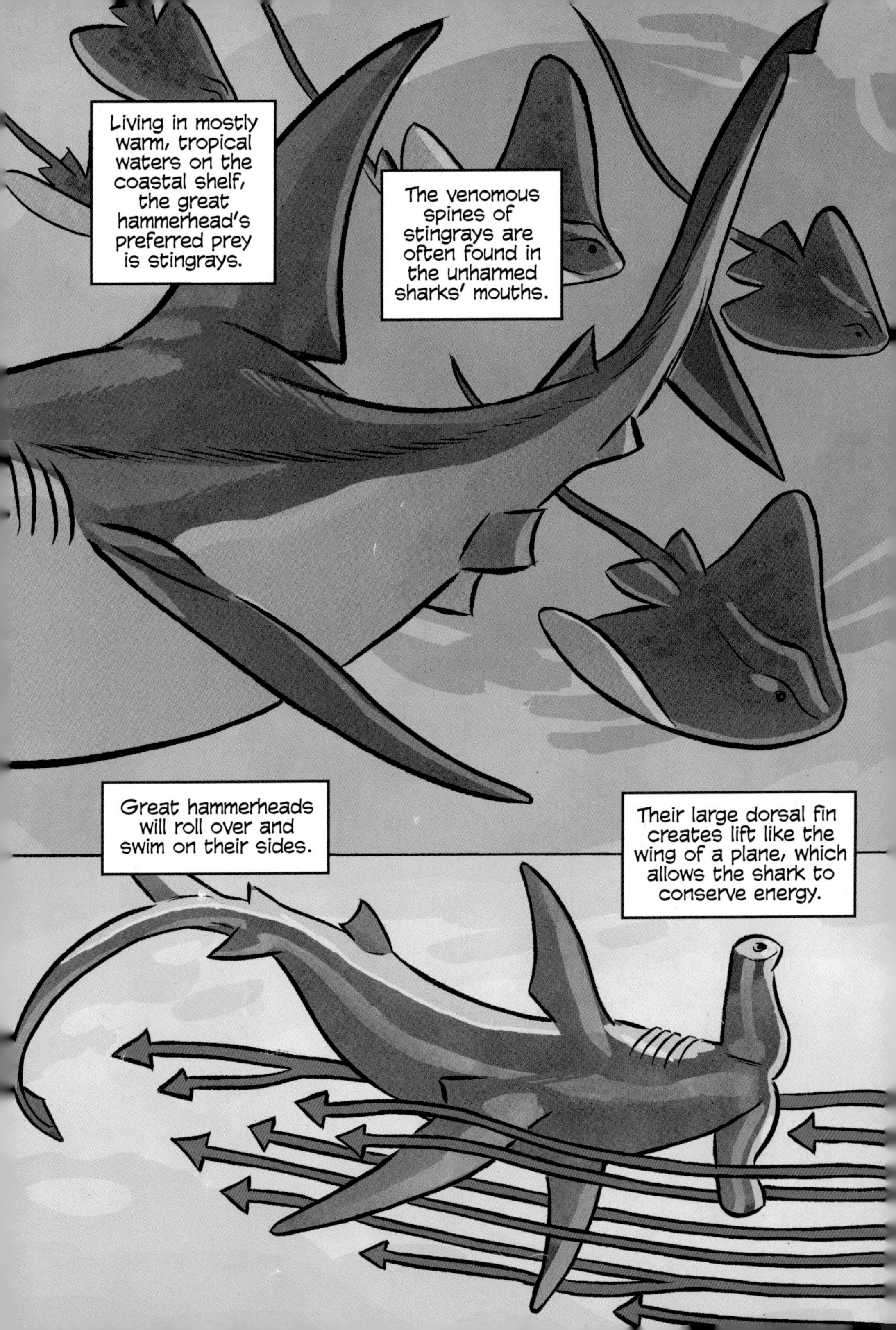
Living in mostly warm, tropical waters on the coastal shelf, the great hammerhead's preferred prey is stingrays.
The venomous spines of stingrays are often found in the unharmed sharks' mouths.
Great hammerheads will roll over and swim on their sides.
Their large dorsal fin creates lift like the wing of a plane, which allows the shark to conserve energy.

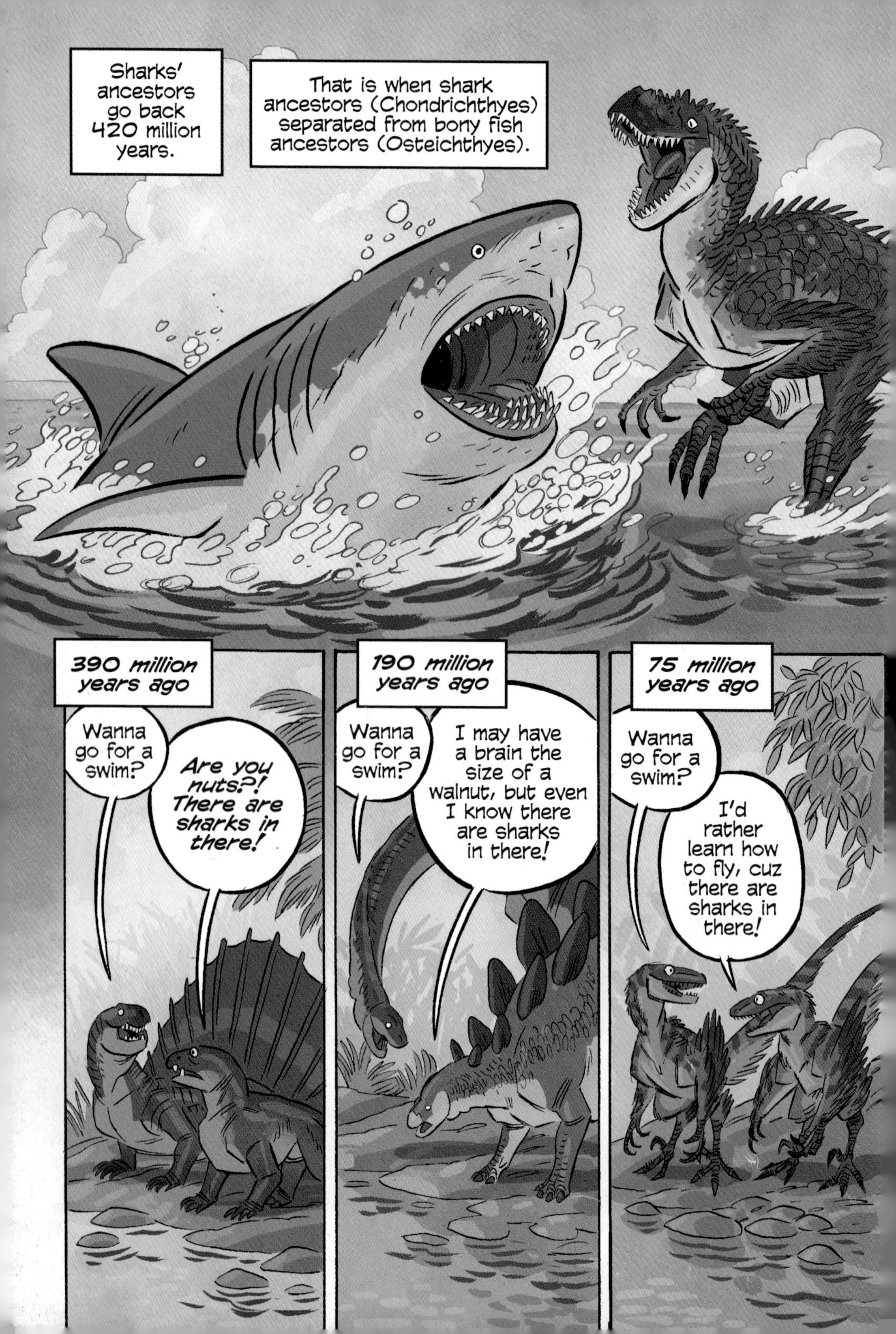
Sharks' ancestors go back 420 million years.
That is when shark ancestors (Chondrichthyes) separated from bony fish ancestors (Osteichthyes).
390 million years ago
Wanna go for a swim?
Are you nuts?! There are sharks in there!
190 million years ago
Wanna go for a swim?
I may have a brain the size of a walnut, but even I know there are sharks in there!
75 million years ago
Wanna go for a swim?
I'd rather learn how to fly, cuz there are sharks in there!

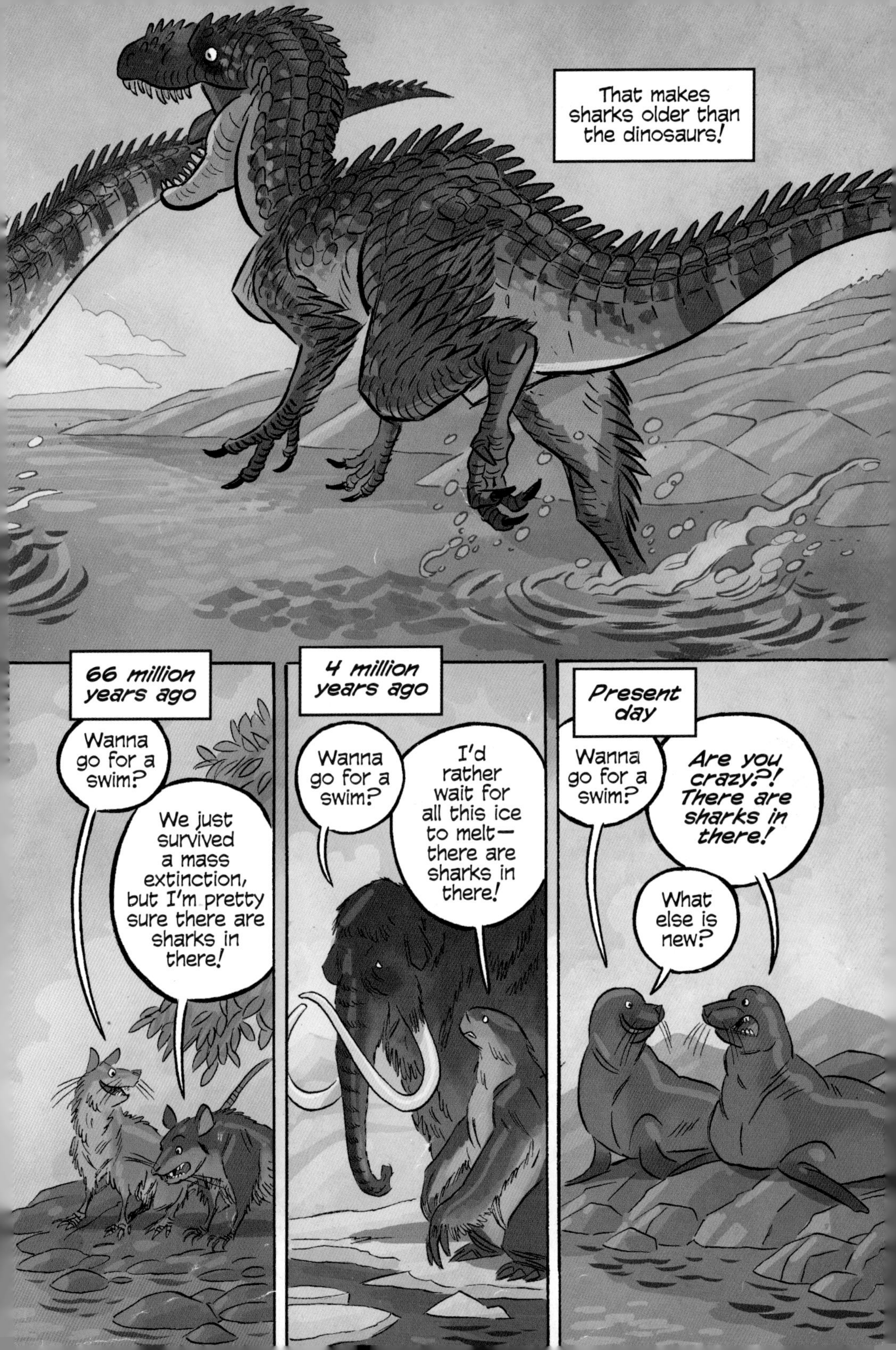
That makes sharks older than the dinosaurs!
66 million years ago
Wanna go for a swim?
We just survived a mass extinction, but I'm pretty sure there are sharks in there!
4 million years ago
Wanna go for a swim?
I'd rather wait for all this ice to melt— there are sharks in there!
Present day
Wanna go for a swim?
Are you crazy?! There are sharks in there!
What else is new?

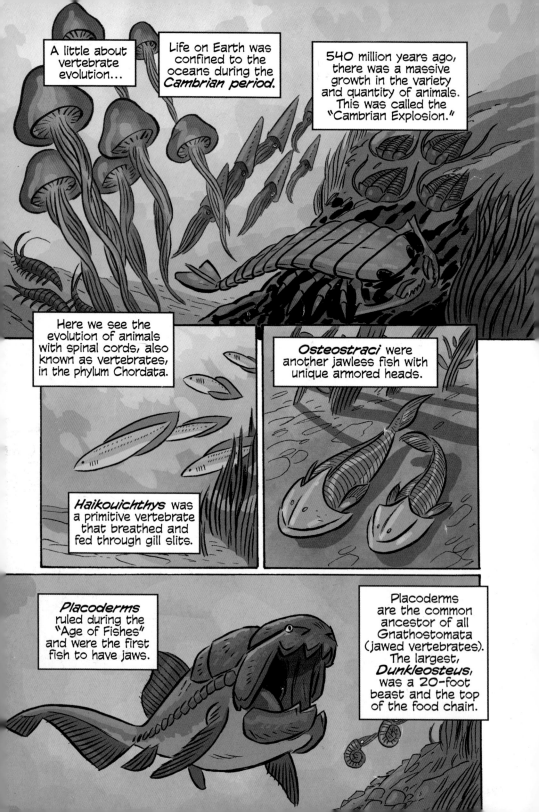

A little about vertebrate evolution…

Life on Earth was confined to the oceans during the *Cambrian period*.

540 million years ago, there was a massive growth in the variety and quantity of animals. This was called the "Cambrian Explosion."

Here we see the evolution of animals with spinal cords, also known as vertebrates, in the phylum Chordata.

Haikouichthys was a primitive vertebrate that breathed and fed through gill slits.

Osteostraci were another jawless fish with unique armored heads.

Placoderms ruled during the "Age of Fishes" and were the first fish to have jaws.

Placoderms are the common ancestor of all Gnathostomata (jawed vertebrates). The largest, *Dunkleosteus*, was a 20-foot beast and the top of the food chain.

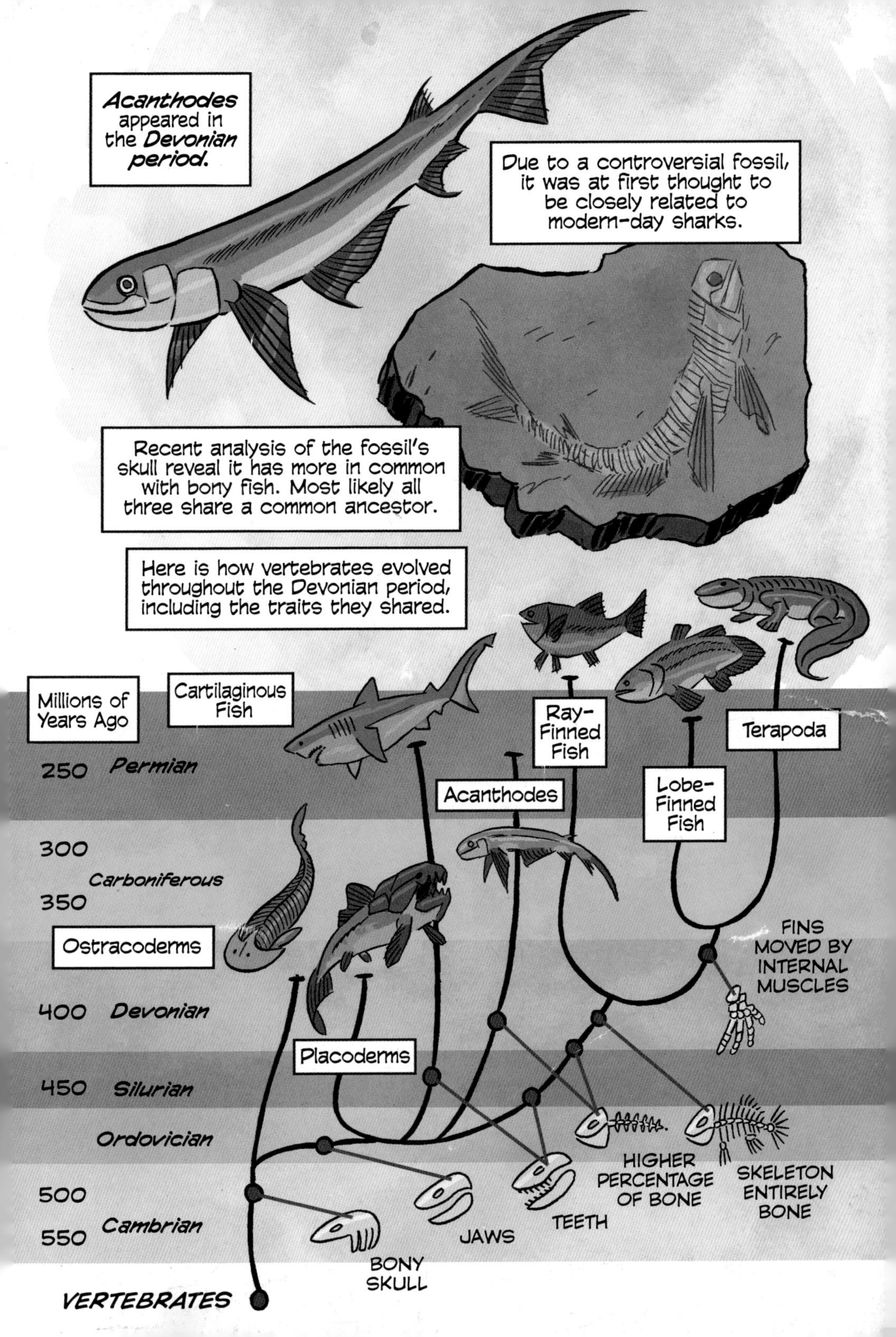
Acanthodes appeared in the *Devonian period.*
Due to a controversial fossil, it was at first thought to be closely related to modern-day sharks.
Recent analysis of the fossil's skull reveal it has more in common with bony fish. Most likely all three share a common ancestor.
Here is how vertebrates evolved throughout the Devonian period, including the traits they shared.
Millions of Years Ago
Cartilaginous Fish
Ray-Finned Fish
Terapoda
250 Permian
Acanthodes
Lobe-Finned Fish
300
Carboniferous
350
Ostracoderms
FINS MOVED BY INTERNAL MUSCLES
400 Devonian
Placoderms
450 Silurian
Ordovician
HIGHER PERCENTAGE OF BONE
SKELETON ENTIRELY BONE
500
550 Cambrian
TEETH
JAWS
BONY SKULL
VERTEBRATES

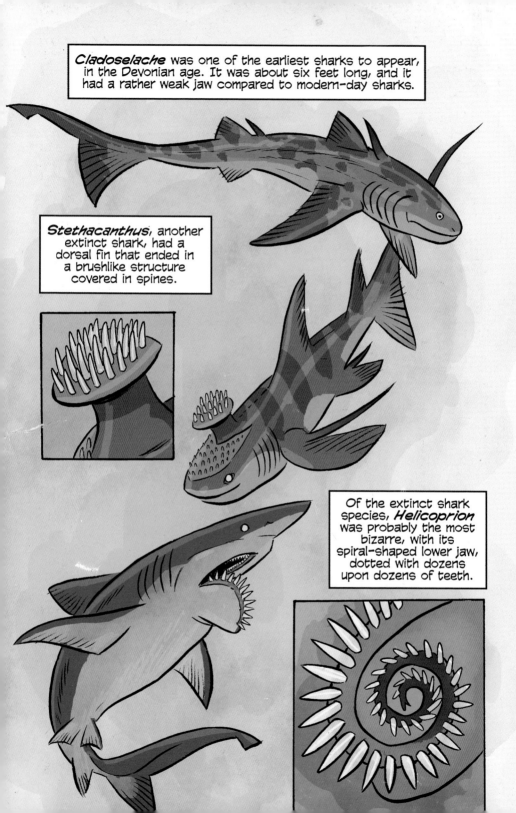

Cladoselache was one of the earliest sharks to appear, in the Devonian age. It was about six feet long, and it had a rather weak jaw compared to modern-day sharks.

Stethacanthus, another extinct shark, had a dorsal fin that ended in a brushlike structure covered in spines.

Of the extinct shark species, **Helicoprion** was probably the most bizarre, with its spiral-shaped lower jaw, dotted with dozens upon dozens of teeth.

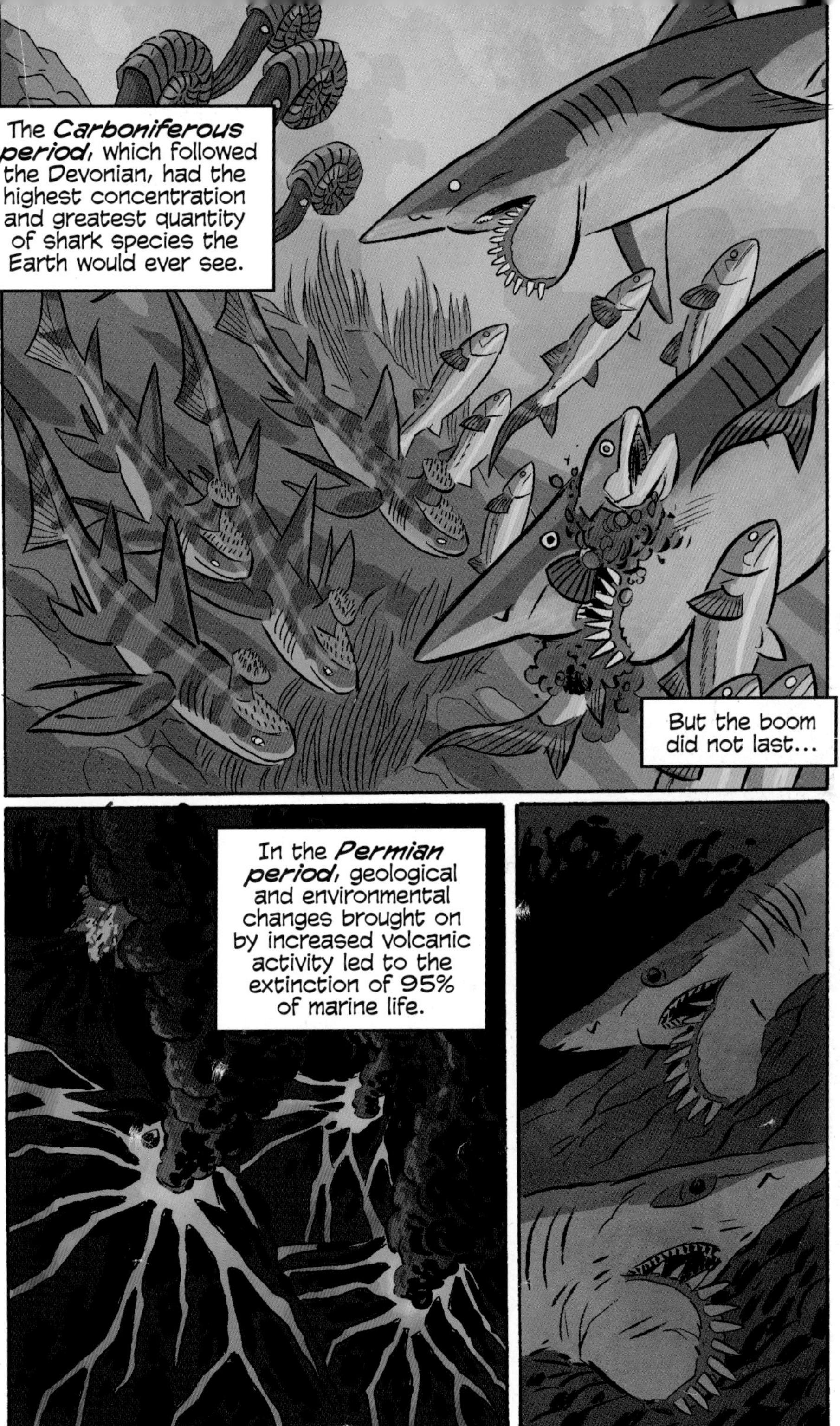
The *Carboniferous period*, which followed the Devonian, had the highest concentration and greatest quantity of shark species the Earth would ever see.
But the boom did not last...
In the *Permian period*, geological and environmental changes brought on by increased volcanic activity led to the extinction of 95% of marine life.

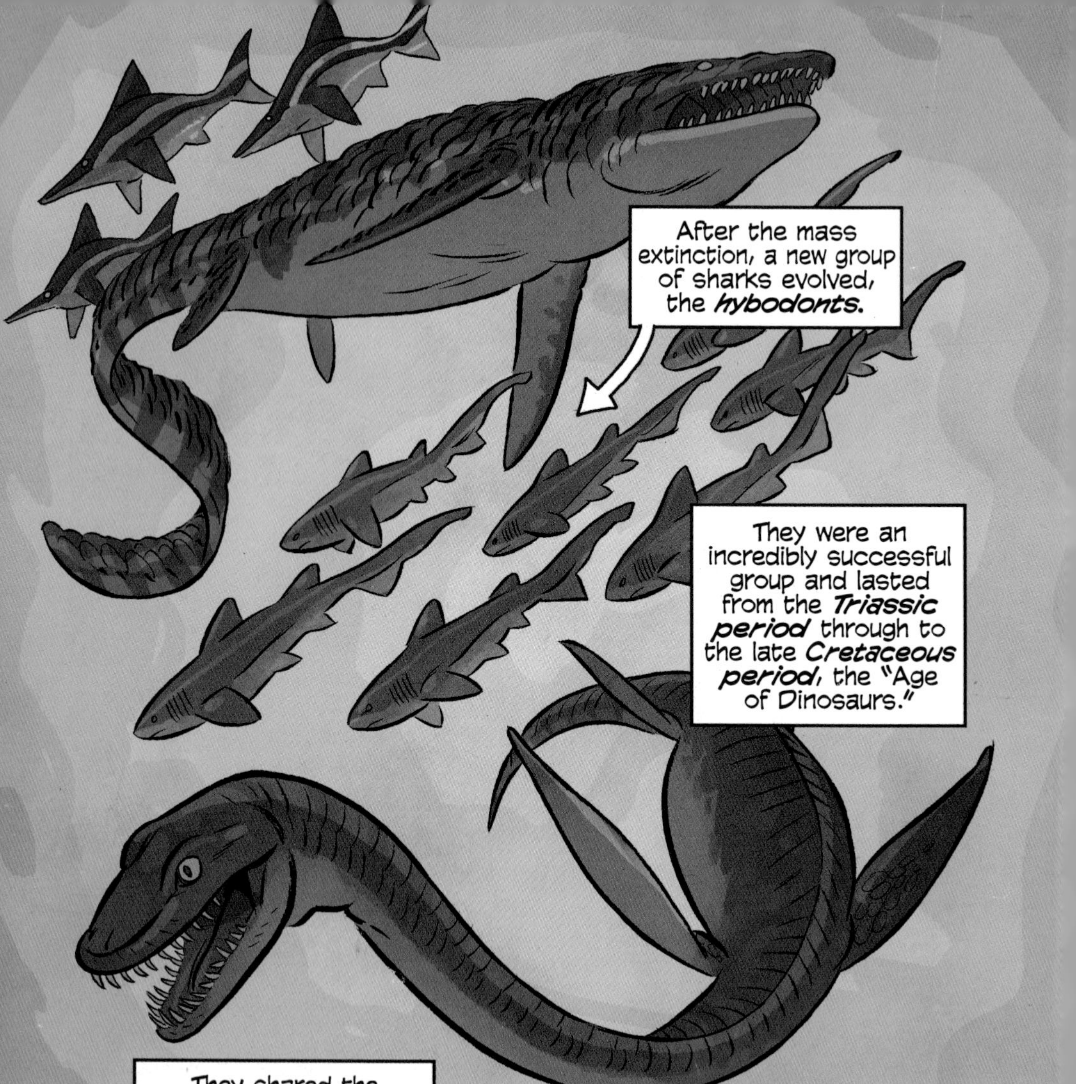
After the mass extinction, a new group of sharks evolved, the *hybodonts.*
They were an incredibly successful group and lasted from the *Triassic period* through to the late *Cretaceous period,* the "Age of Dinosaurs."
They shared the ocean with much larger aquatic reptiles.

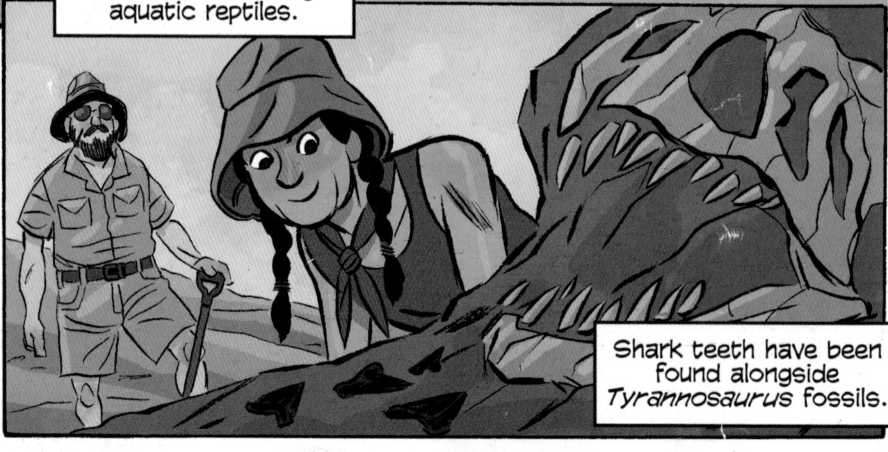
Shark teeth have been found alongside *Tyrannosaurus* fossils.

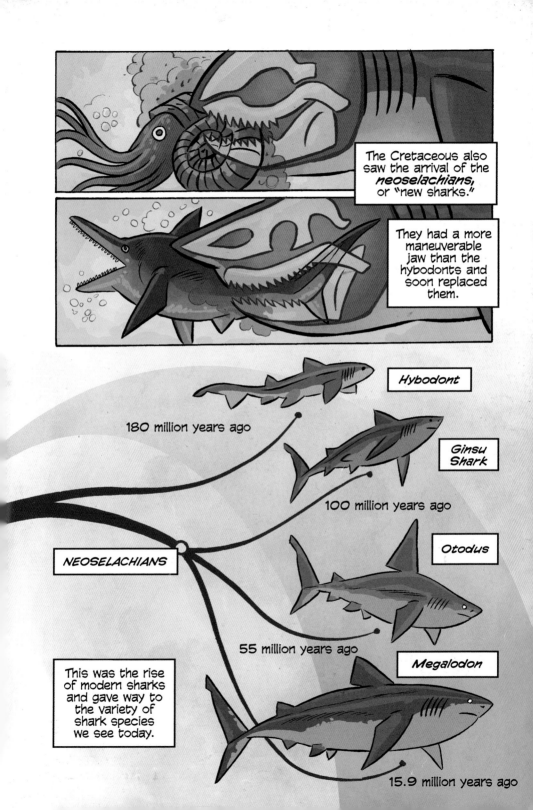

The Cretaceous also saw the arrival of the *neoselachians,* or "new sharks."

They had a more maneuverable jaw than the hybodonts and soon replaced them.

Hybodont

180 million years ago

Ginsu Shark

100 million years ago

NEOSELACHIANS

Otodus

55 million years ago

This was the rise of modern sharks and gave way to the variety of shark species we see today.

Megalodon

15.9 million years ago

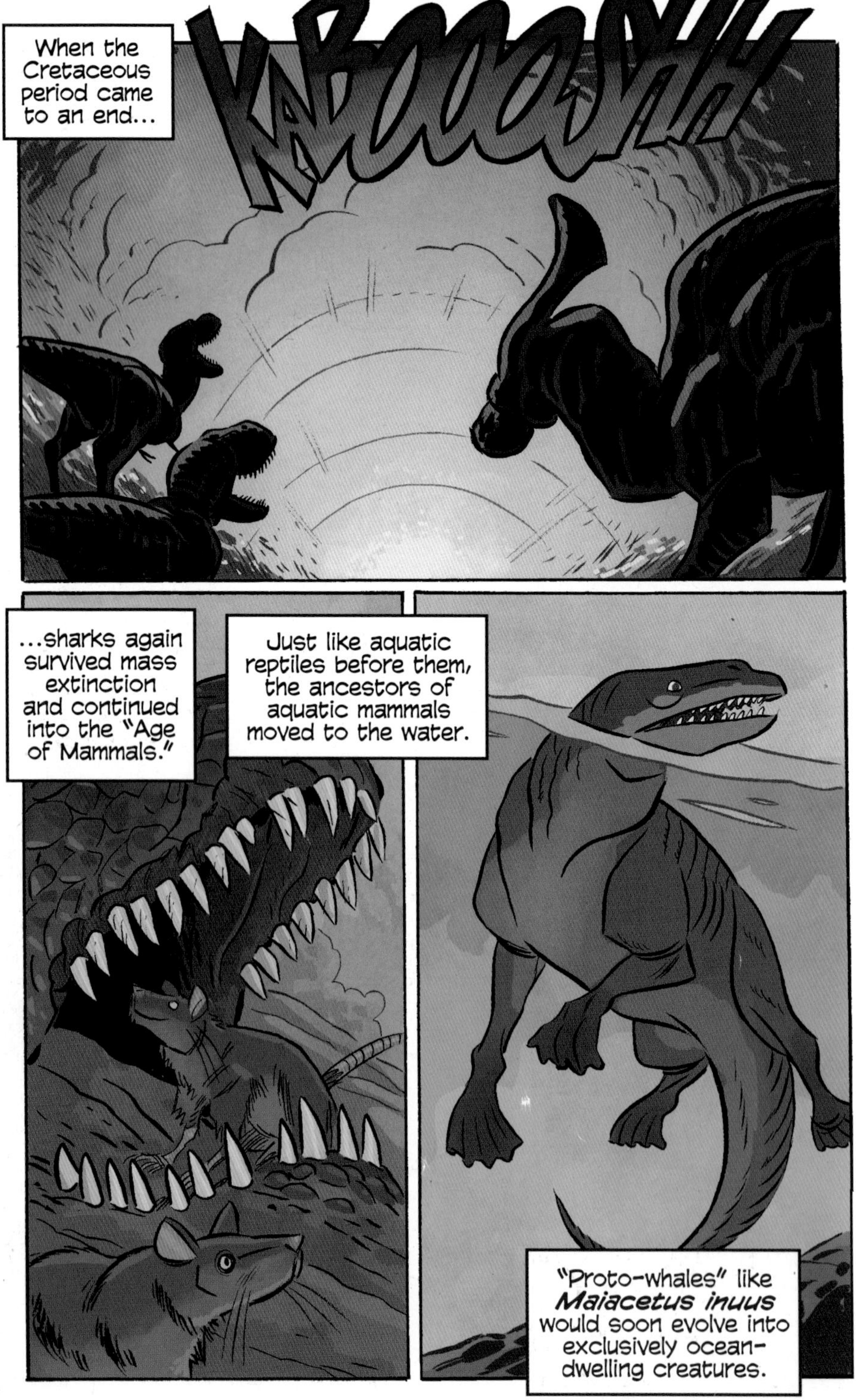
When the Cretaceous period came to an end...
KABOOOSHH
...sharks again survived mass extinction and continued into the "Age of Mammals."
Just like aquatic reptiles before them, the ancestors of aquatic mammals moved to the water.
"Proto-whales" like *Maiacetus inuus* would soon evolve into exclusively ocean-dwelling creatures.

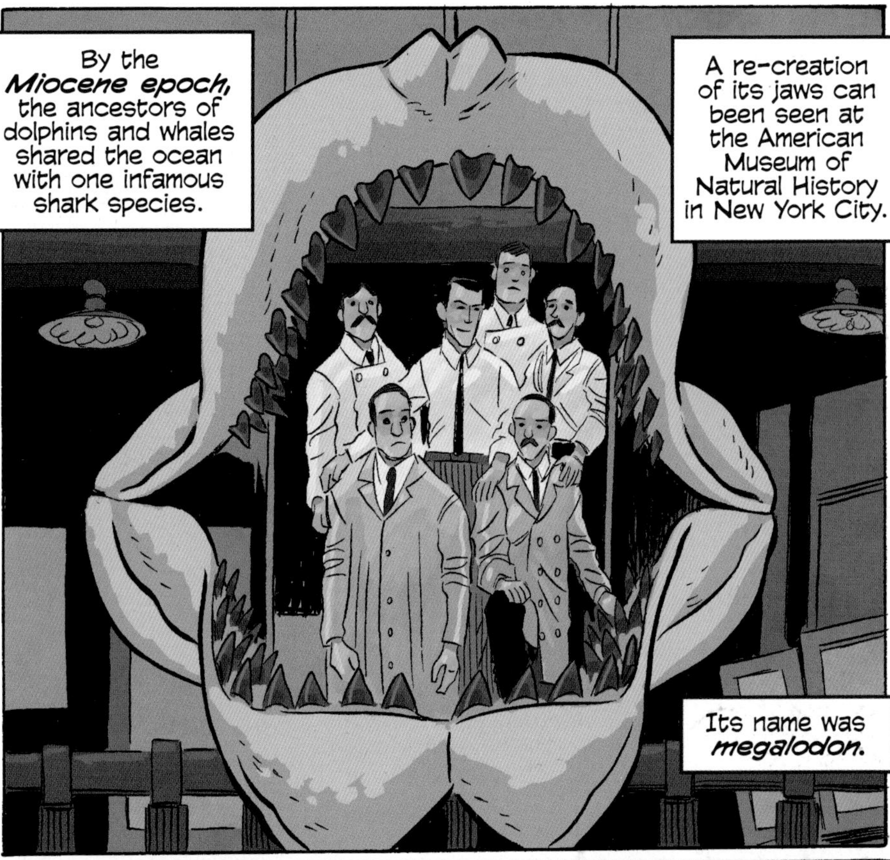
By the *Miocene epoch,* the ancestors of dolphins and whales shared the ocean with one infamous shark species.
A re-creation of its jaws can been seen at the American Museum of Natural History in New York City.
Its name was *megalodon.*

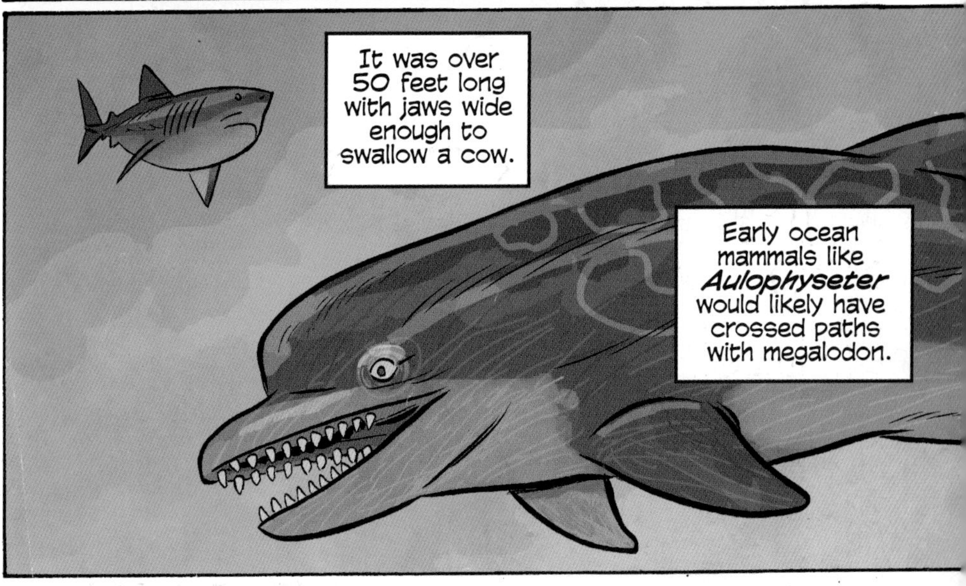
It was over 50 feet long with jaws wide enough to swallow a cow.
Early ocean mammals like *Aulophyseter* would likely have crossed paths with megalodon.

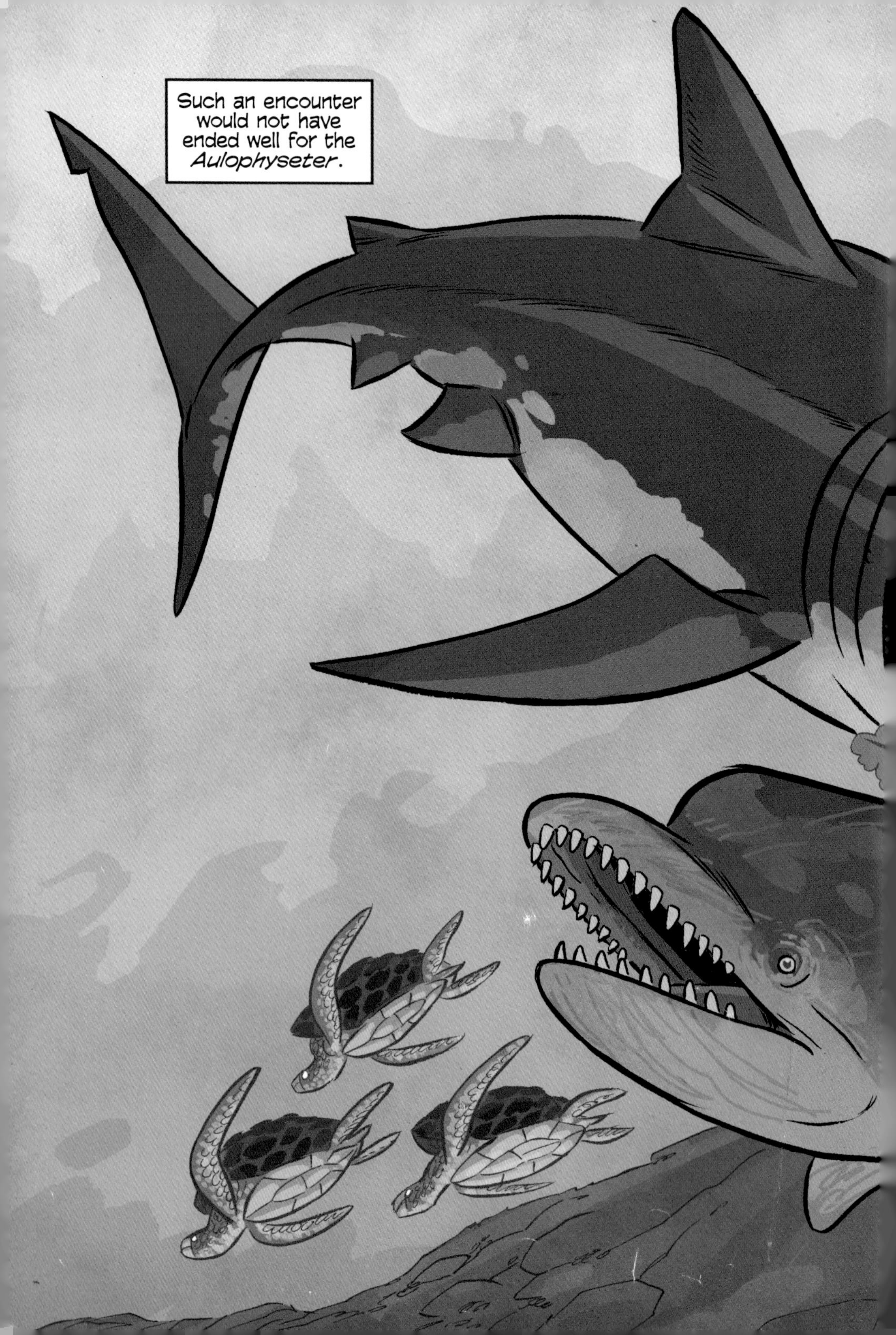
Such an encounter would not have ended well for the *Aulophyseter*.

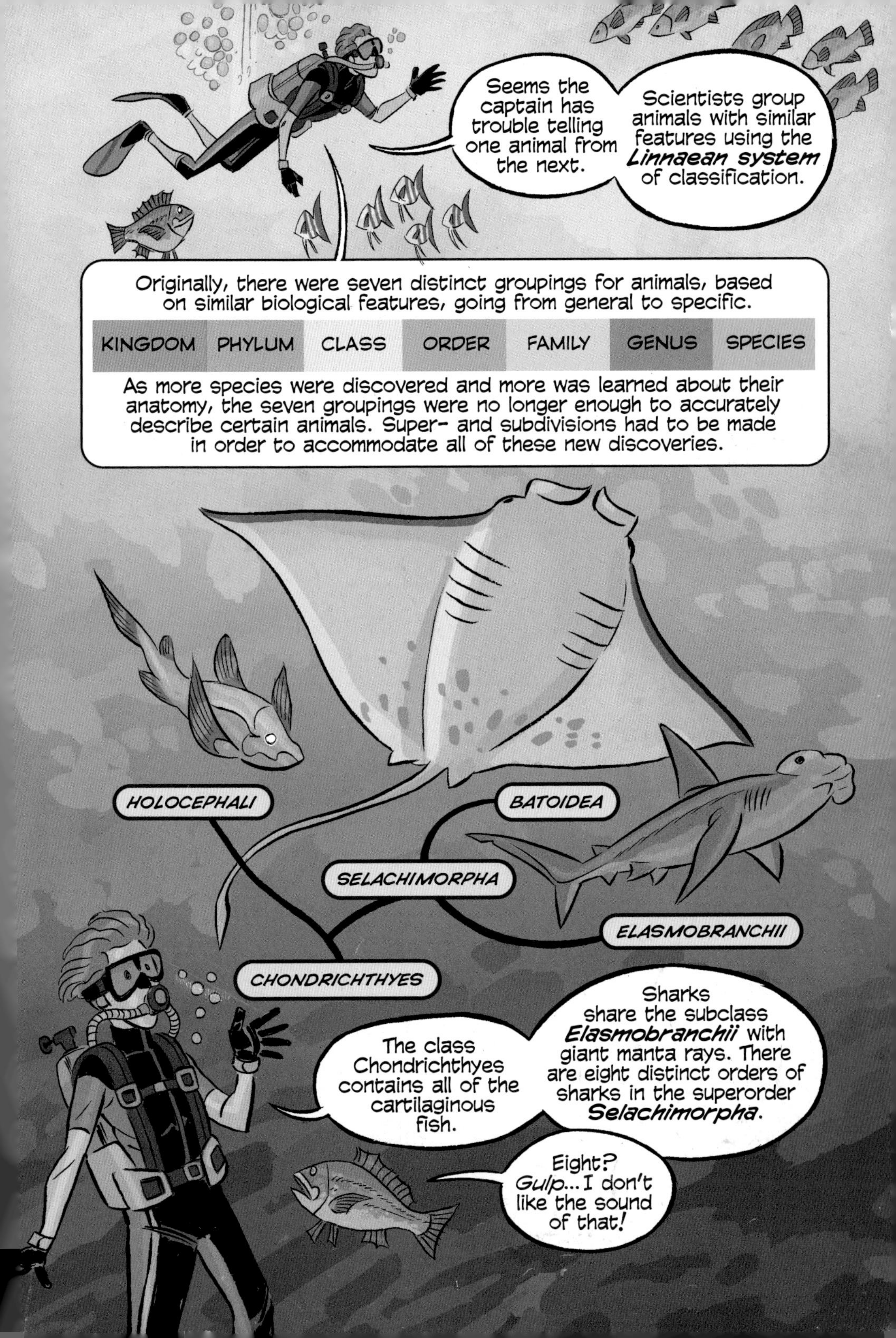
Seems the captain has trouble telling one animal from the next.
Scientists group animals with similar features using the *Linnaean system* of classification.
Originally, there were seven distinct groupings for animals, based on similar biological features, going from general to specific.
KINGDOM PHYLUM CLASS ORDER FAMILY GENUS SPECIES
As more species were discovered and more was learned about their anatomy, the seven groupings were no longer enough to accurately describe certain animals. Super- and subdivisions had to be made in order to accommodate all of these new discoveries.
HOLOCEPHALI
BATOIDEA
SELACHIMORPHA
ELASMOBRANCHII
CHONDRICHTHYES
The class Chondrichthyes contains all of the cartilaginous fish.
Sharks share the subclass *Elasmobranchii* with giant manta rays. There are eight distinct orders of sharks in the superorder *Selachimorpha*.
Eight? *Gulp*... I don't like the sound of that!

SUPERORDER SELACHIMORPHA

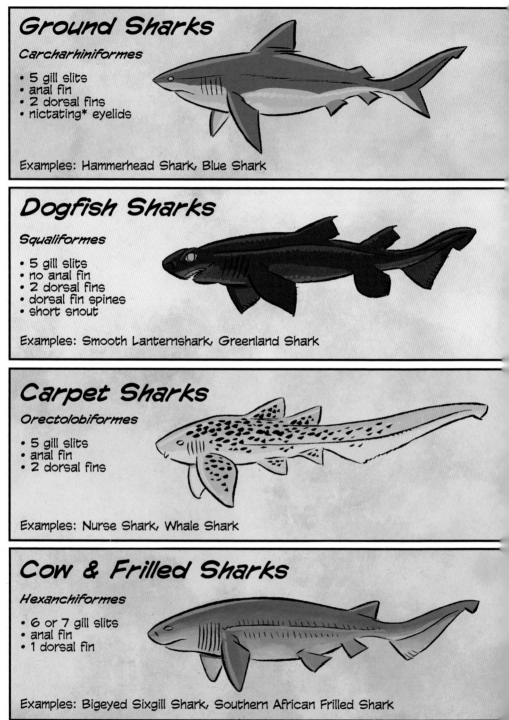

Ground Sharks

Carcharhiniformes

- 5 gill slits
- anal fin
- 2 dorsal fins
- nictating* eyelids

Examples: Hammerhead Shark, Blue Shark

Dogfish Sharks

Squaliformes

- 5 gill slits
- no anal fin
- 2 dorsal fins
- dorsal fin spines
- short snout

Examples: Smooth Lanternshark, Greenland Shark

Carpet Sharks

Orectolobiformes

- 5 gill slits
- anal fin
- 2 dorsal fins

Examples: Nurse Shark, Whale Shark

Cow & Frilled Sharks

Hexanchiformes

- 6 or 7 gill slits
- anal fin
- 1 dorsal fin

Examples: Bigeyed Sixgill Shark, Southern African Frilled Shark

*transparent eyelid used to protect the eye

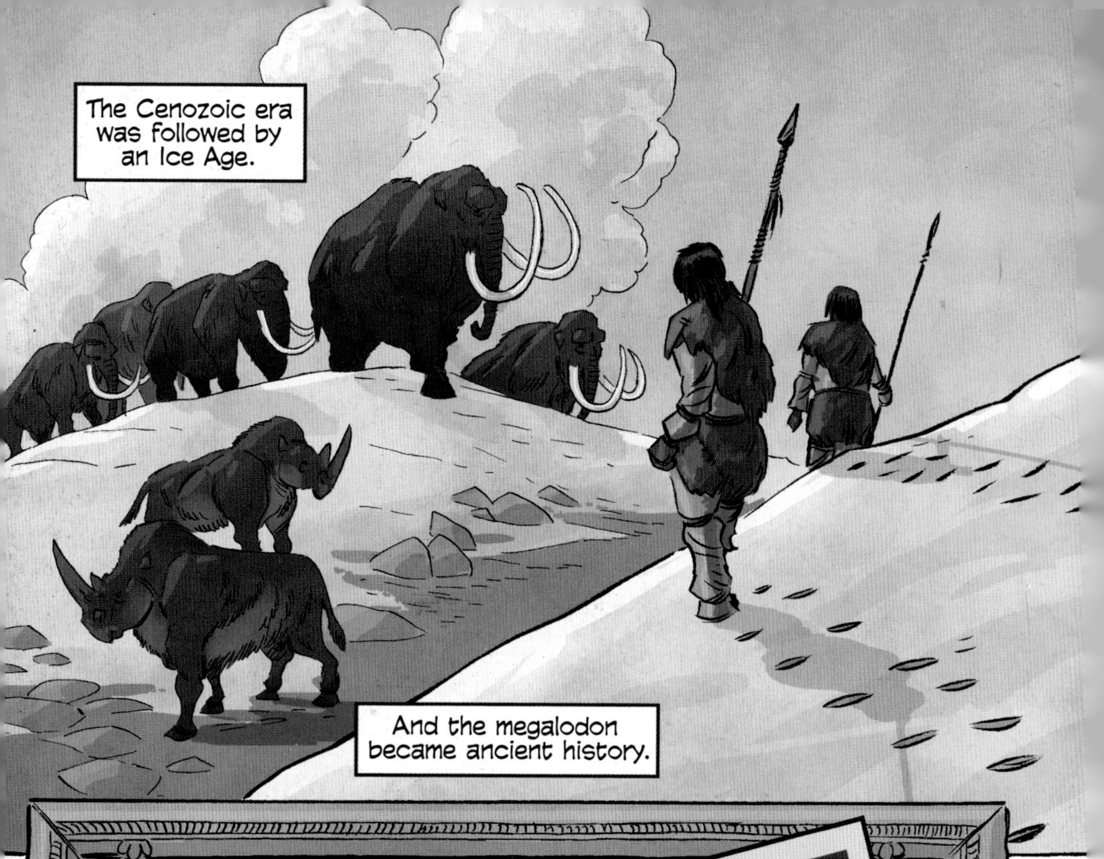
The Cenozoic era was followed by an Ice Age.
And the megalodon became ancient history.

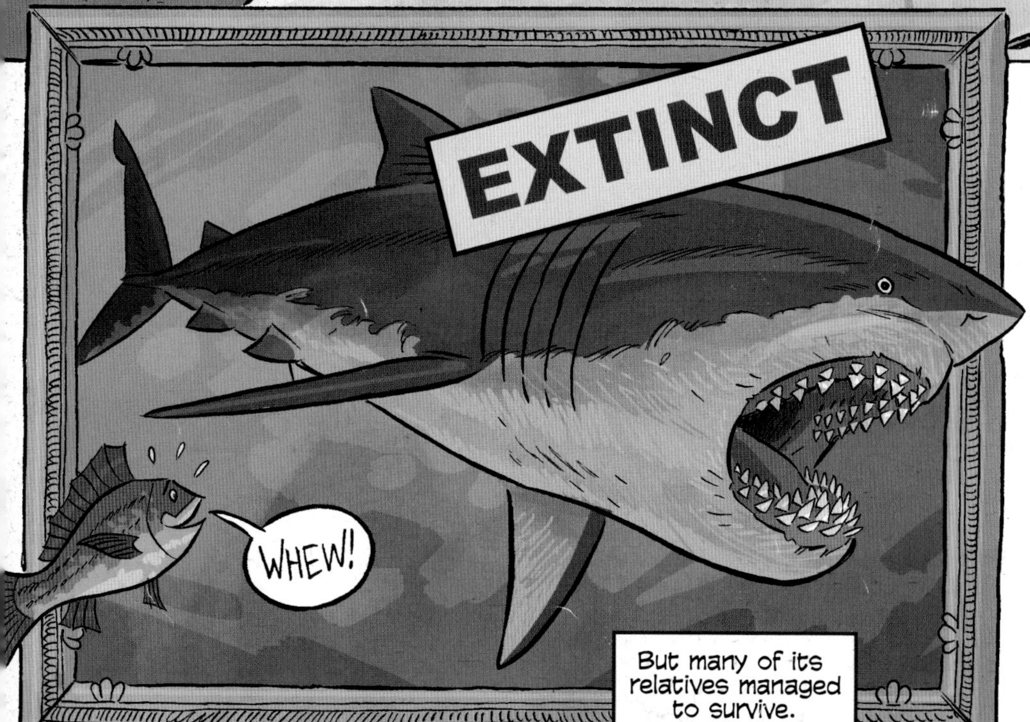
EXTINCT
WHEW!
But many of its relatives managed to survive.

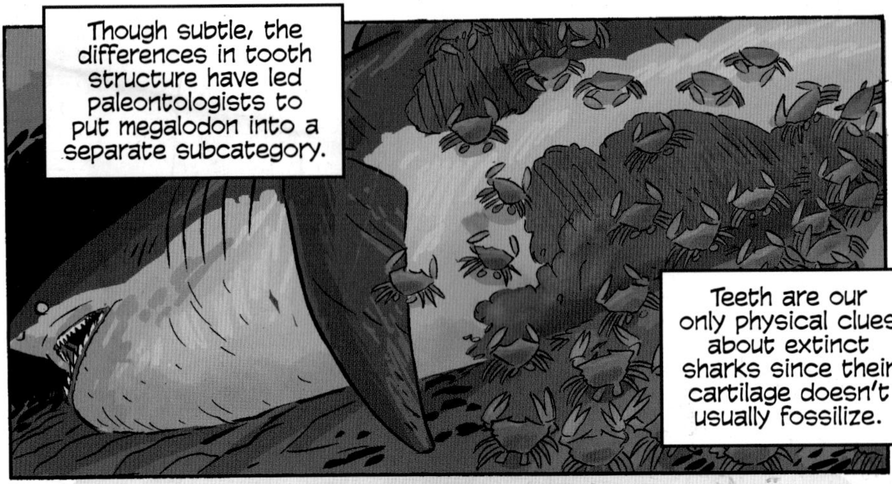
Though subtle, the differences in tooth structure have led paleontologists to put megalodon into a separate subcategory.
Teeth are our only physical clues about extinct sharks since their cartilage doesn't usually fossilize.

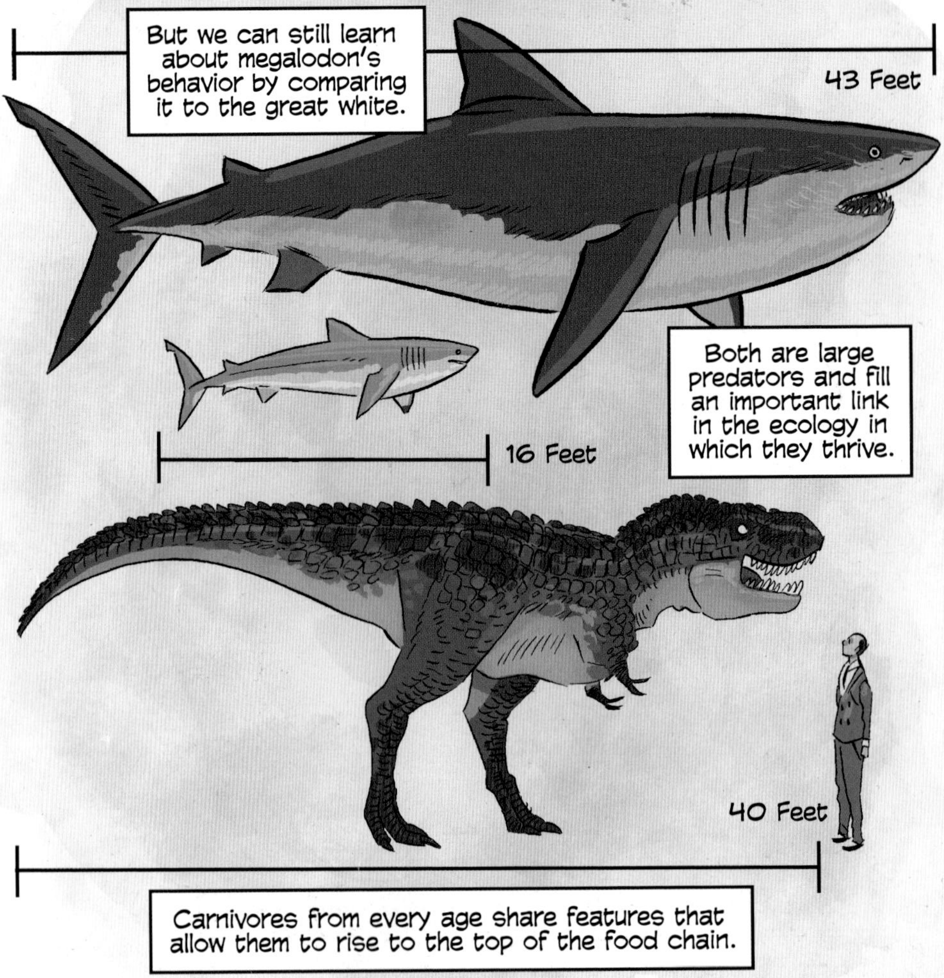
But we can still learn about megalodon's behavior by comparing it to the great white.
43 Feet
16 Feet
Both are large predators and fill an important link in the ecology in which they thrive.
40 Feet
Carnivores from every age share features that allow them to rise to the top of the food chain.

GOBLIN SHARK

Latin name: *Mitsukurina owstoni*

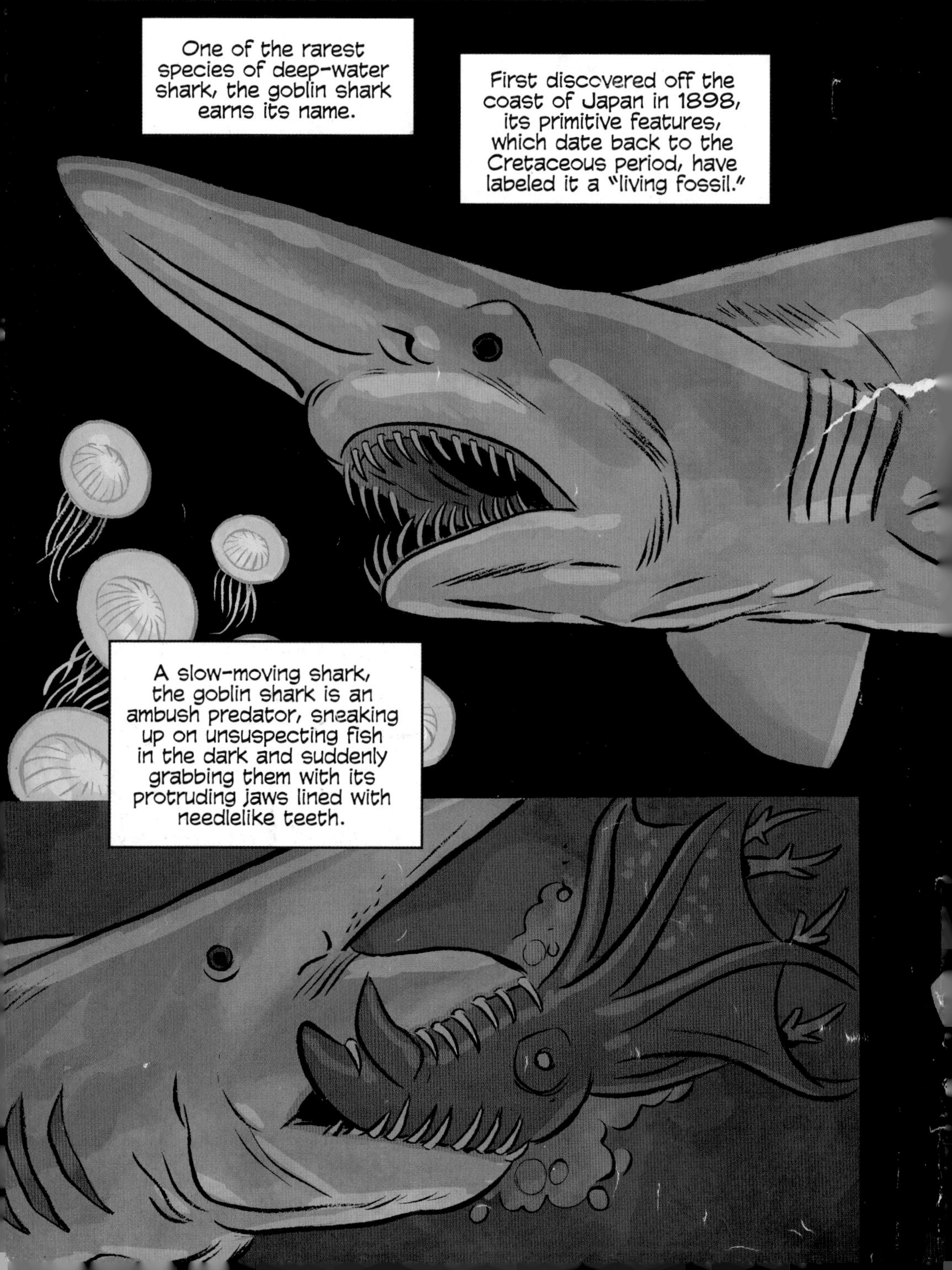
One of the rarest species of deep-water shark, the goblin shark earns its name.
First discovered off the coast of Japan in 1898, its primitive features, which date back to the Cretaceous period, have labeled it a "living fossil."
A slow-moving shark, the goblin shark is an ambush predator, sneaking up on unsuspecting fish in the dark and suddenly grabbing them with its protruding jaws lined with needlelike teeth.

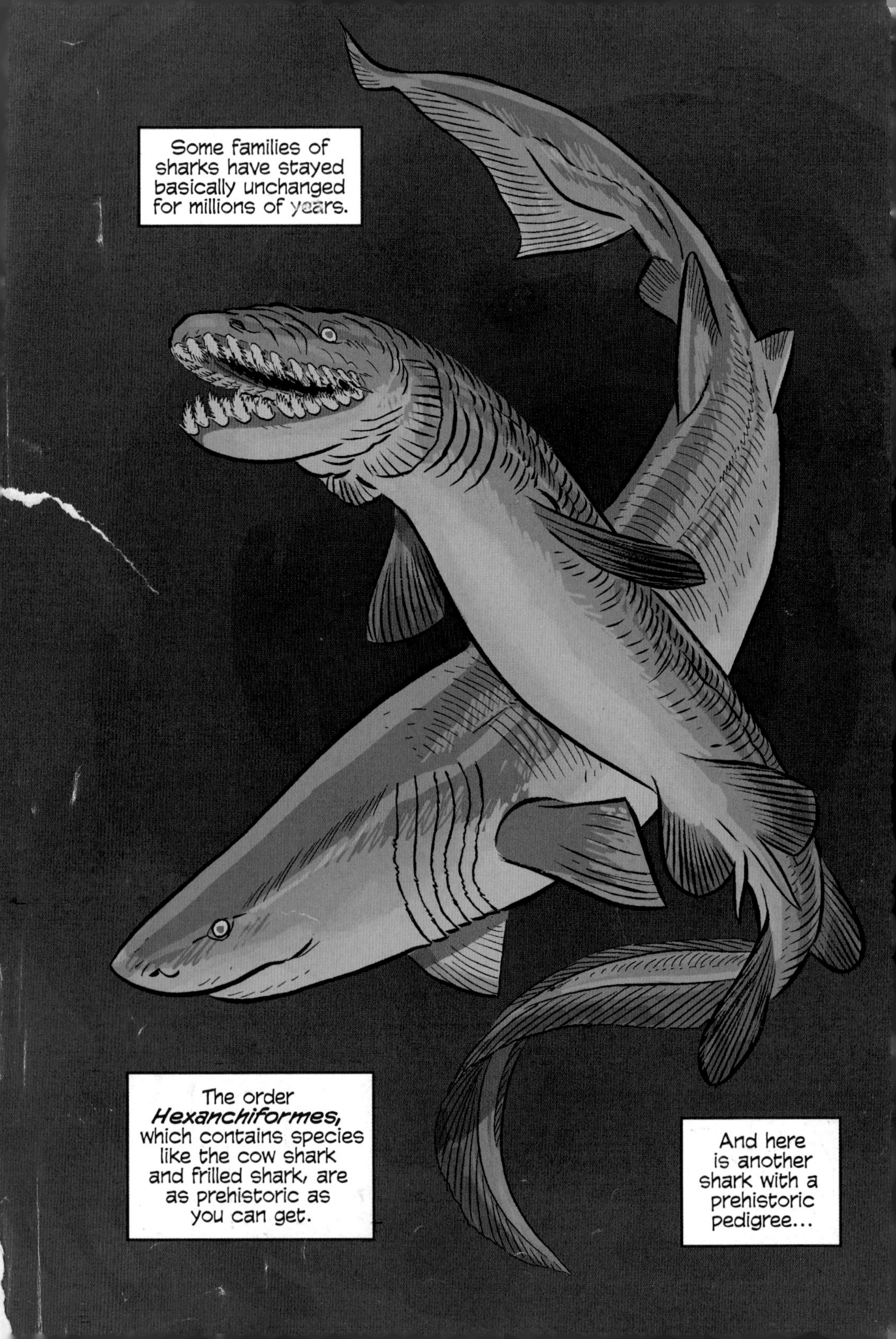
Some families of sharks have stayed basically unchanged for millions of years.
The order *Hexanchiformes,* which contains species like the cow shark and frilled shark, are as prehistoric as you can get.
And here is another shark with a prehistoric pedigree...

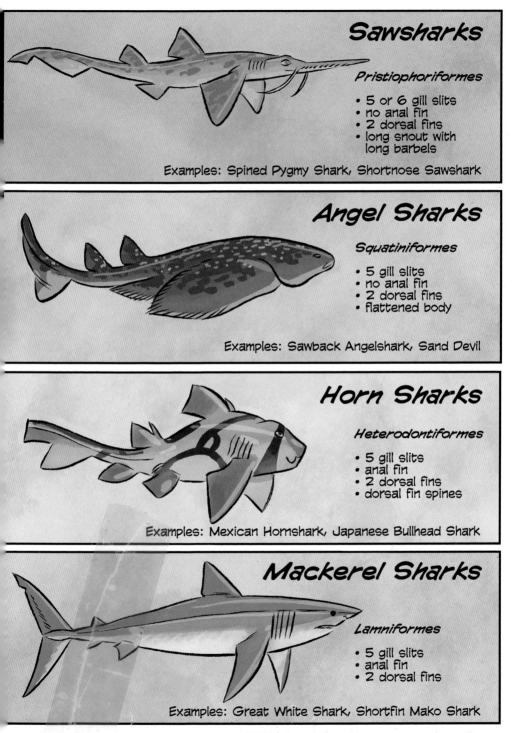

Sawsharks

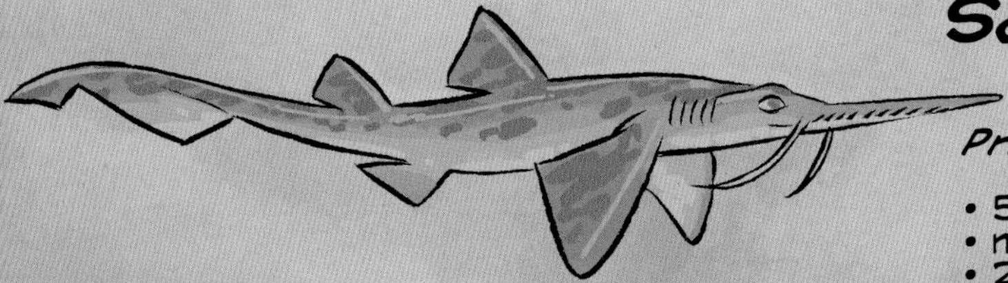

Pristiophoriformes

- 5 or 6 gill slits
- no anal fin
- 2 dorsal fins
- long snout with long barbels

Examples: Spined Pygmy Shark, Shortnose Sawshark

Angel Sharks

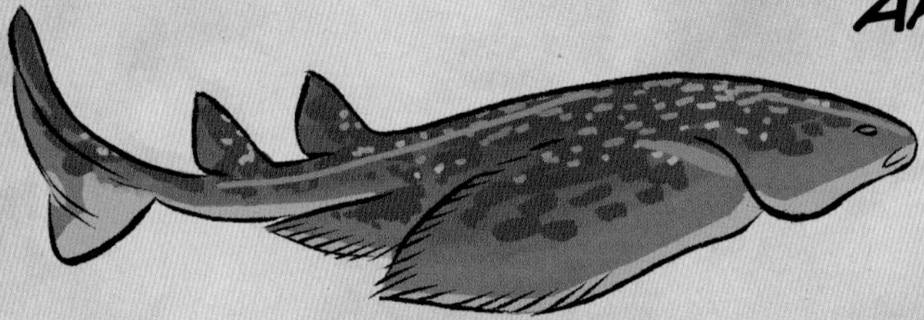

Squatiniformes

- 5 gill slits
- no anal fin
- 2 dorsal fins
- flattened body

Examples: Sawback Angelshark, Sand Devil

Horn Sharks

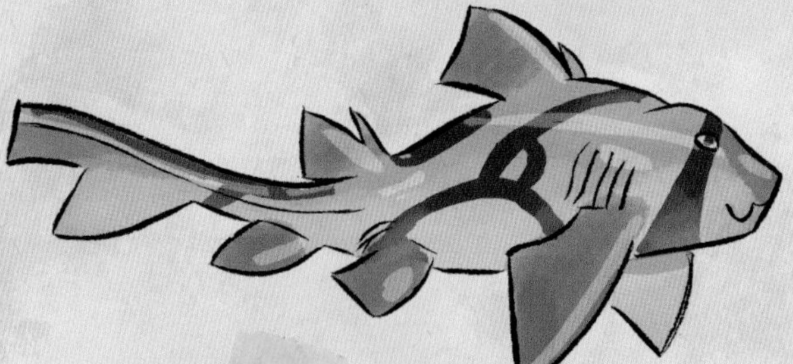

Heterodontiformes

- 5 gill slits
- anal fin
- 2 dorsal fins
- dorsal fin spines

Examples: Mexican Hornshark, Japanese Bullhead Shark

Mackerel Sharks

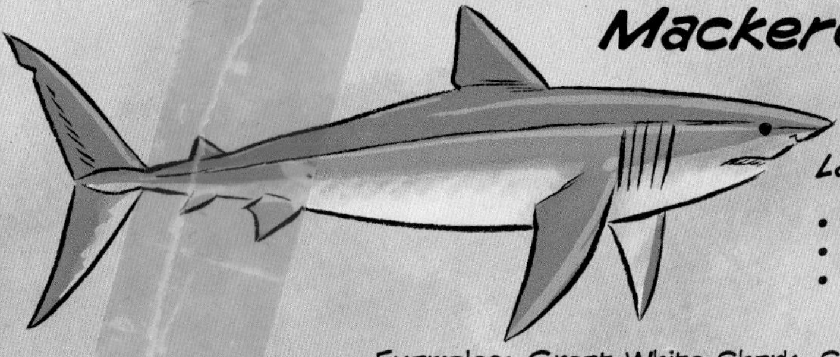

Lamniformes

- 5 gill slits
- anal fin
- 2 dorsal fins

Examples: Great White Shark, Shortfin Mako Shark

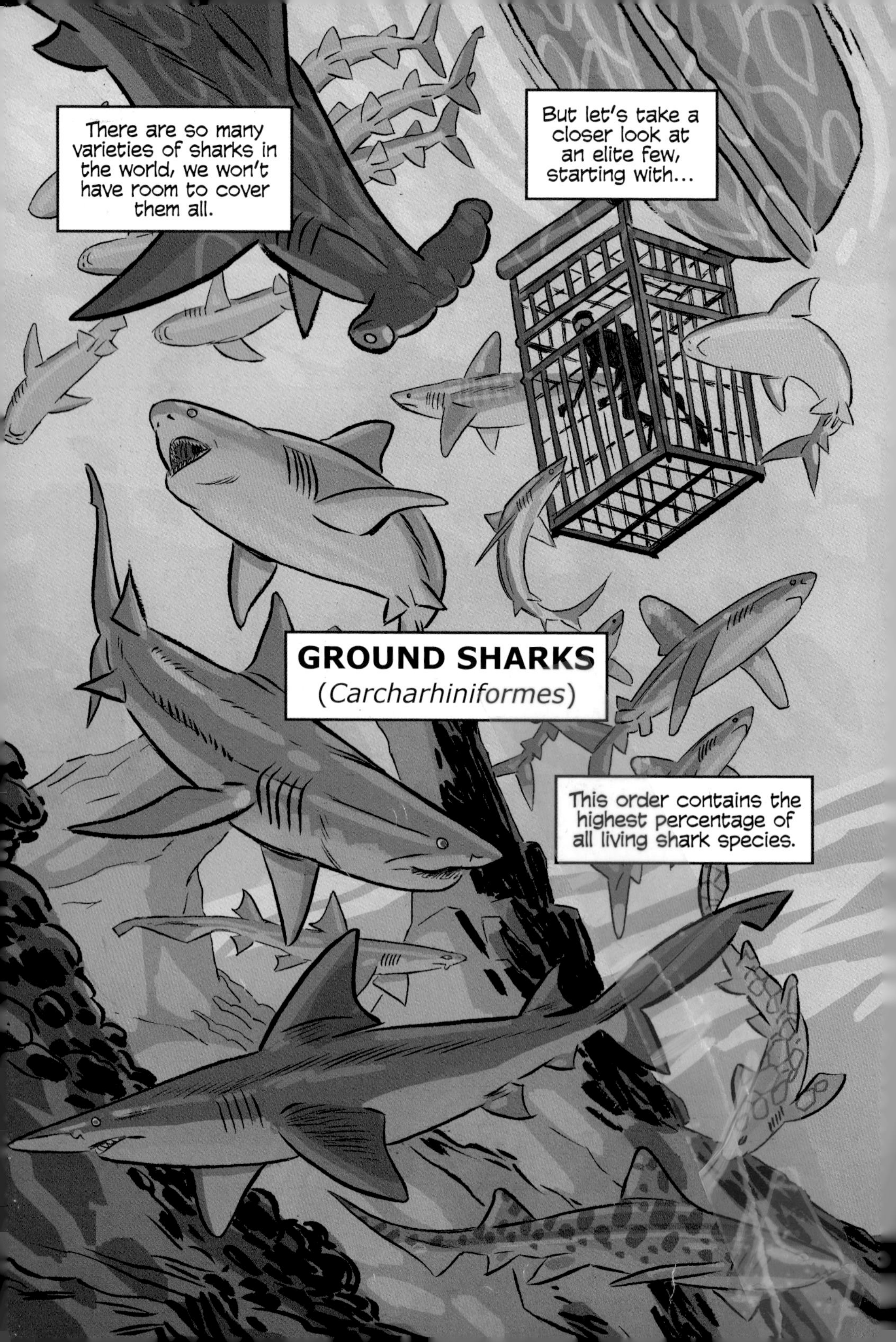
There are so many varieties of sharks in the world, we won't have room to cover them all.
But let's take a closer look at an elite few, starting with...
GROUND SHARKS
(Carcharhiniformes)
This order contains the highest percentage of all living shark species.

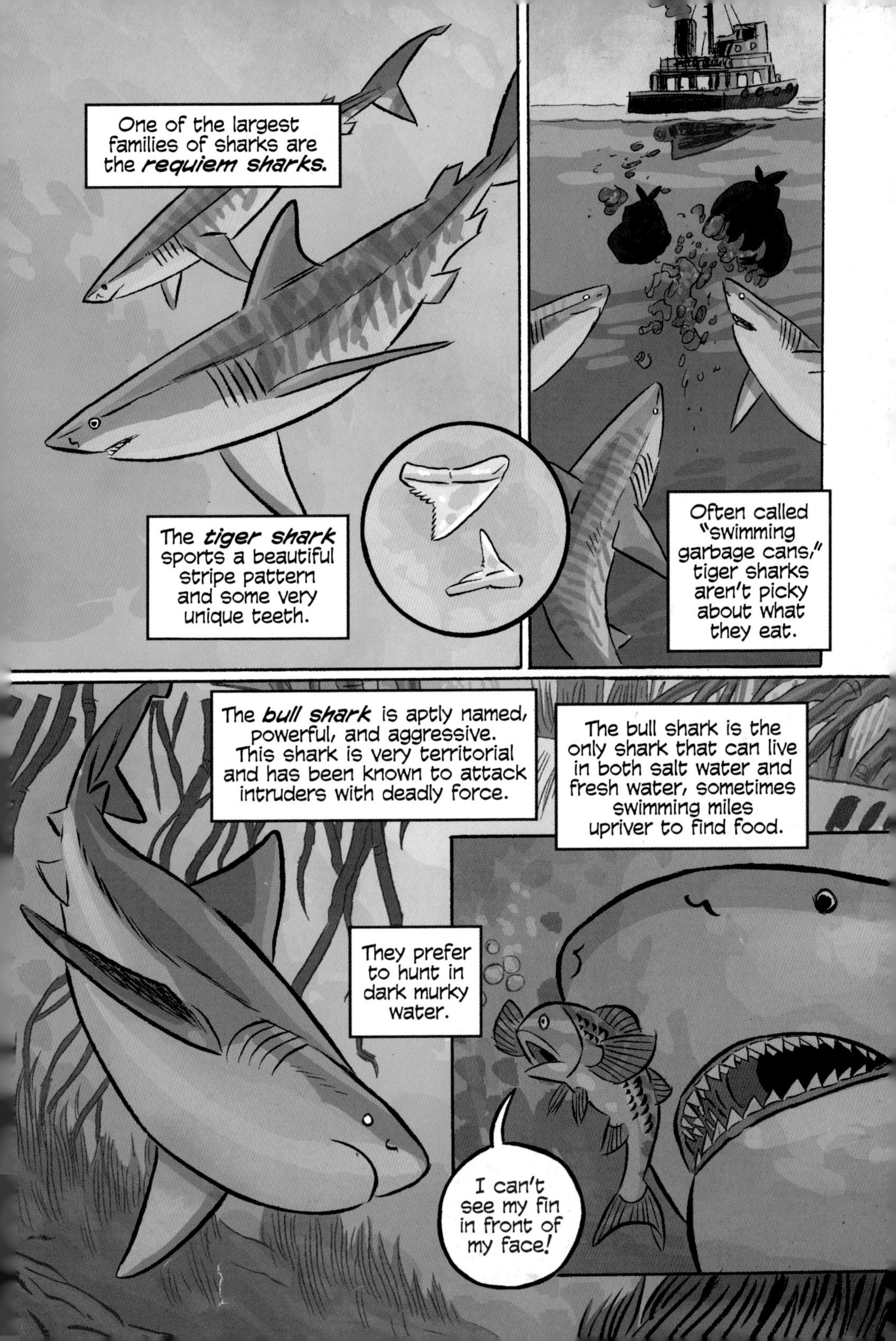

One of the largest families of sharks are the *requiem sharks.*
The *tiger shark* sports a beautiful stripe pattern and some very unique teeth.
Often called "swimming garbage cans," tiger sharks aren't picky about what they eat.
The *bull shark* is aptly named, powerful, and aggressive. This shark is very territorial and has been known to attack intruders with deadly force.
The bull shark is the only shark that can live in both salt water and fresh water, sometimes swimming miles upriver to find food.
They prefer to hunt in dark murky water.
I can't see my fin in front of my face!

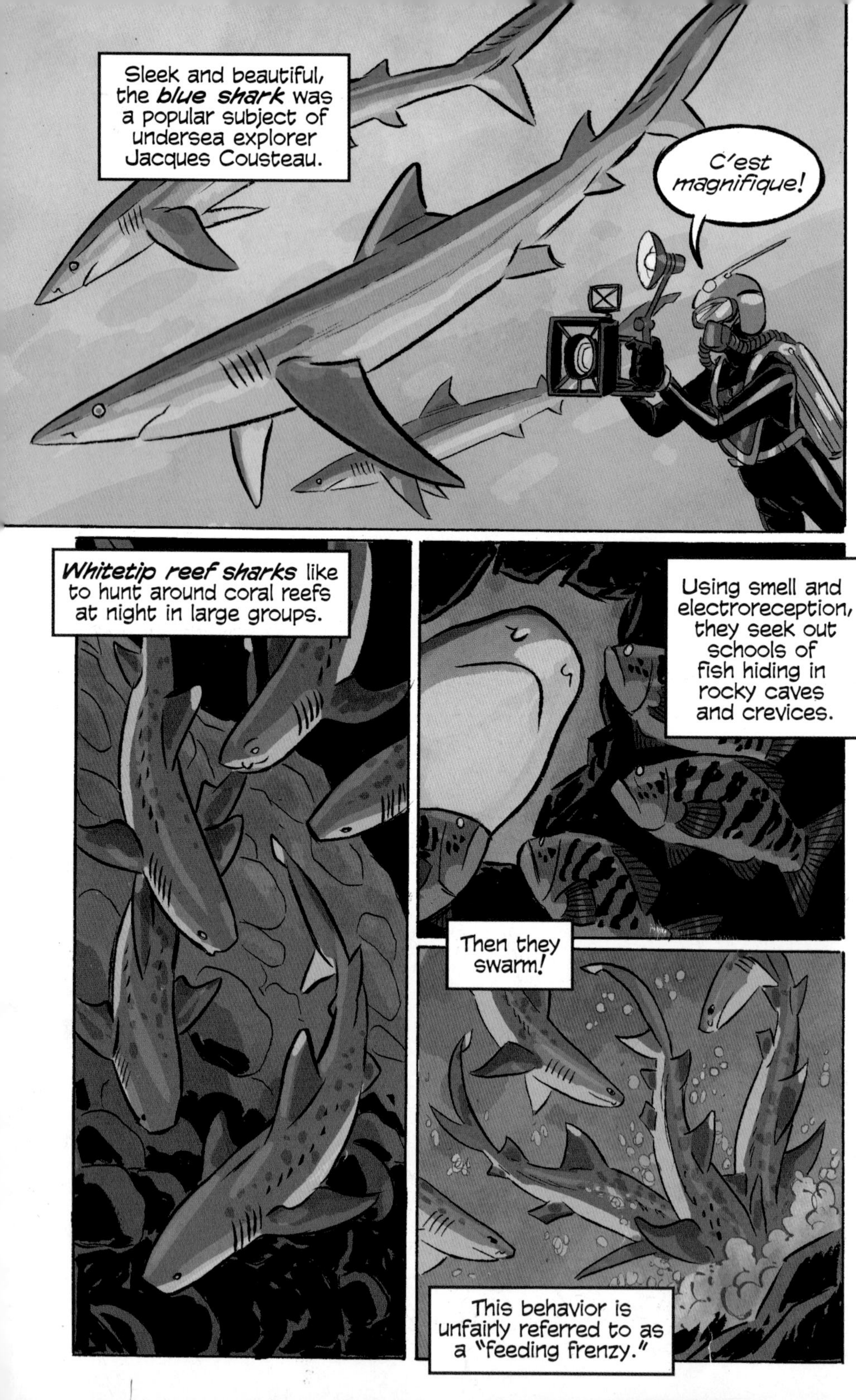
Sleek and beautiful, the *blue shark* was a popular subject of undersea explorer Jacques Cousteau.
C'est magnifique!
Whitetip reef sharks like to hunt around coral reefs at night in large groups.
Using smell and electroreception, they seek out schools of fish hiding in rocky caves and crevices.
Then they swarm!
This behavior is unfairly referred to as a "feeding frenzy."

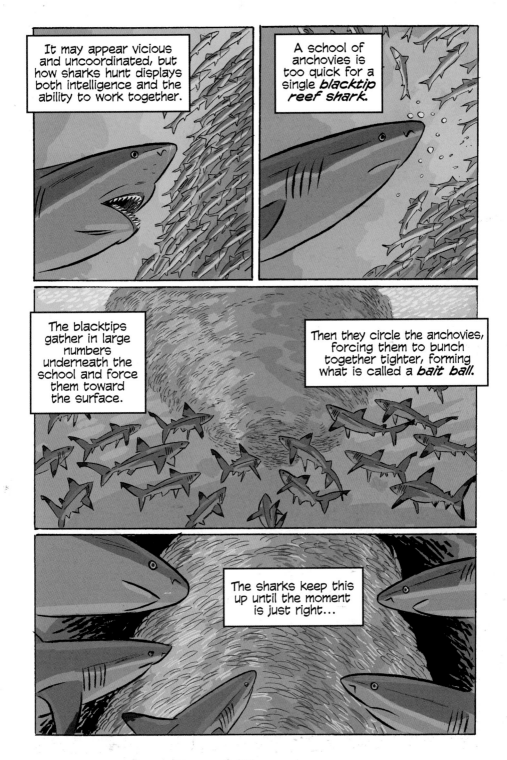

It may appear vicious and uncoordinated, but how sharks hunt displays both intelligence and the ability to work together.

A school of anchovies is too quick for a single *blacktip reef shark*.

The blacktips gather in large numbers underneath the school and force them toward the surface.

Then they circle the anchovies, forcing them to bunch together tighter, forming what is called a *bait ball*.

The sharks keep this up until the moment is just right...

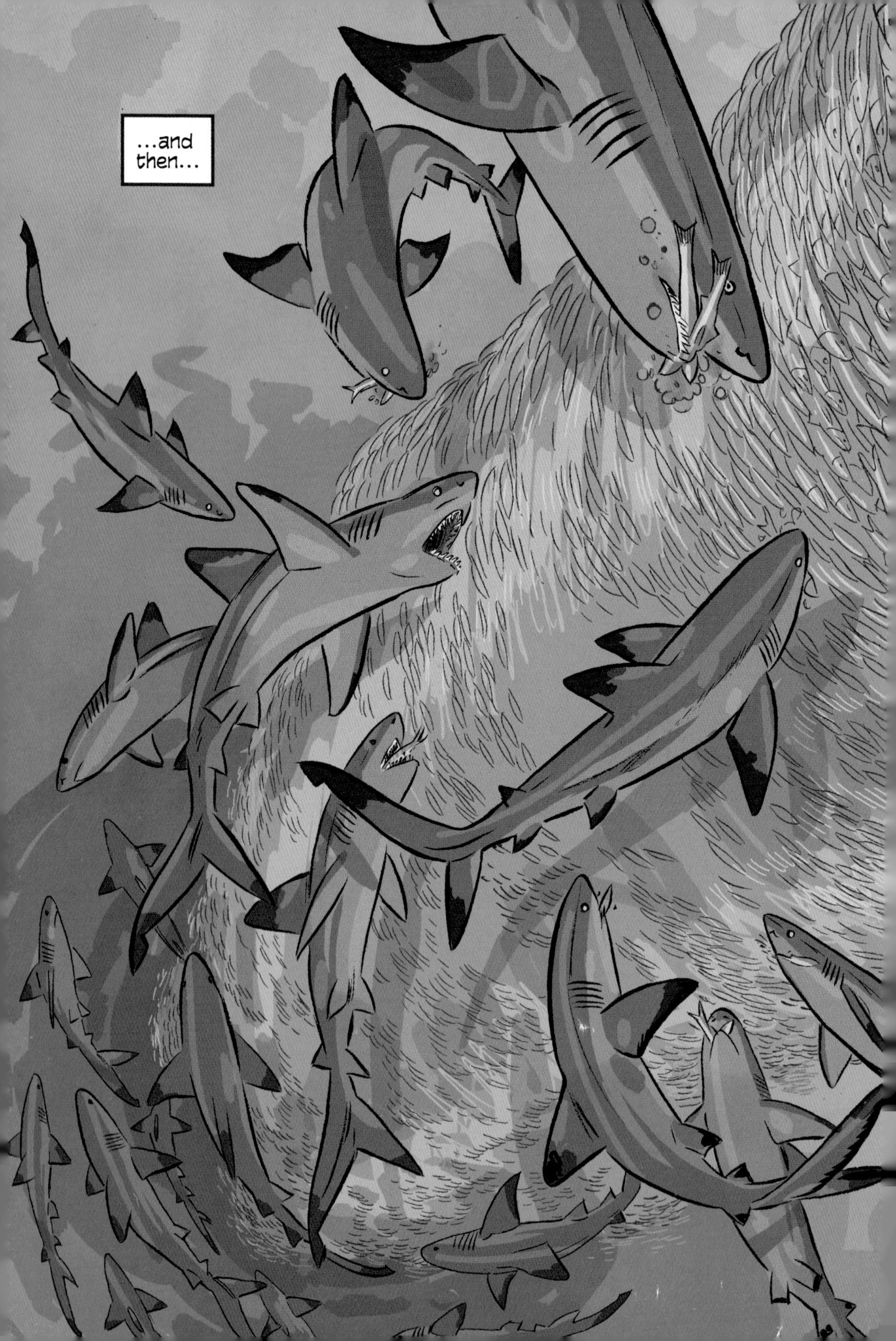
...and then...

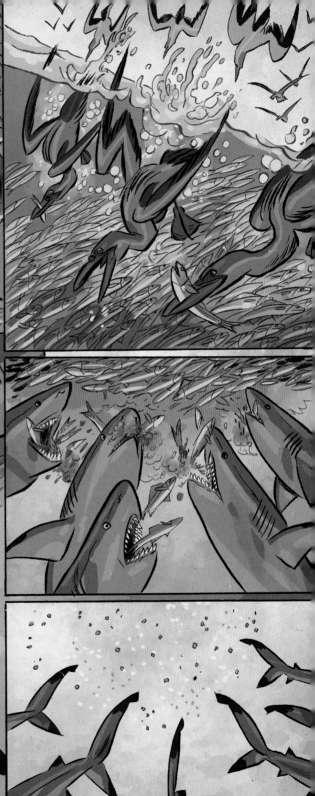

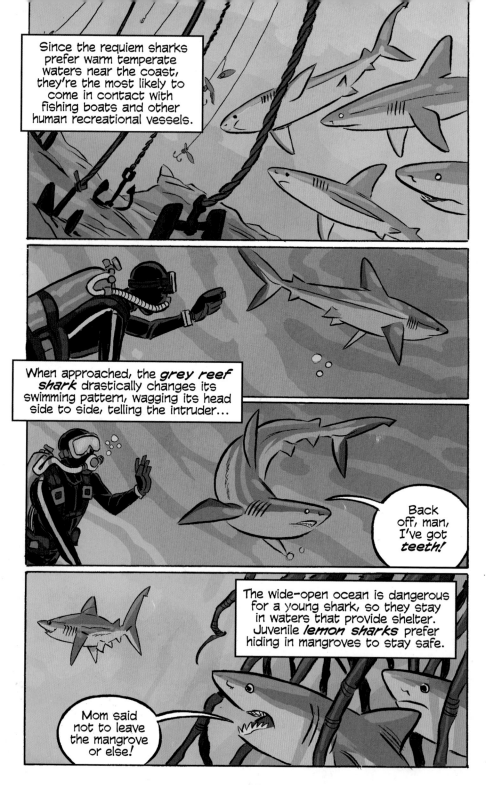

Since the requiem sharks prefer warm temperate waters near the coast, they're the most likely to come in contact with fishing boats and other human recreational vessels.

When approached, the *grey reef shark* drastically changes its swimming pattern, wagging its head side to side, telling the intruder...

Back off, man, I've got *teeth!*

The wide-open ocean is dangerous for a young shark, so they stay in waters that provide shelter. Juvenile *lemon sharks* prefer hiding in mangroves to stay safe.

Mom said not to leave the mangrove or else!

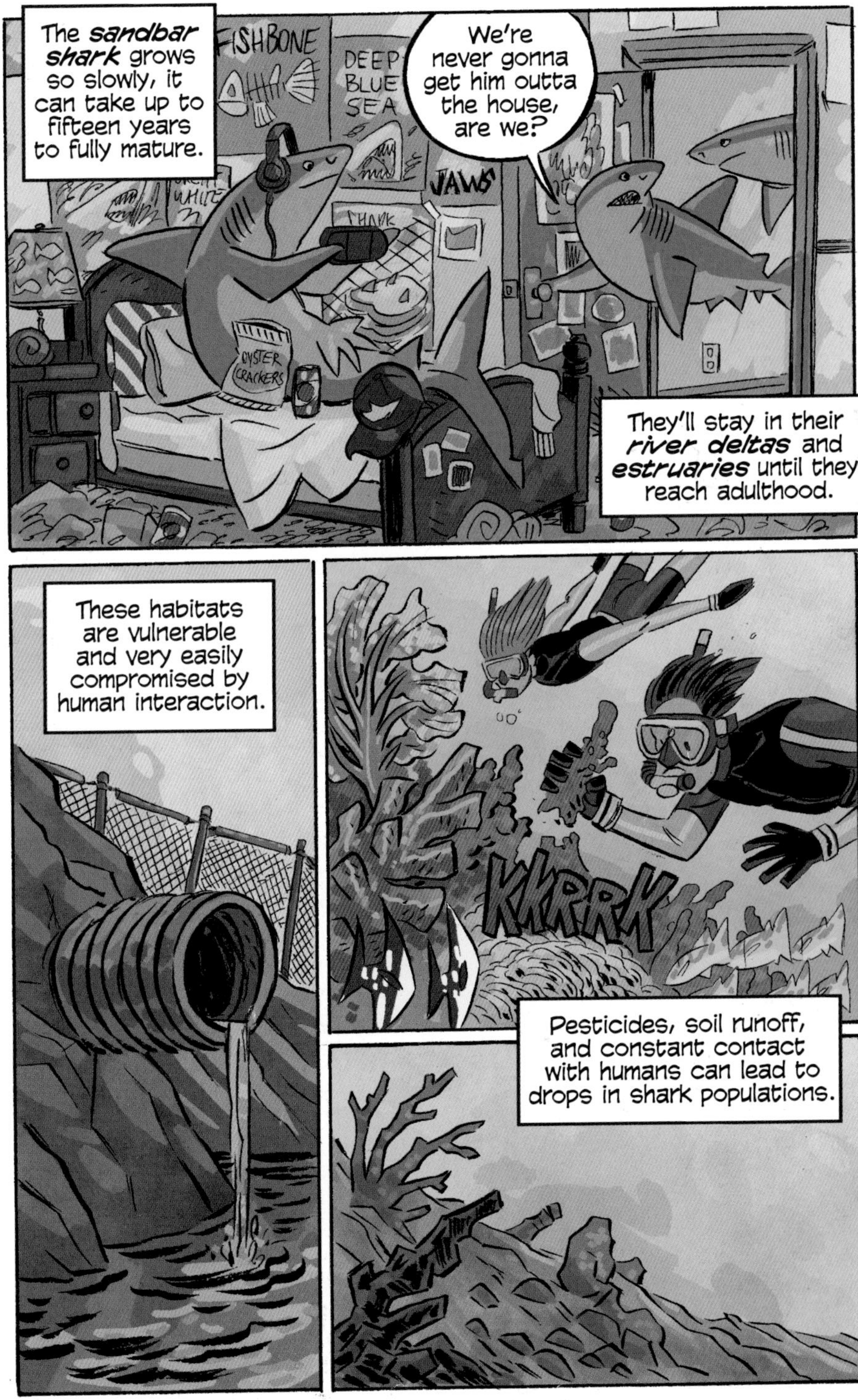
The *sandbar shark* grows so slowly, it can take up to fifteen years to fully mature.
FISHBONE
DEEP BLUE SEA
We're never gonna get him outta the house, are we?
JAWS
OYSTER CRACKERS
They'll stay in their *river deltas* and *estruaries* until they reach adulthood.
These habitats are vulnerable and very easily compromised by human interaction.
KKRRK
Pesticides, soil runoff, and constant contact with humans can lead to drops in shark populations.

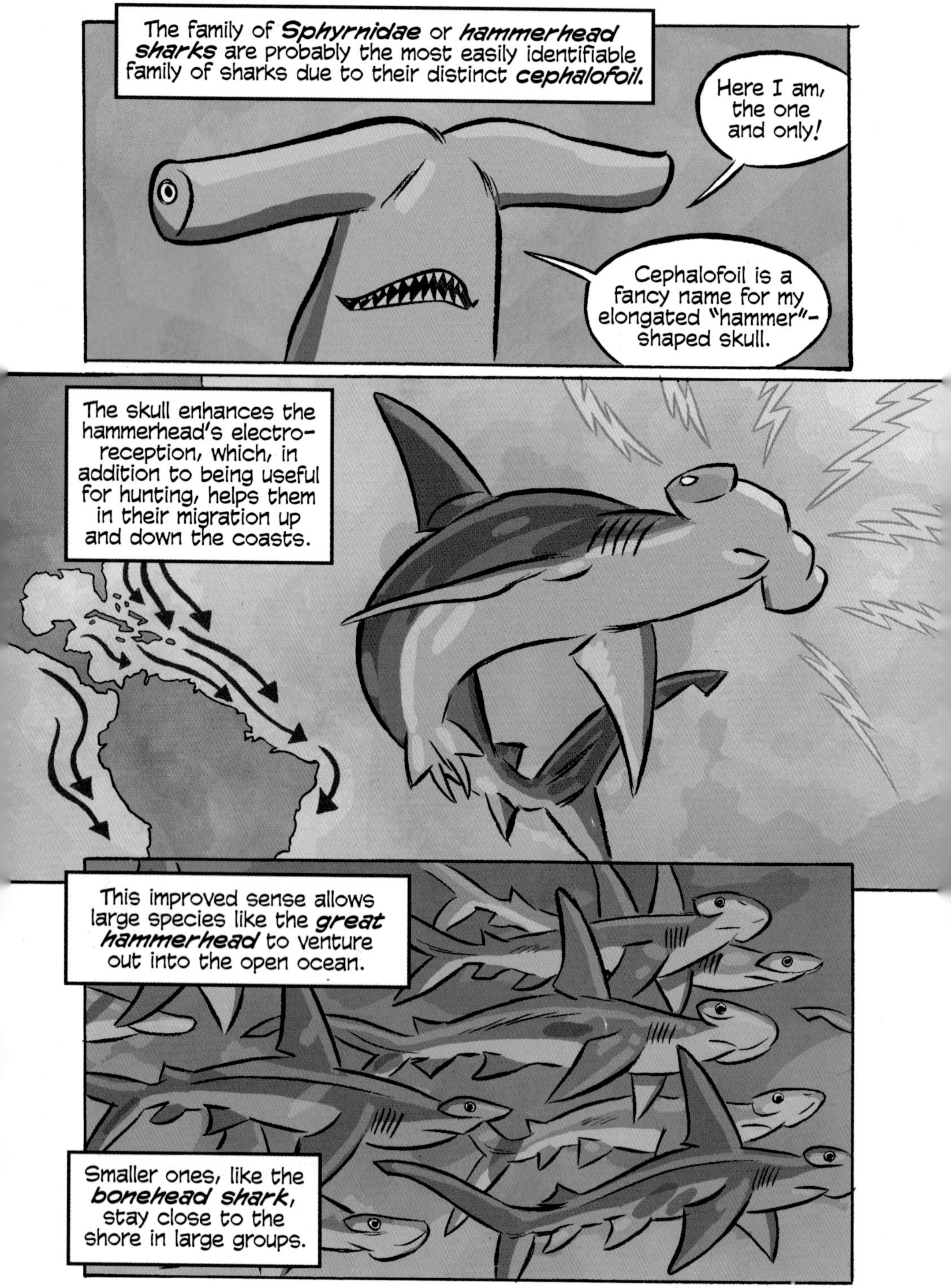

The family of *Sphyrnidae* or *hammerhead sharks* are probably the most easily identifiable family of sharks due to their distinct *cephalofoil.*
Here I am, the one and only!
Cephalofoil is a fancy name for my elongated "hammer"-shaped skull.
The skull enhances the hammerhead's electroreception, which, in addition to being useful for hunting, helps them in their migration up and down the coasts.
This improved sense allows large species like the *great hammerhead* to venture out into the open ocean.
Smaller ones, like the *bonehead shark*, stay close to the shore in large groups.

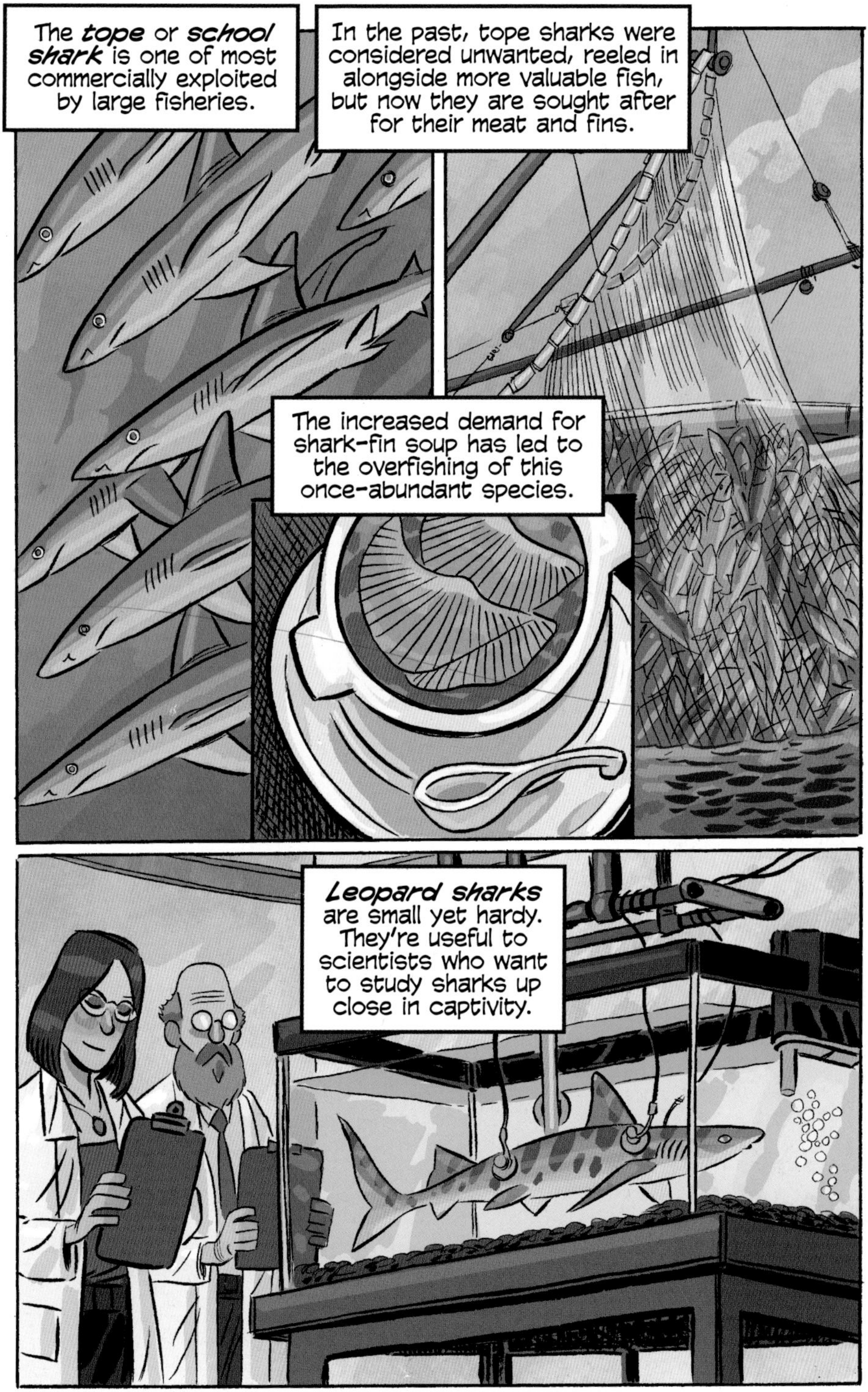
The *tope* or *school shark* is one of most commercially exploited by large fisheries.
In the past, tope sharks were considered unwanted, reeled in alongside more valuable fish, but now they are sought after for their meat and fins.
The increased demand for shark-fin soup has led to the overfishing of this once-abundant species.
Leopard sharks are small yet hardy. They're useful to scientists who want to study sharks up close in captivity.

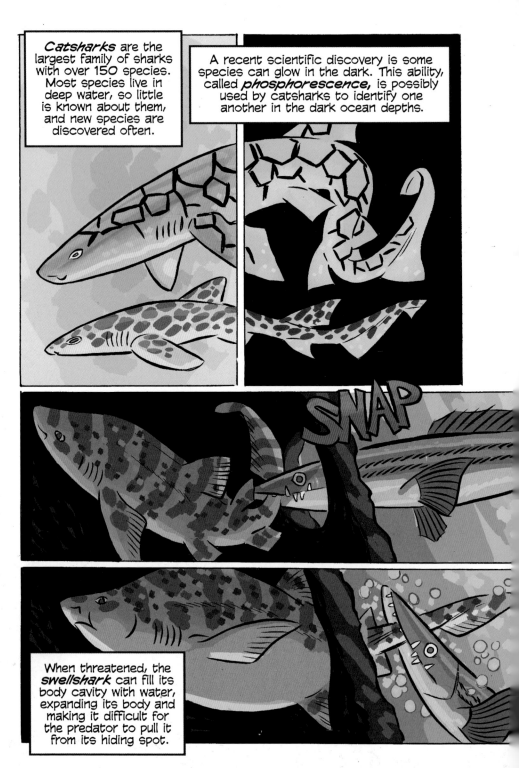

Catsharks are the largest family of sharks with over 150 species. Most species live in deep water, so little is known about them, and new species are discovered often.

A recent scientific discovery is some species can glow in the dark. This ability, called *phosphorescence,* is possibly used by catsharks to identify one another in the dark ocean depths.

SNAP

When threatened, the *swellshark* can fill its body cavity with water, expanding its body and making it difficult for the predator to pull it from its hiding spot.

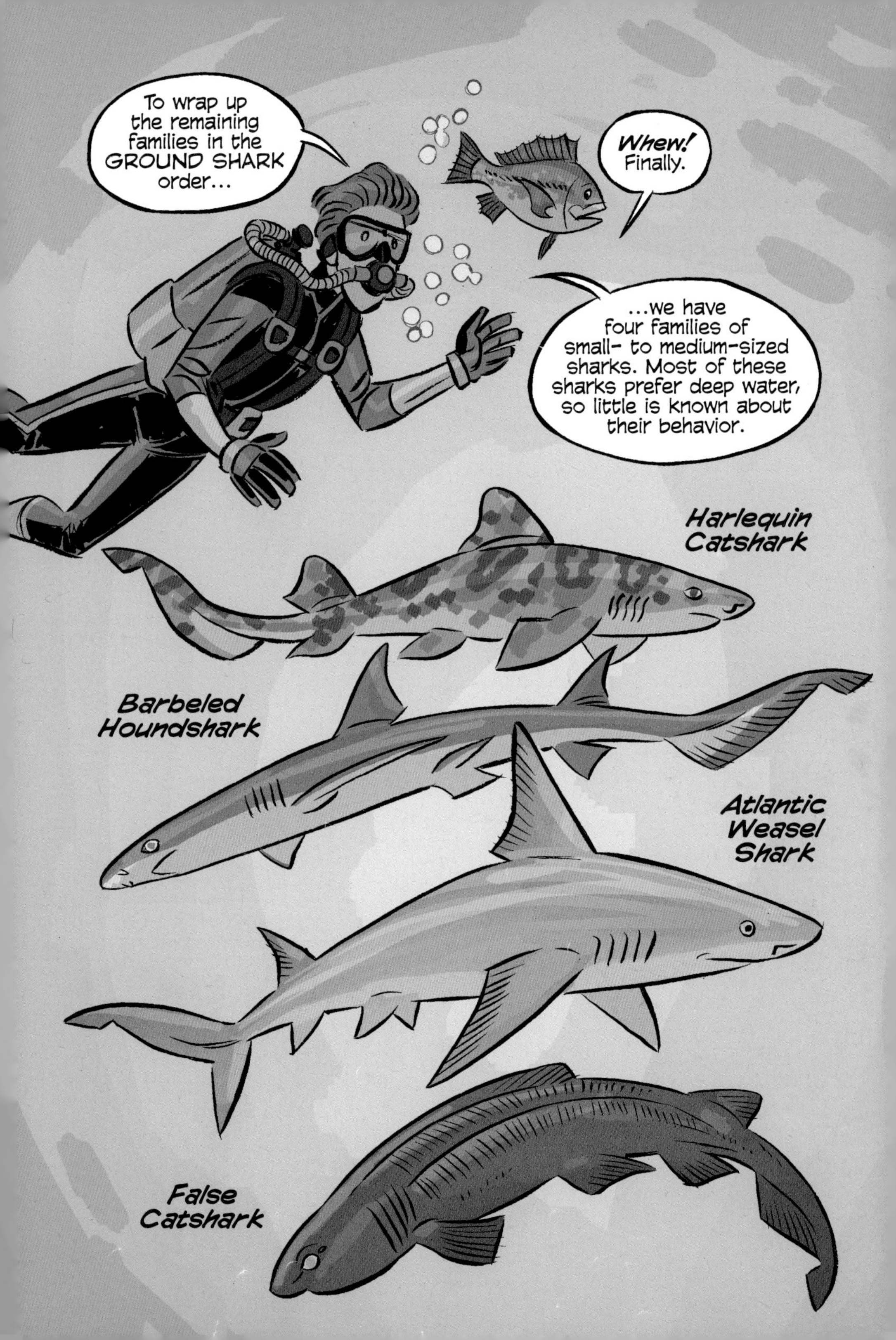
To wrap up the remaining families in the GROUND SHARK order...
Whew! Finally.
...we have four families of small- to medium-sized sharks. Most of these sharks prefer deep water, so little is known about their behavior.
Harlequin Catshark
Barbeled Houndshark
Atlantic Weasel Shark
False Catshark

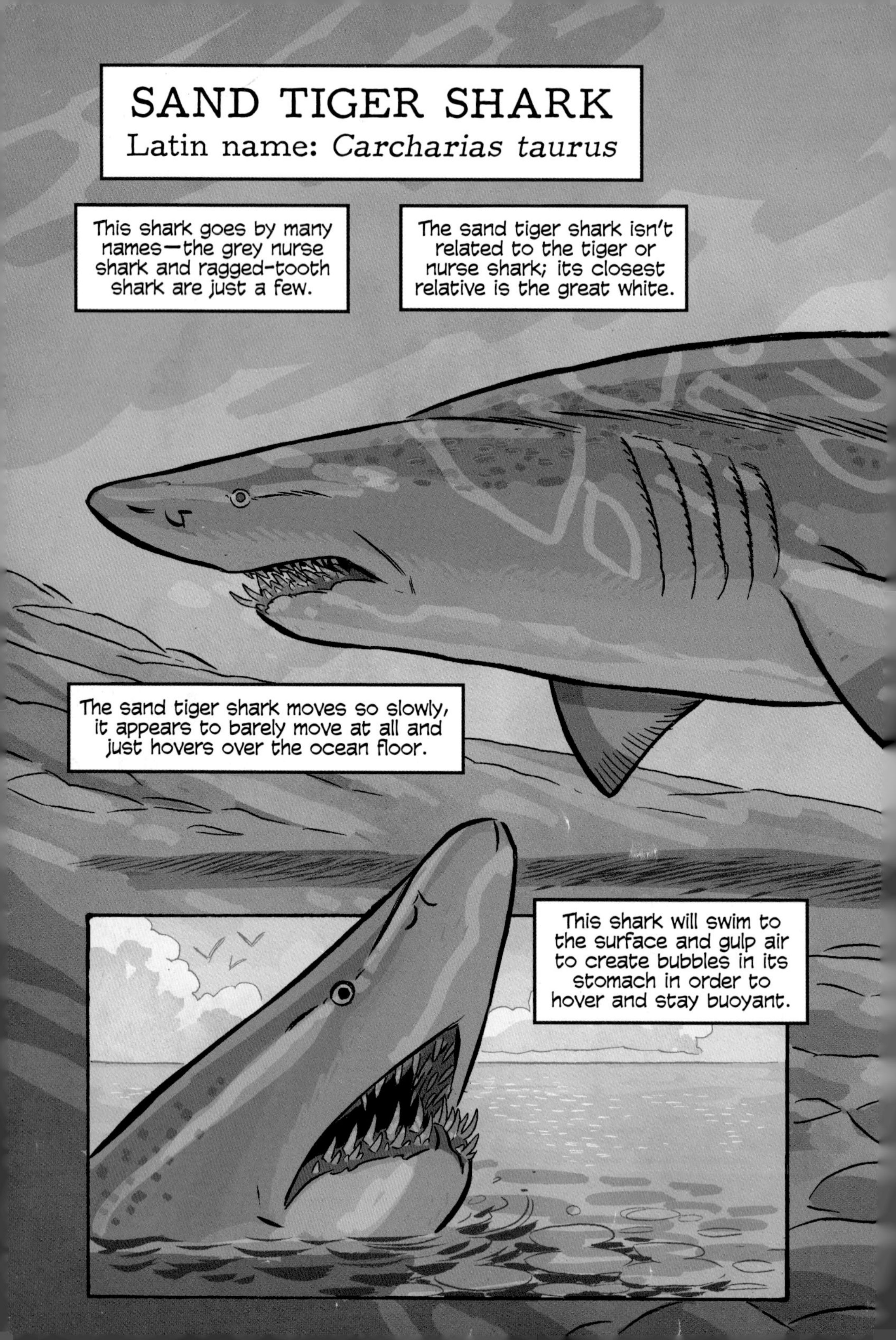
SAND TIGER SHARK
Latin name: *Carcharias taurus*
This shark goes by many names—the grey nurse shark and ragged-tooth shark are just a few.
The sand tiger shark isn't related to the tiger or nurse shark; its closest relative is the great white.
The sand tiger shark moves so slowly, it appears to barely move at all and just hovers over the ocean floor.
This shark will swim to the surface and gulp air to create bubbles in its stomach in order to hover and stay buoyant.

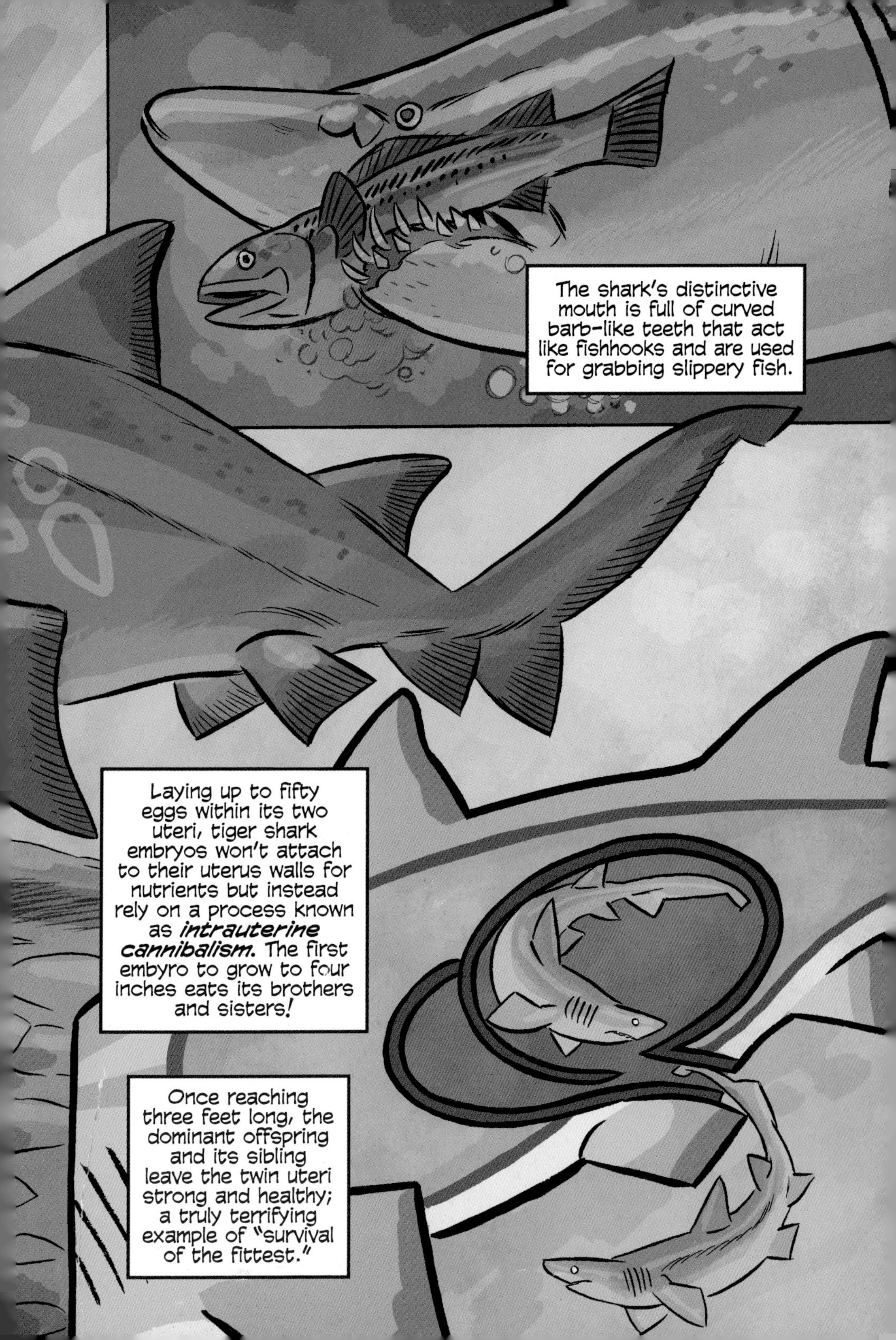
The shark's distinctive mouth is full of curved barb-like teeth that act like fishhooks and are used for grabbing slippery fish.
Laying up to fifty eggs within its two uteri, tiger shark embryos won't attach to their uterus walls for nutrients but instead rely on a process known as *intrauterine cannibalism.* The first embyro to grow to four inches eats its brothers and sisters!
Once reaching three feet long, the dominant offspring and its sibling leave the twin uteri strong and healthy; a truly terrifying example of "survival of the fittest."

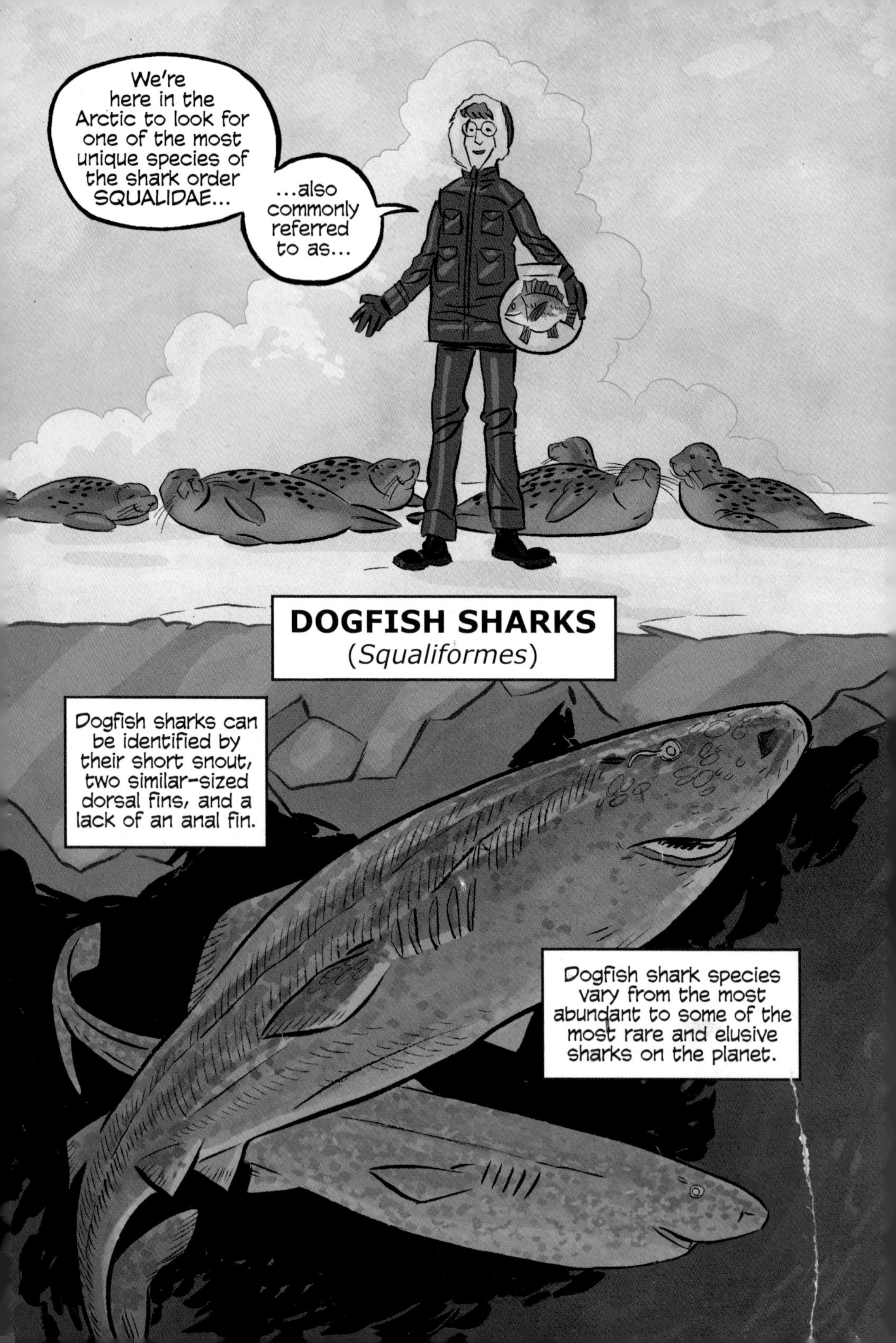
We're here in the Arctic to look for one of the most unique species of the shark order SQUALIDAE...
...also commonly referred to as...
DOGFISH SHARKS
(Squaliformes)
Dogfish sharks can be identified by their short snout, two similar-sized dorsal fins, and a lack of an anal fin.
Dogfish shark species vary from the most abundant to some of the most rare and elusive sharks on the planet.

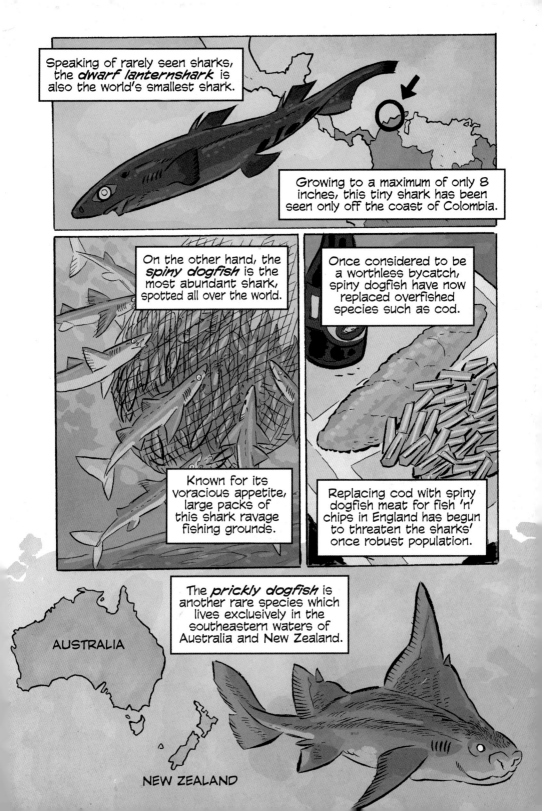

Speaking of rarely seen sharks, the *dwarf lanternshark* is also the world's smallest shark.

Growing to a maximum of only 8 inches, this tiny shark has been seen only off the coast of Colombia.

On the other hand, the *spiny dogfish* is the most abundant shark, spotted all over the world.

Once considered to be a worthless bycatch, spiny dogfish have now replaced overfished species such as cod.

Known for its voracious appetite, large packs of this shark ravage fishing grounds.

Replacing cod with spiny dogfish meat for fish 'n' chips in England has begun to threaten the sharks' once robust population.

The *prickly dogfish* is another rare species which lives exclusively in the southeastern waters of Australia and New Zealand.

AUSTRALIA

NEW ZEALAND

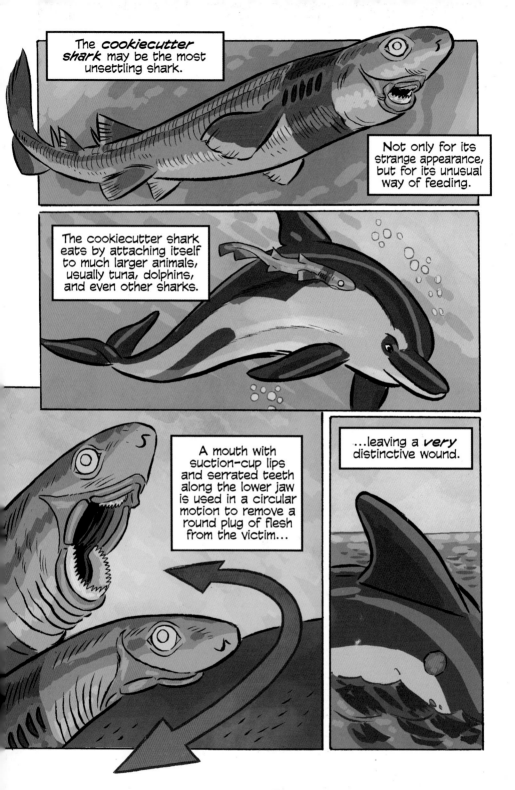

The *cookiecutter shark* may be the most unsettling shark.

Not only for its strange appearance, but for its unusual way of feeding.

The cookiecutter shark eats by attaching itself to much larger animals, usually tuna, dolphins, and even other sharks.

A mouth with suction-cup lips and serrated teeth along the lower jaw is used in a circular motion to remove a round plug of flesh from the victim...

...leaving a *very* distinctive wound.

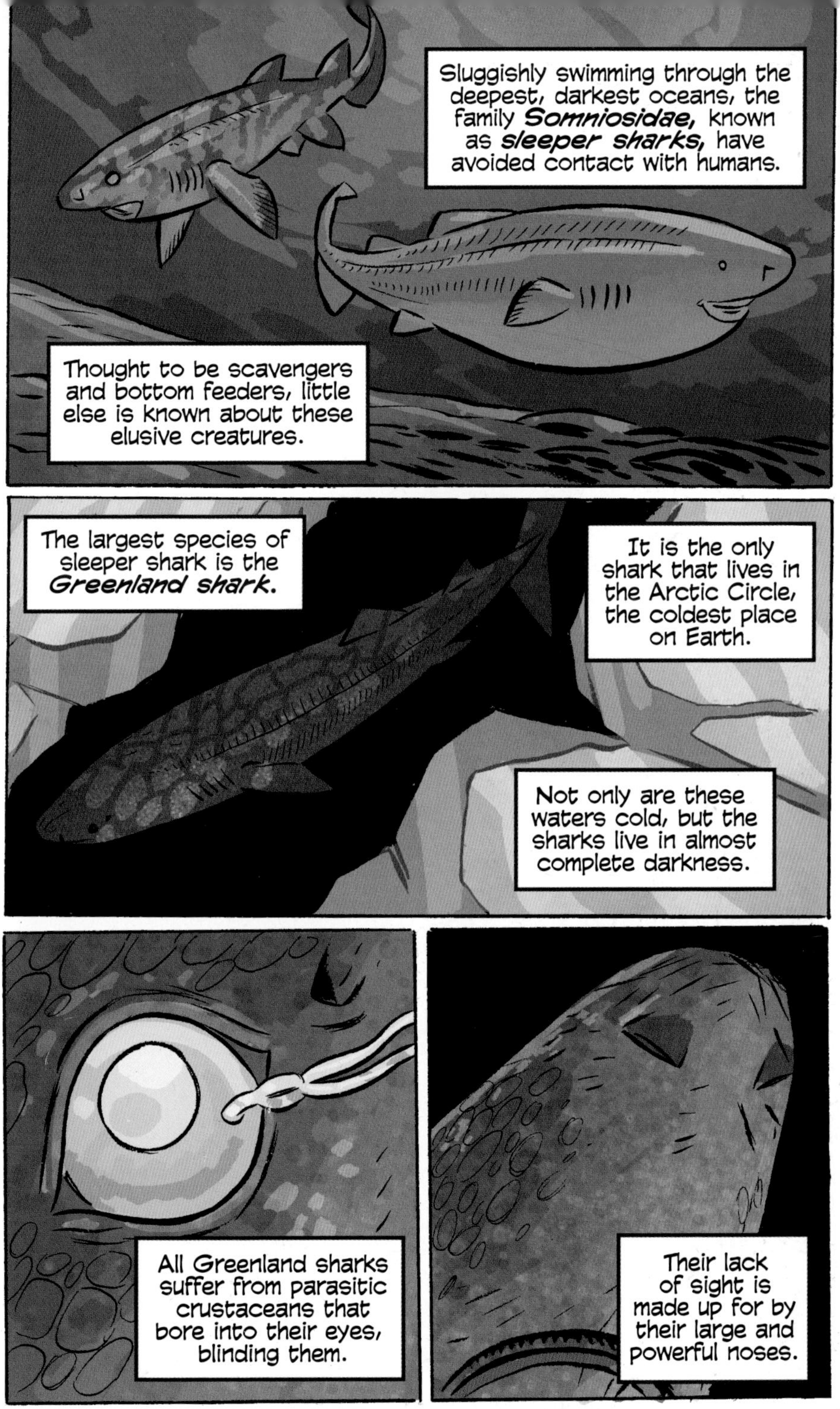
Sluggishly swimming through the deepest, darkest oceans, the family *Somniosidae,* known as *sleeper sharks,* have avoided contact with humans.
Thought to be scavengers and bottom feeders, little else is known about these elusive creatures.
The largest species of sleeper shark is the *Greenland shark*.
It is the only shark that lives in the Arctic Circle, the coldest place on Earth.
Not only are these waters cold, but the sharks live in almost complete darkness.
All Greenland sharks suffer from parasitic crustaceans that bore into their eyes, blinding them.
Their lack of sight is made up for by their large and powerful noses.

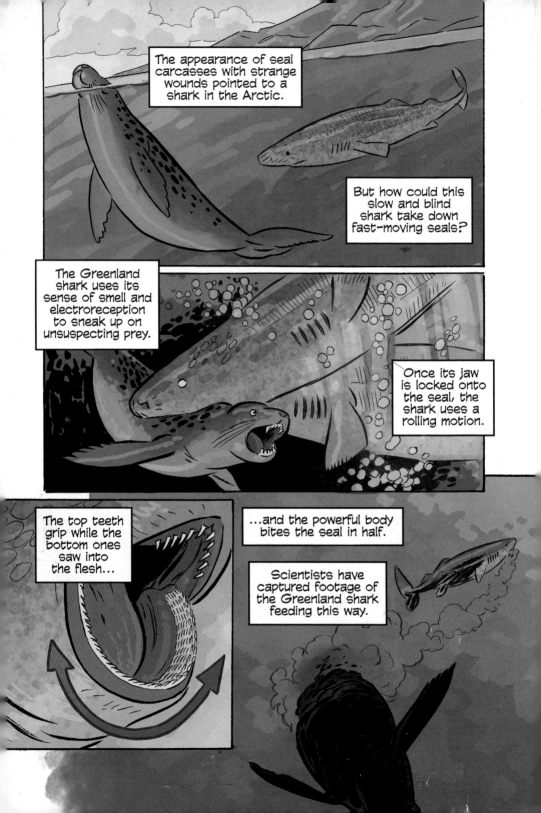

The appearance of seal carcasses with strange wounds pointed to a shark in the Arctic.

But how could this slow and blind shark take down fast-moving seals?

The Greenland shark uses its sense of smell and electroreception to sneak up on unsuspecting prey.

Once its jaw is locked onto the seal, the shark uses a rolling motion.

The top teeth grip while the bottom ones saw into the flesh...

...and the powerful body bites the seal in half.

Scientists have captured footage of the Greenland shark feeding this way.

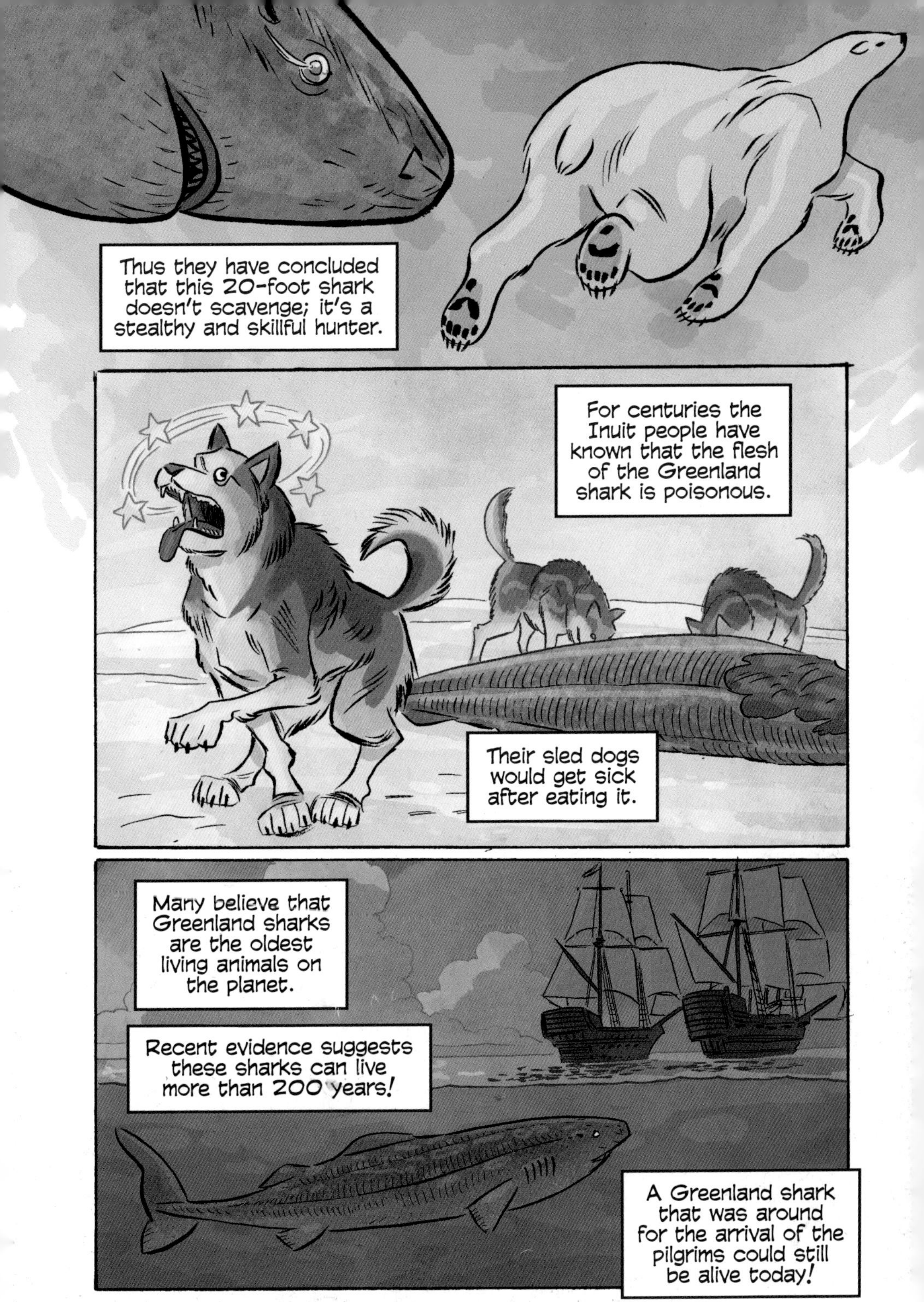
Thus they have concluded that this 20-foot shark doesn't scavenge; it's a stealthy and skillful hunter.
For centuries the Inuit people have known that the flesh of the Greenland shark is poisonous.
Their sled dogs would get sick after eating it.
Many believe that Greenland sharks are the oldest living animals on the planet.
Recent evidence suggests these sharks can live more than 200 years!
A Greenland shark that was around for the arrival of the pilgrims could still be alive today!

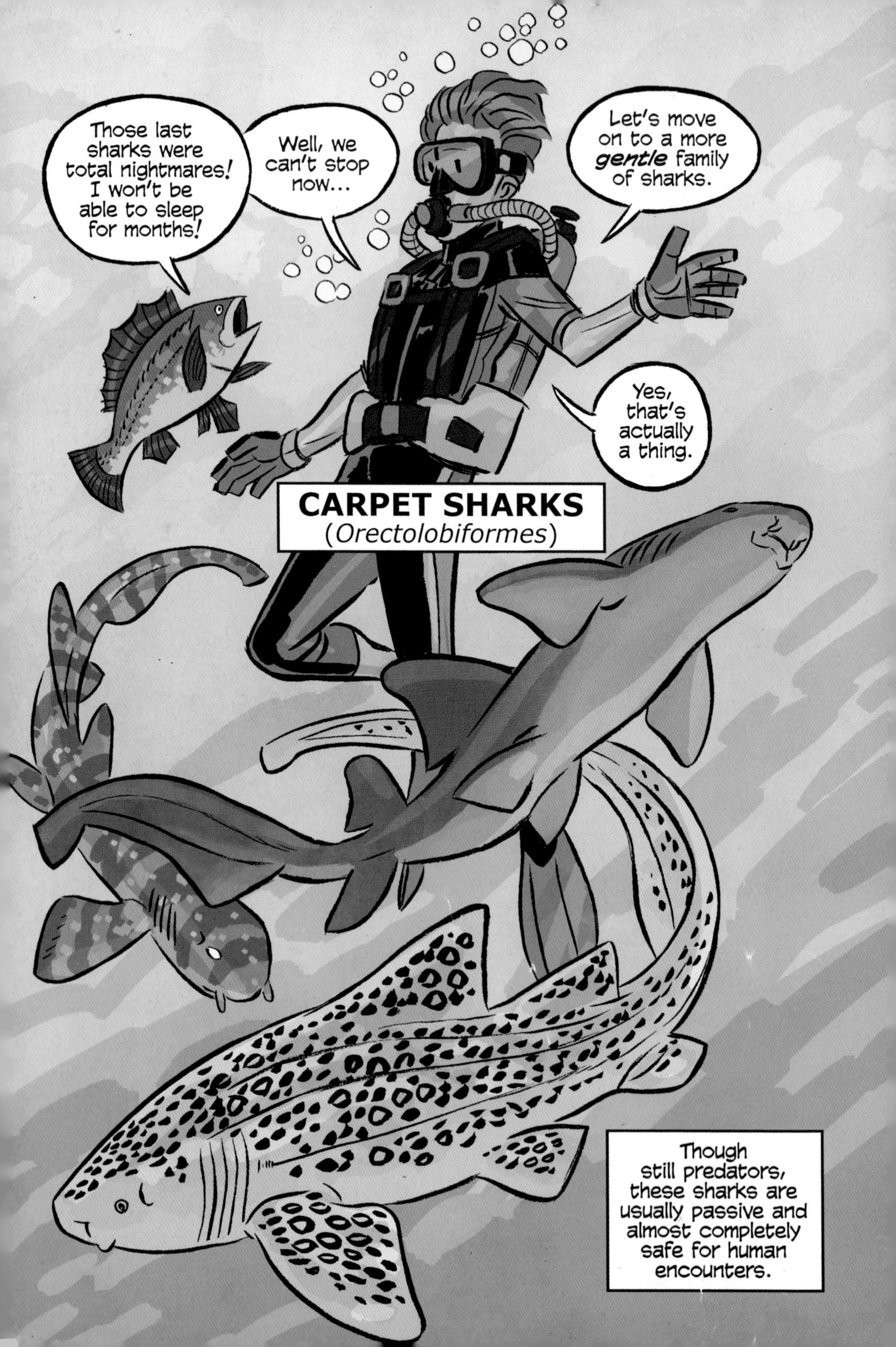
Those last sharks were total nightmares! I won't be able to sleep for months!
Well, we can't stop now...
Let's move on to a more gentle family of sharks.
Yes, that's actually a thing.
CARPET SHARKS (Orectolobiformes)
Though still predators, these sharks are usually passive and almost completely safe for human encounters.

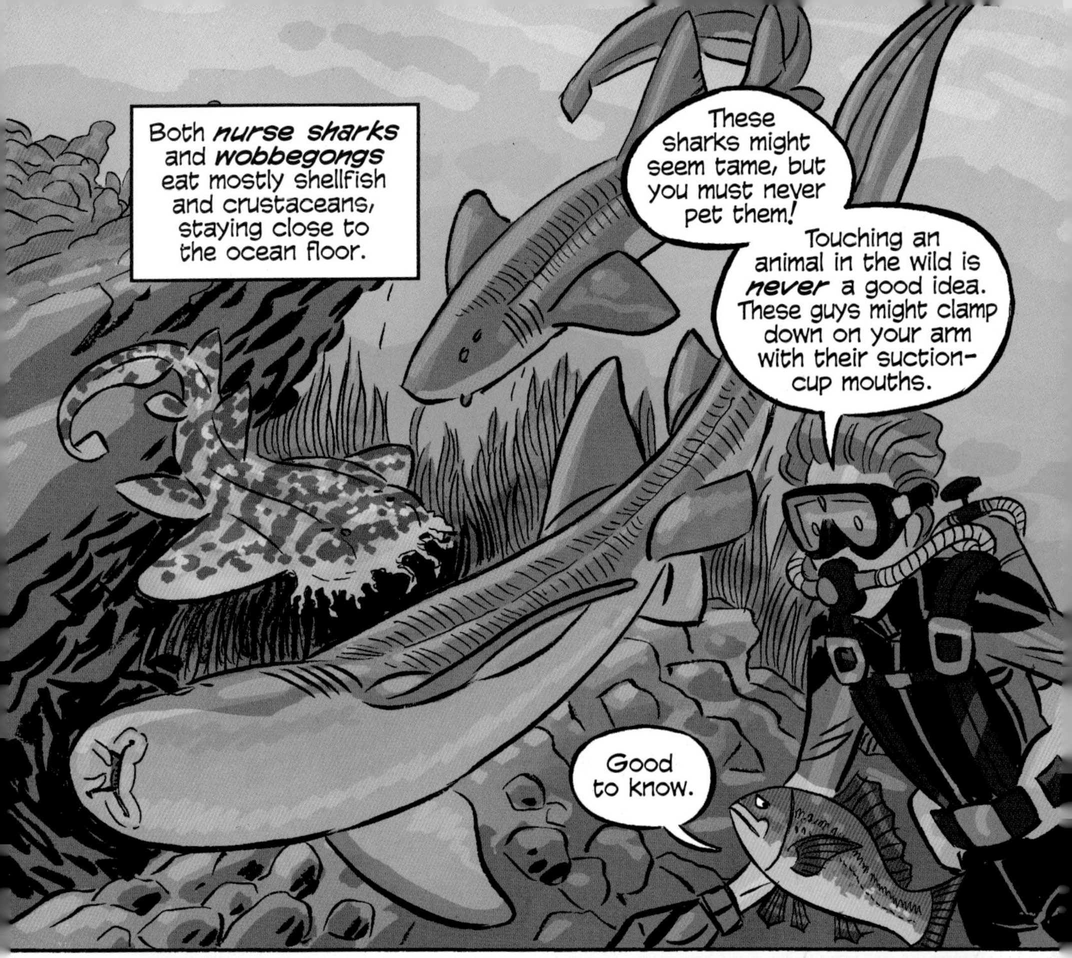
Both ***nurse sharks*** and ***wobbegongs*** eat mostly shellfish and crustaceans, staying close to the ocean floor.
These sharks might seem tame, but you must never pet them!
Touching an animal in the wild is ***never*** a good idea. These guys might clamp down on your arm with their suction-cup mouths.
Good to know.

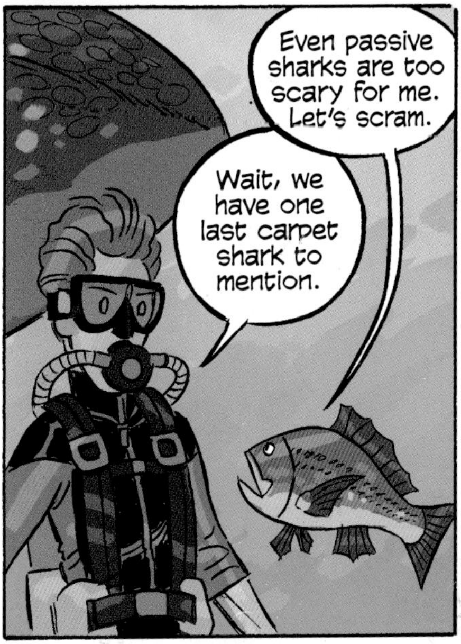
Even passive sharks are too scary for me. Let's scram.
Wait, we have one last carpet shark to mention.

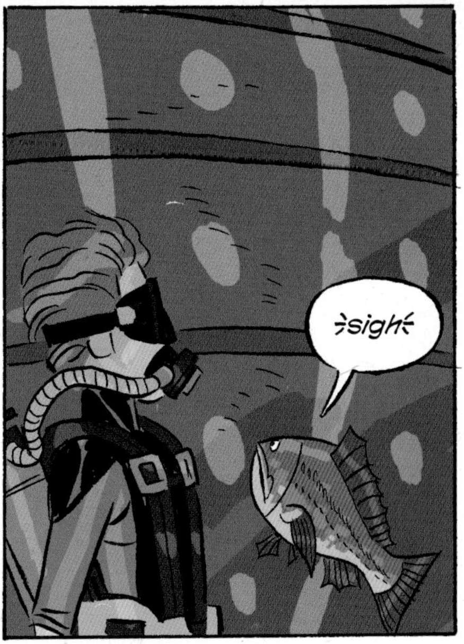
sigh

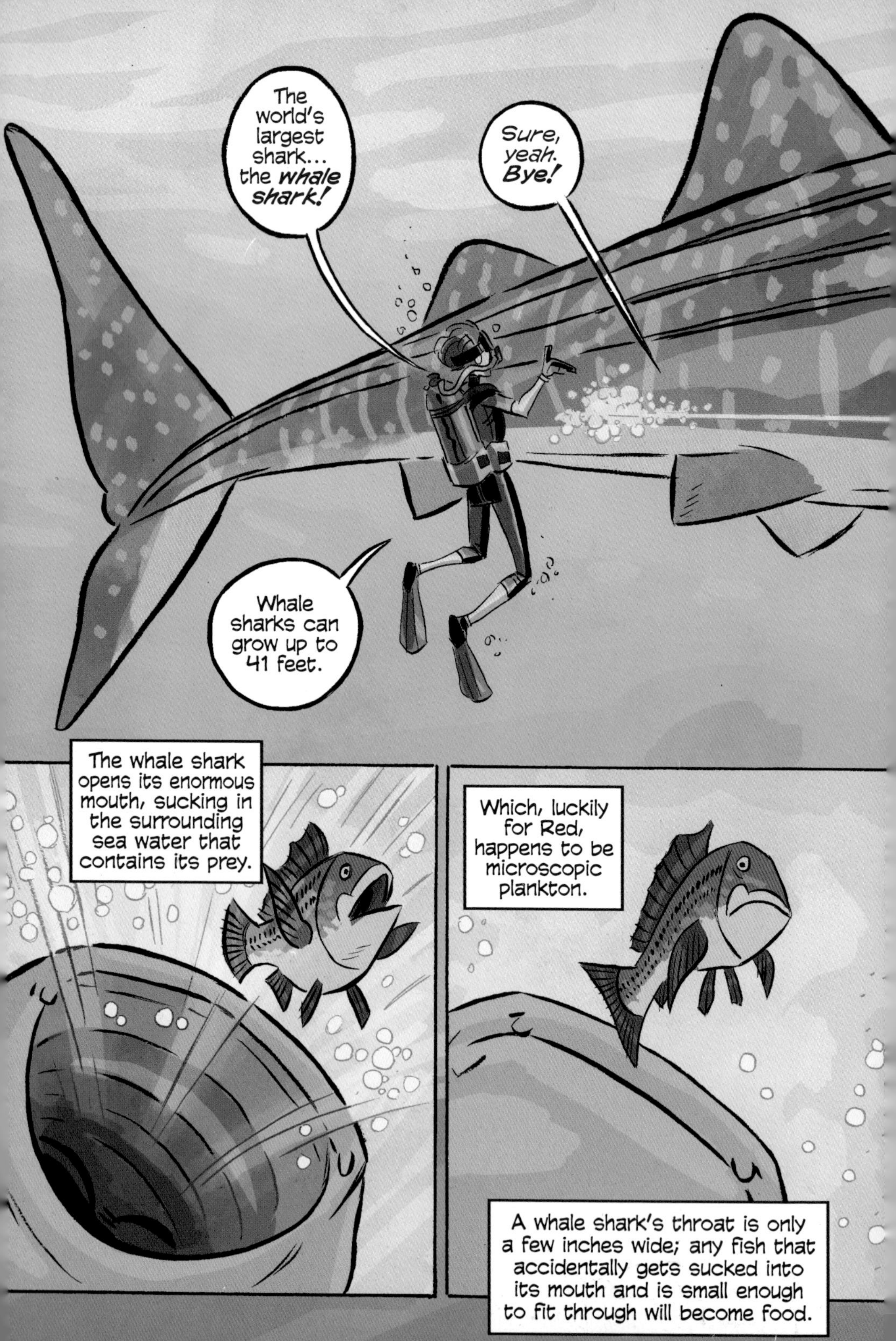
The world's largest shark... the whale shark!
Sure, yeah. Bye!
Whale sharks can grow up to 41 feet.
The whale shark opens its enormous mouth, sucking in the surrounding sea water that contains its prey.
Which, luckily for Red, happens to be microscopic plankton.
A whale shark's throat is only a few inches wide; any fish that accidentally gets sucked into its mouth and is small enough to fit through will become food.

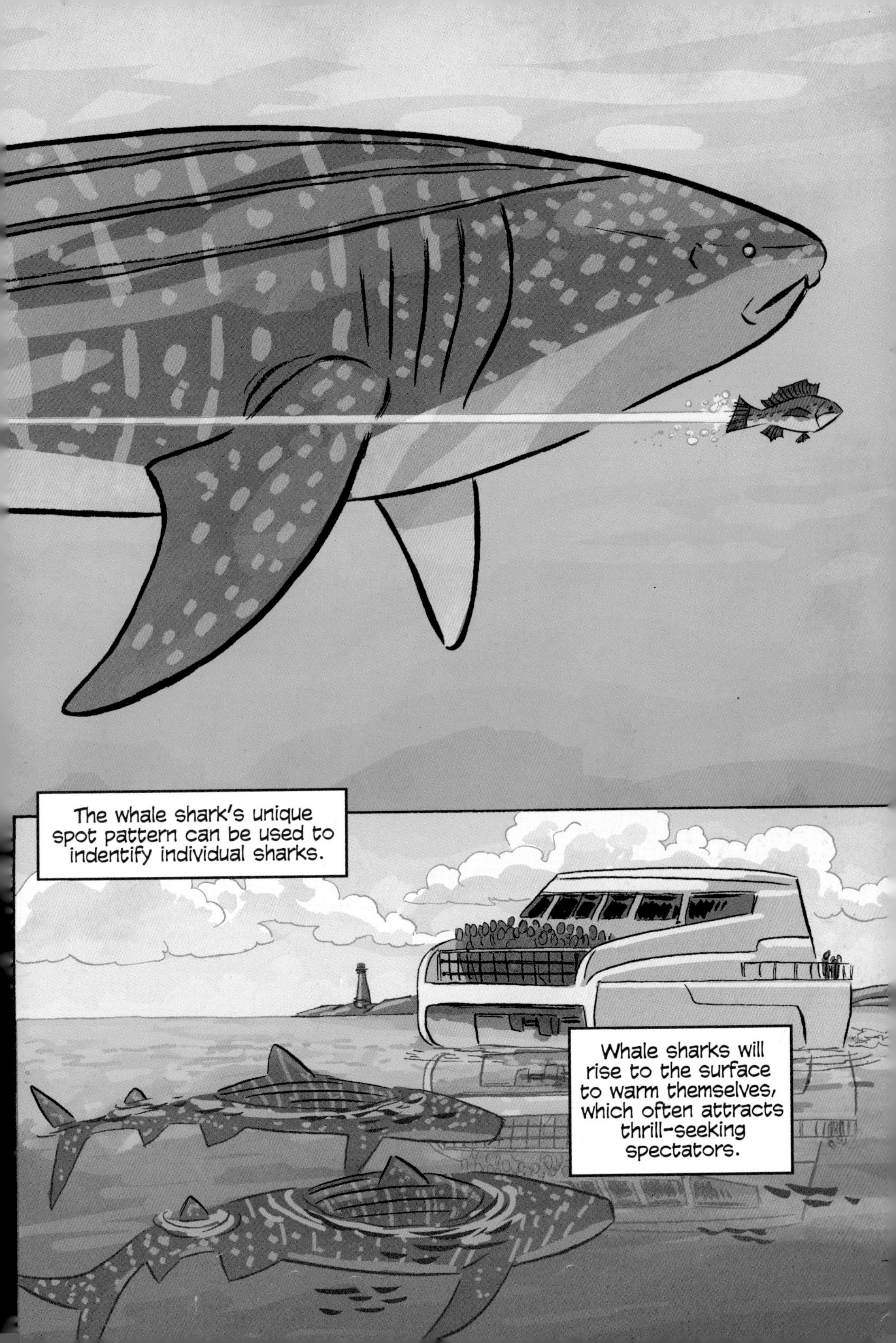
The whale shark's unique spot pattern can be used to indentify individual sharks.
Whale sharks will rise to the surface to warm themselves, which often attracts thrill-seeking spectators.

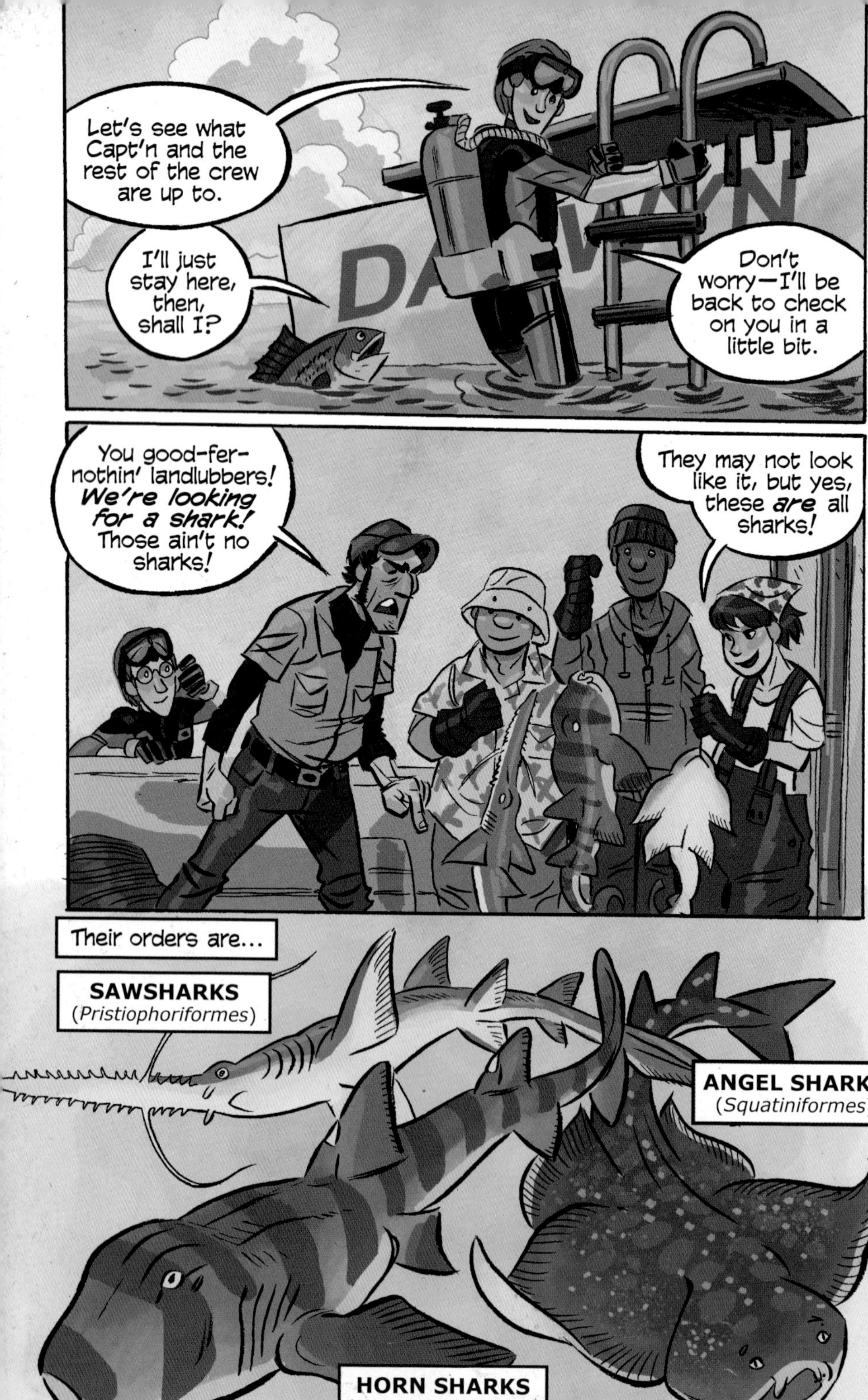

Let's see what Capt'n and the rest of the crew are up to.
I'll just stay here, then, shall I?
Don't worry—I'll be back to check on you in a little bit.
You good-fer-nothin' landlubbers! *We're looking for a shark!* Those ain't no sharks!
They may not look like it, but yes, these *are* all sharks!
Their orders are...
SAWSHARKS (*Pristiophoriformes*)
ANGEL SHARKS (*Squatiniformes*)
HORN SHARKS (*Heterodontiformes*)

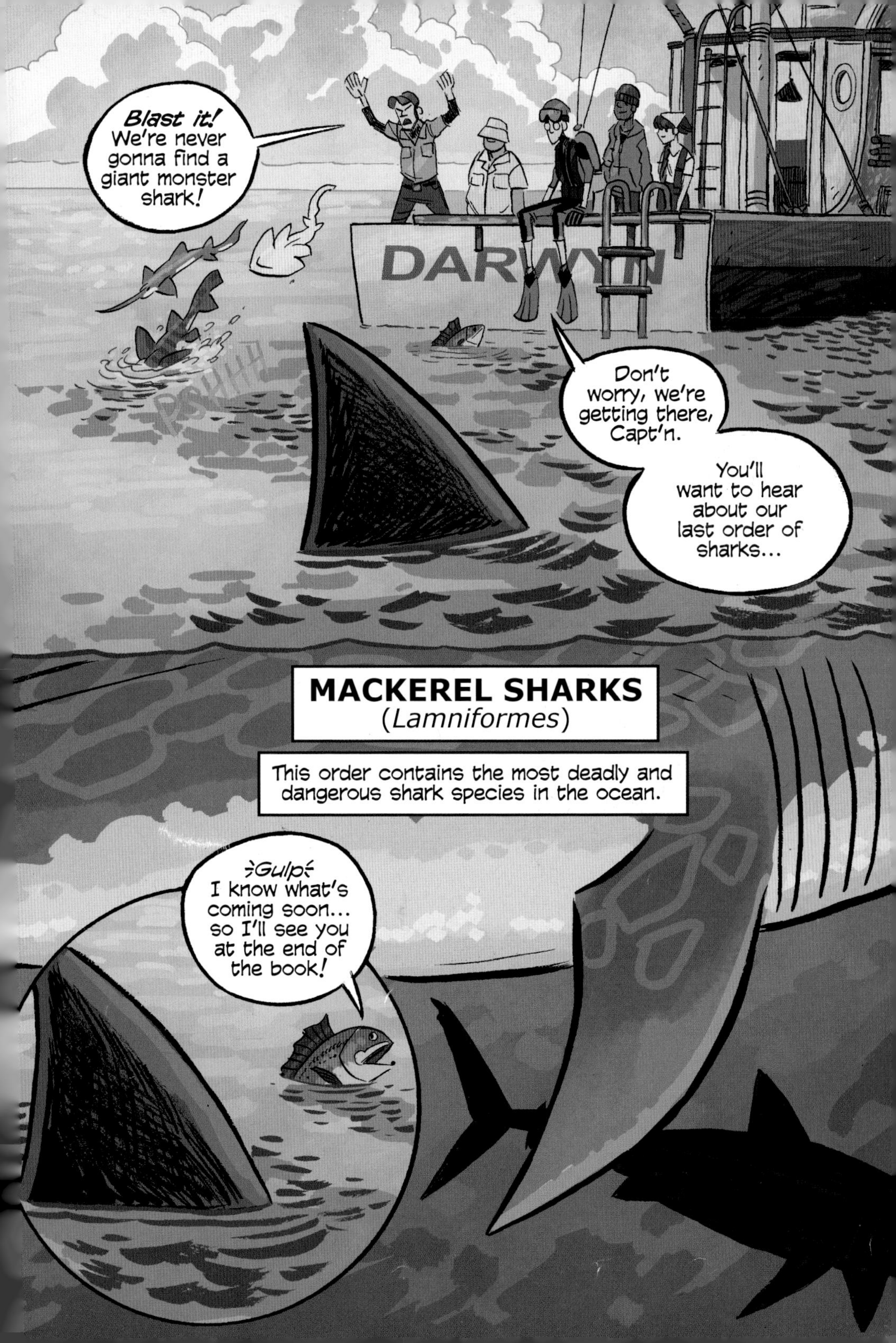

Blast it! We're never gonna find a giant monster shark!
DARWYN
PSHHH
Don't worry, we're getting there, Capt'n.
You'll want to hear about our last order of sharks...
MACKEREL SHARKS (*Lamniformes*)
This order contains the most deadly and dangerous shark species in the ocean.
Gulp I know what's coming soon... so I'll see you at the end of the book!

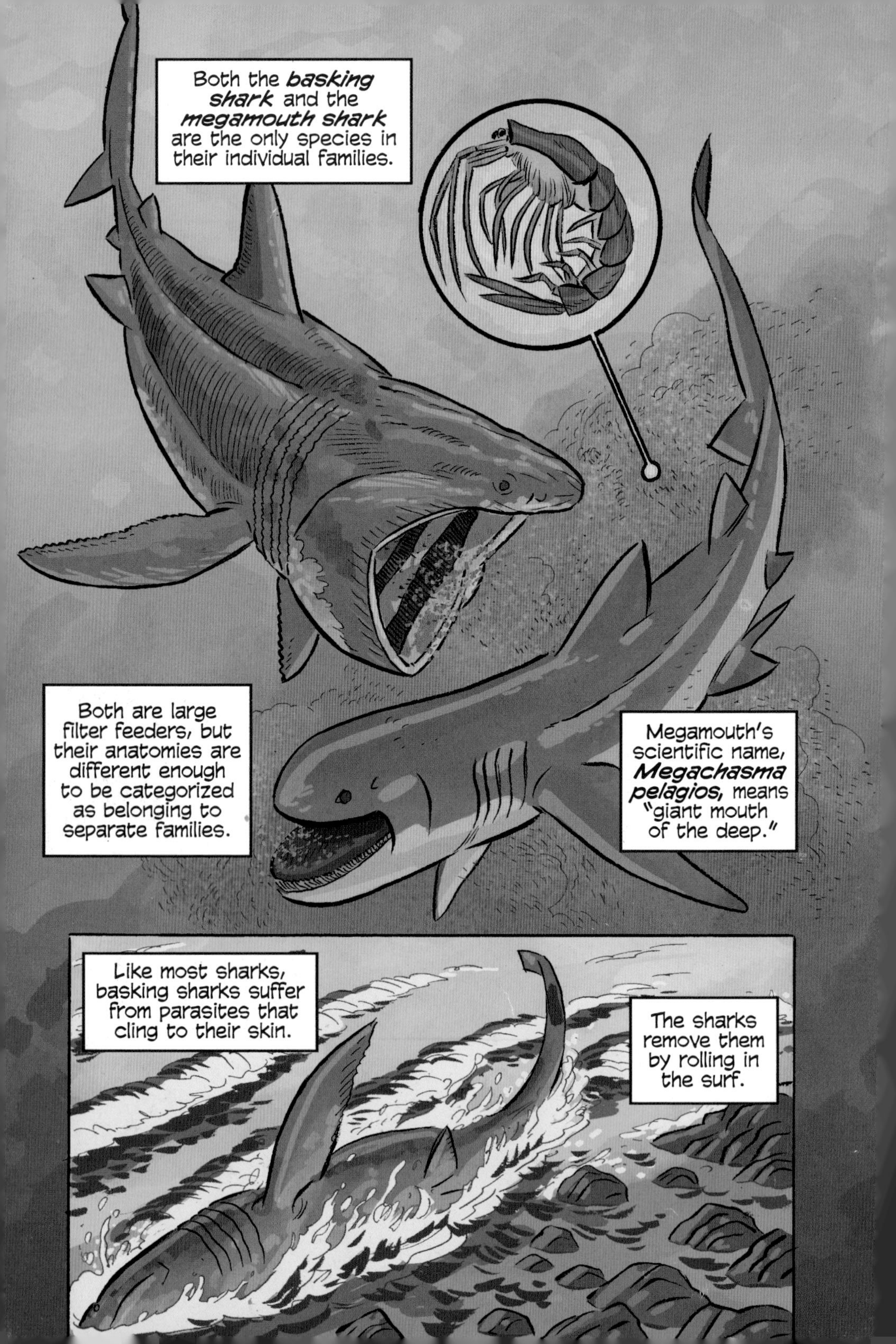

Both the *basking shark* and the *megamouth shark* are the only species in their individual families.
Both are large filter feeders, but their anatomies are different enough to be categorized as belonging to separate families.
Megamouth's scientific name, ***Megachasma pelagios,*** means "giant mouth of the deep."
Like most sharks, basking sharks suffer from parasites that cling to their skin.
The sharks remove them by rolling in the surf.

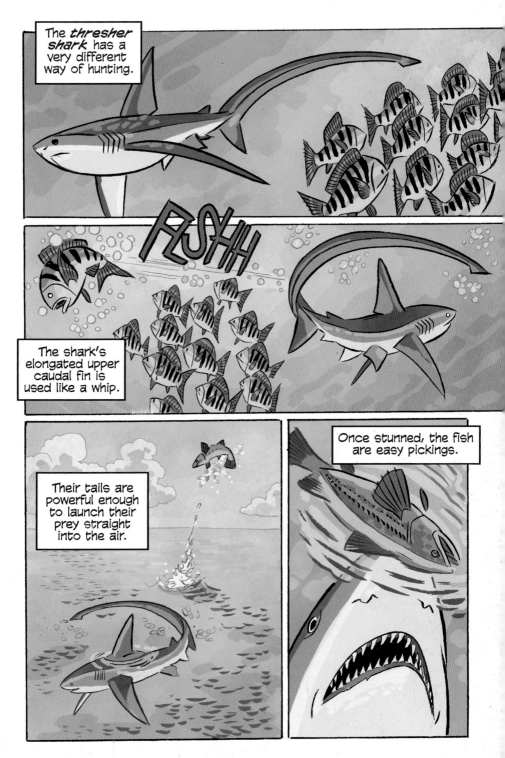

The *thresher shark* has a very different way of hunting.

FISHH

The shark's elongated upper caudal fin is used like a whip.

Their tails are powerful enough to launch their prey straight into the air.

Once stunned, the fish are easy pickings.

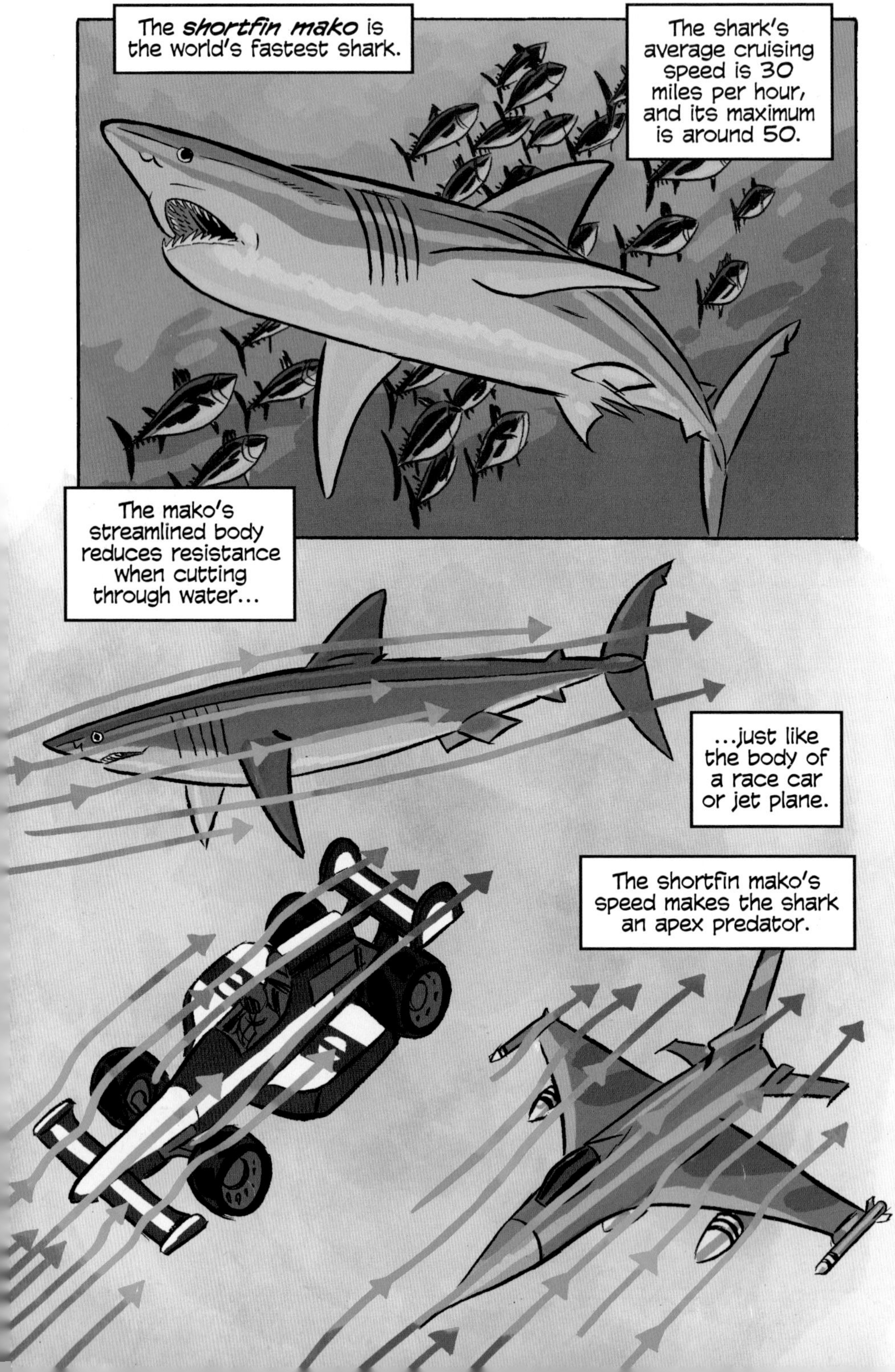
The *shortfin mako* is the world's fastest shark.
The shark's average cruising speed is 30 miles per hour, and its maximum is around 50.
The mako's streamlined body reduces resistance when cutting through water...
...just like the body of a race car or jet plane.
The shortfin mako's speed makes the shark an apex predator.

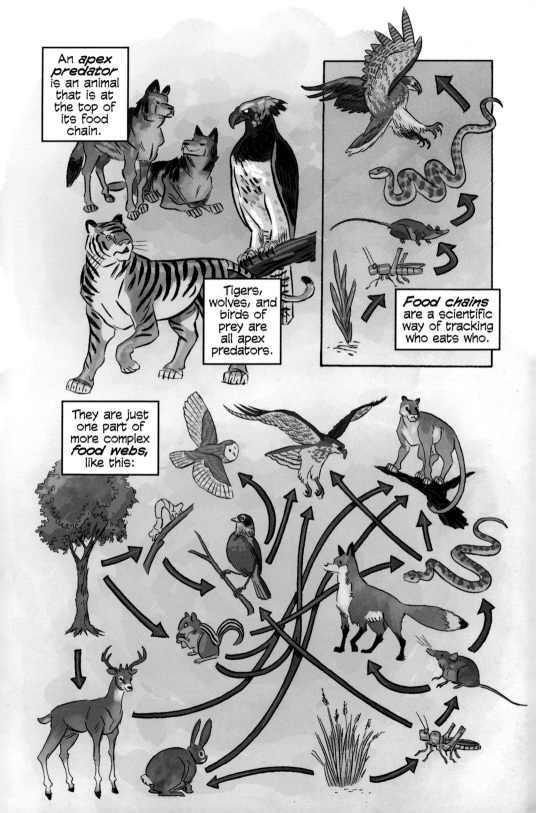

An **apex predator** is an animal that is at the top of its food chain.

Tigers, wolves, and birds of prey are all apex predators.

Food chains are a scientific way of tracking who eats who.

They are just one part of more complex **food webs**, like this:

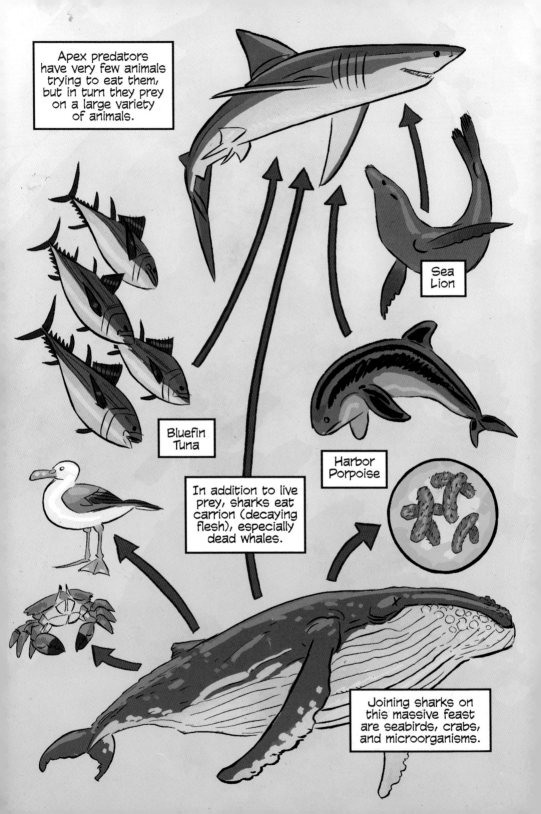

Apex predators have very few animals trying to eat them, but in turn they prey on a large variety of animals.

Sea Lion

Bluefin Tuna

Harbor Porpoise

In addition to live prey, sharks eat carrion (decaying flesh), especially dead whales.

Joining sharks on this massive feast are seabirds, crabs, and microorganisms.

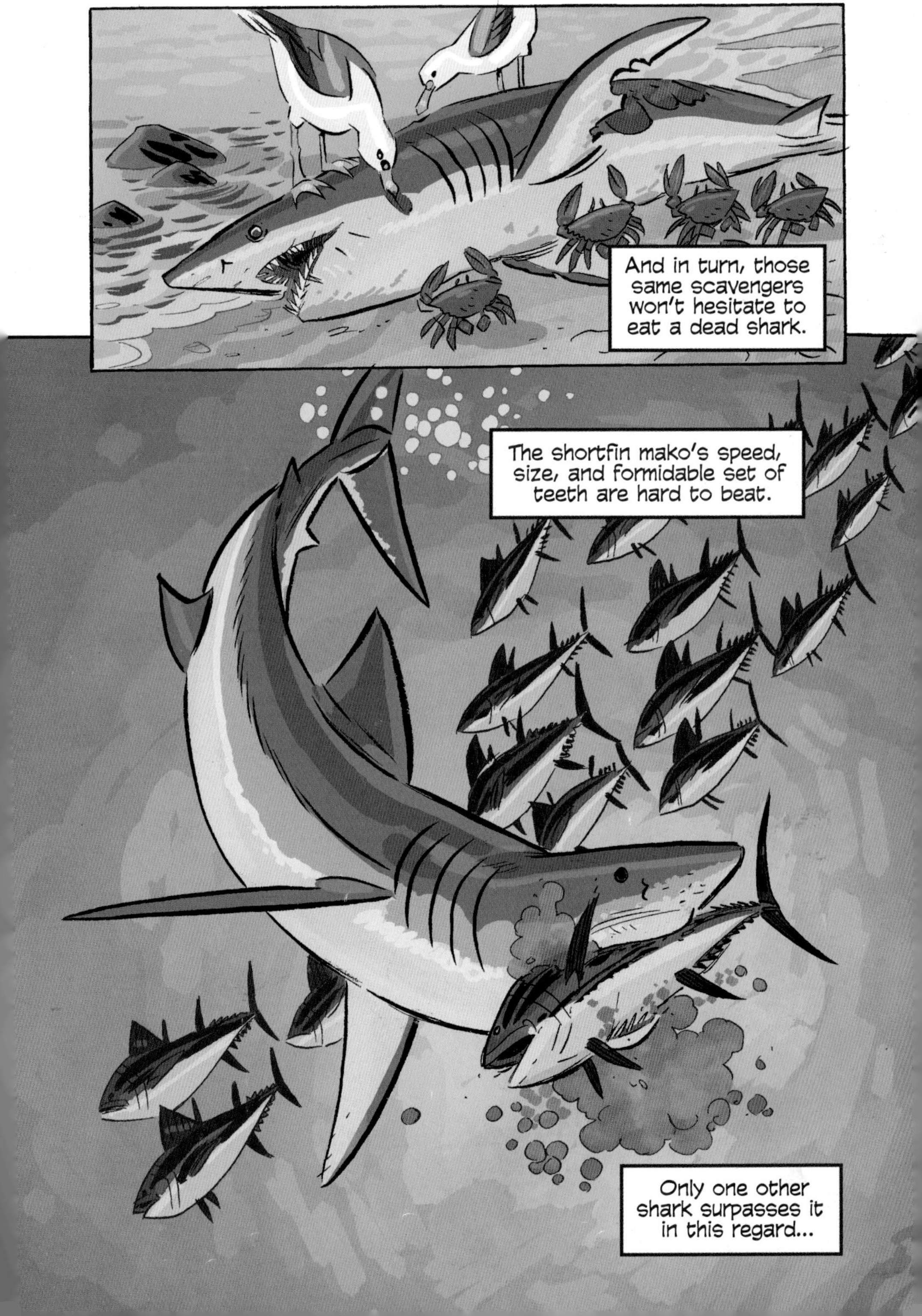
And in turn, those same scavengers won't hesitate to eat a dead shark.
The shortfin mako's speed, size, and formidable set of teeth are hard to beat.
Only one other shark surpasses it in this regard...

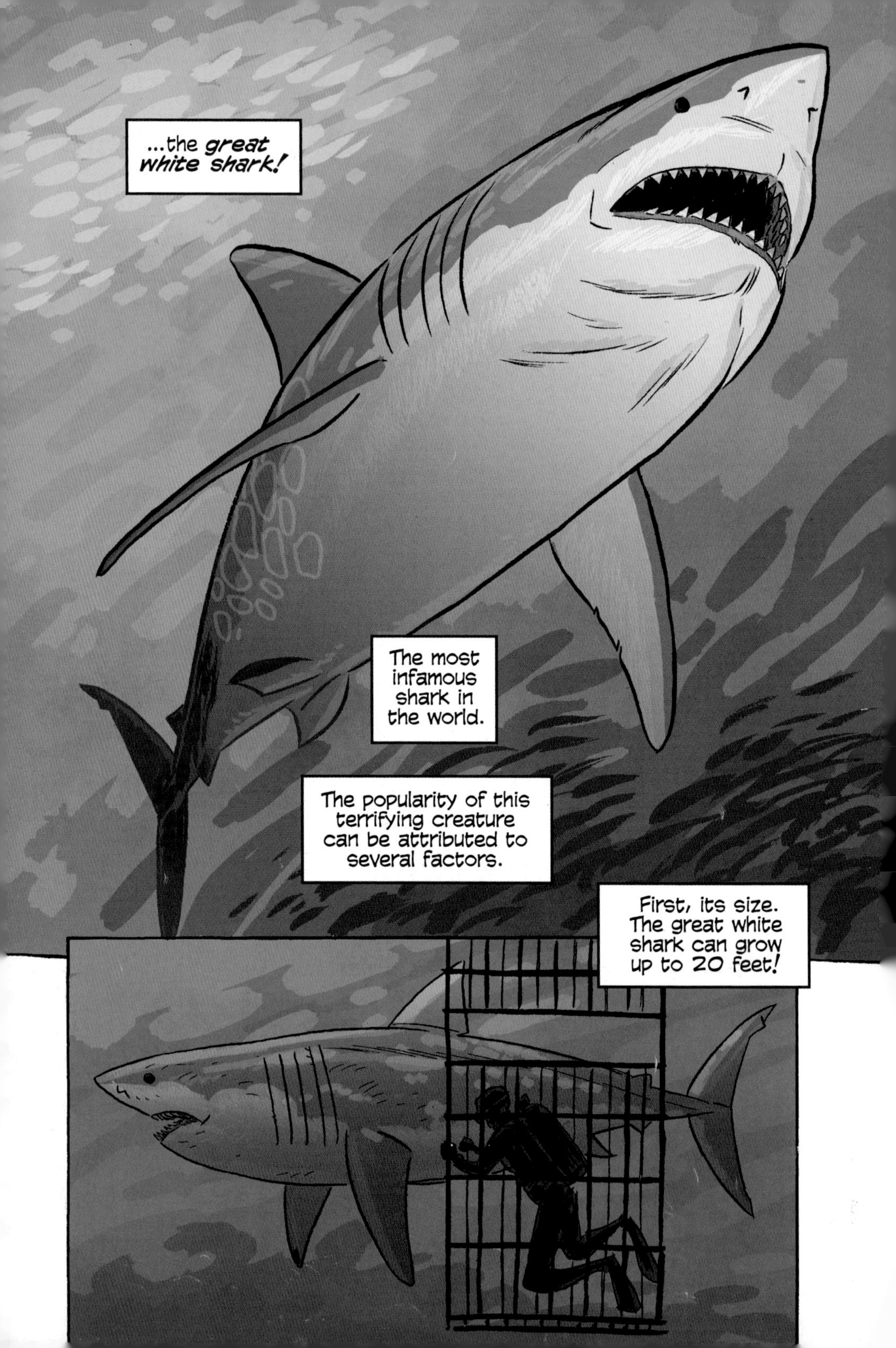
...the *great white shark!*
The most infamous shark in the world.
The popularity of this terrifying creature can be attributed to several factors.
First, its size. The great white shark can grow up to 20 feet!

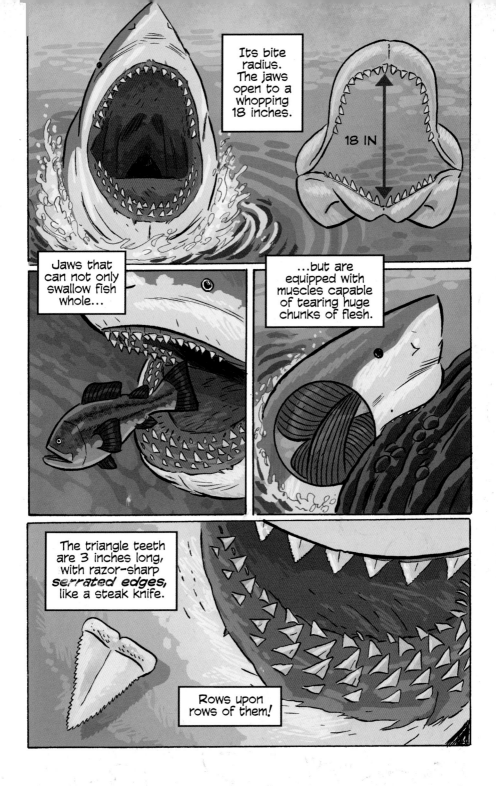

Its bite radius. The jaws open to a whopping 18 inches.

18 IN

Jaws that can not only swallow fish whole...

...but are equipped with muscles capable of tearing huge chunks of flesh.

The triangle teeth are 3 inches long, with razor-sharp *serrated edges*, like a steak knife.

Rows upon rows of them!

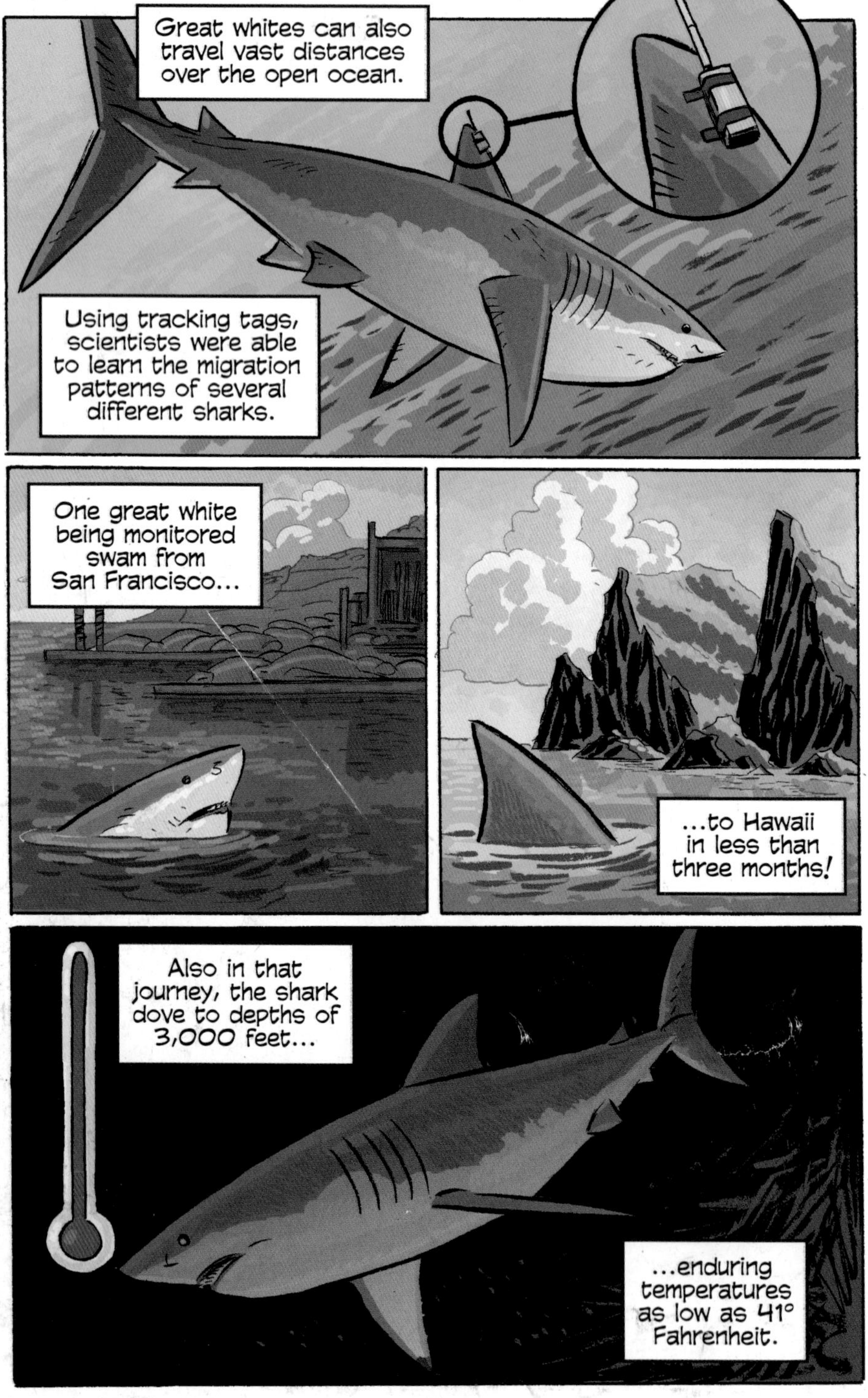
Great whites can also travel vast distances over the open ocean.
Using tracking tags, scientists were able to learn the migration patterns of several different sharks.
One great white being monitored swam from San Francisco...
...to Hawaii in less than three months!
Also in that journey, the shark dove to depths of 3,000 feet...
...enduring temperatures as low as 41° Fahrenheit.

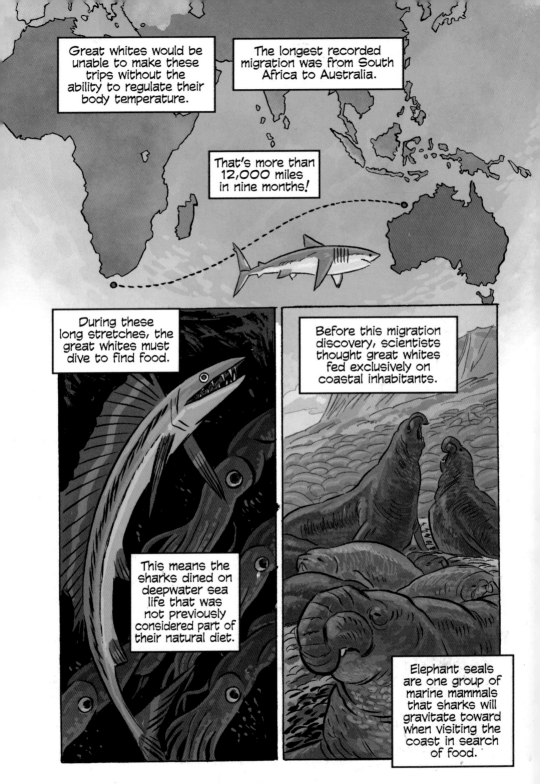

Great whites would be unable to make these trips without the ability to regulate their body temperature.

The longest recorded migration was from South Africa to Australia.

That's more than 12,000 miles in nine months!

During these long stretches, the great whites must dive to find food.

This means the sharks dined on deepwater sea life that was not previously considered part of their natural diet.

Before this migration discovery, scientists thought great whites fed exclusively on coastal inhabitants.

Elephant seals are one group of marine mammals that sharks will gravitate toward when visiting the coast in search of food.

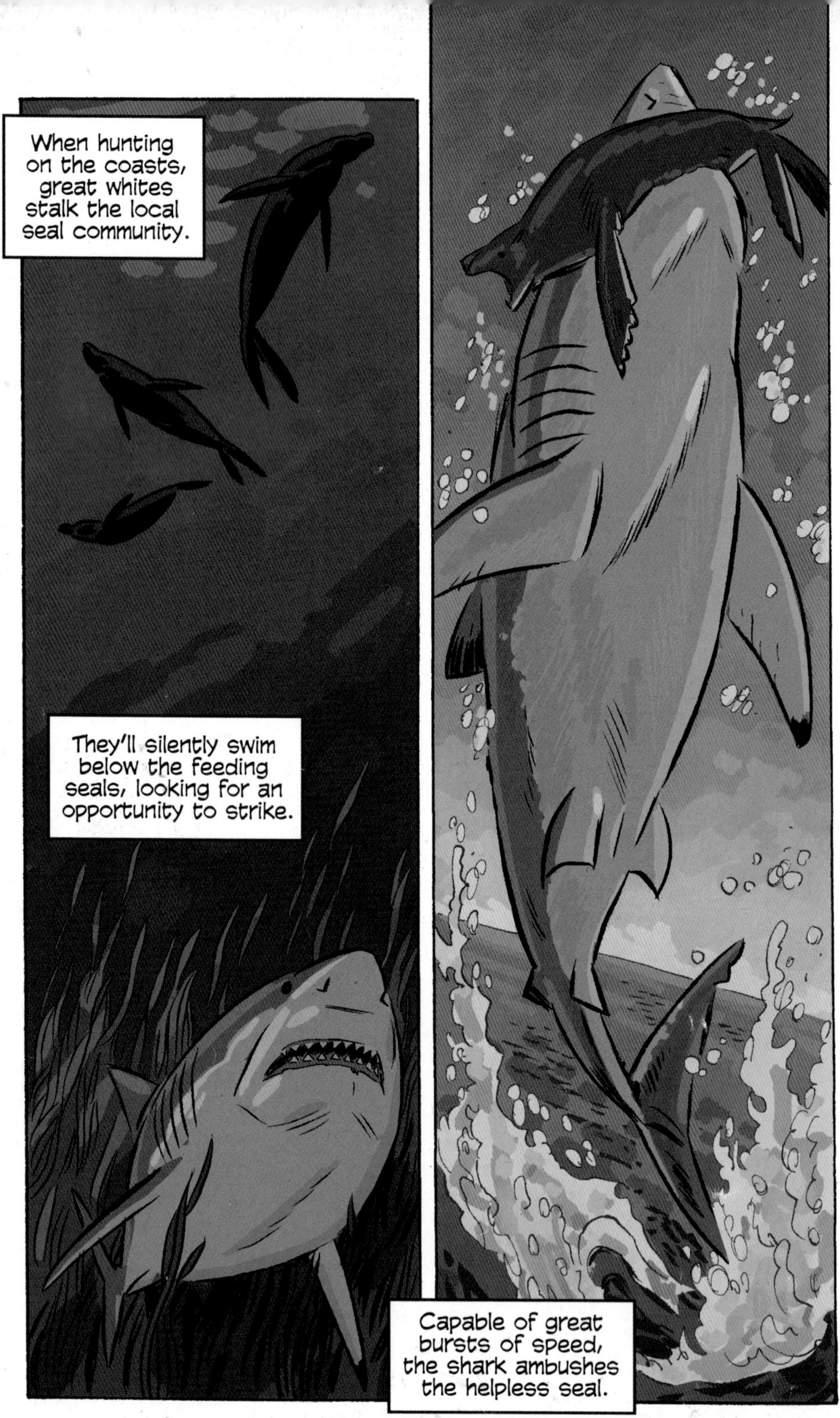
When hunting on the coasts, great whites stalk the local seal community.
They'll silently swim below the feeding seals, looking for an opportunity to strike.
Capable of great bursts of speed, the shark ambushes the helpless seal.

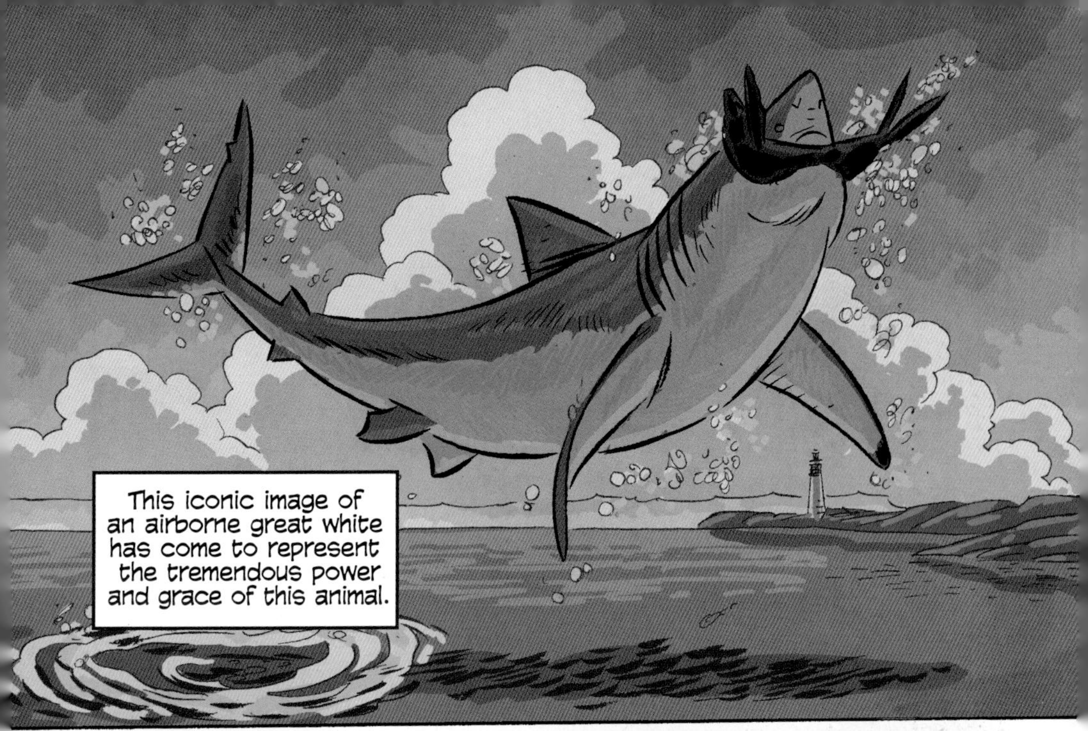
This iconic image of an airborne great white has come to represent the tremendous power and grace of this animal.

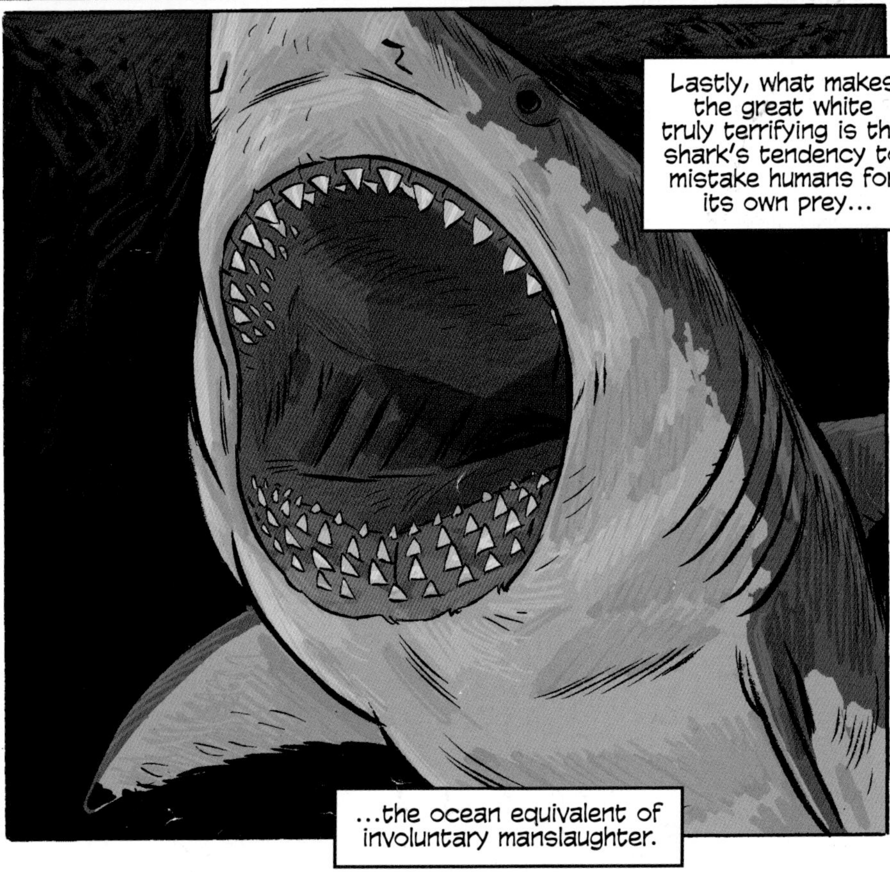
Lastly, what makes the great white truly terrifying is the shark's tendency to mistake humans for its own prey...
...the ocean equivalent of involuntary manslaughter.

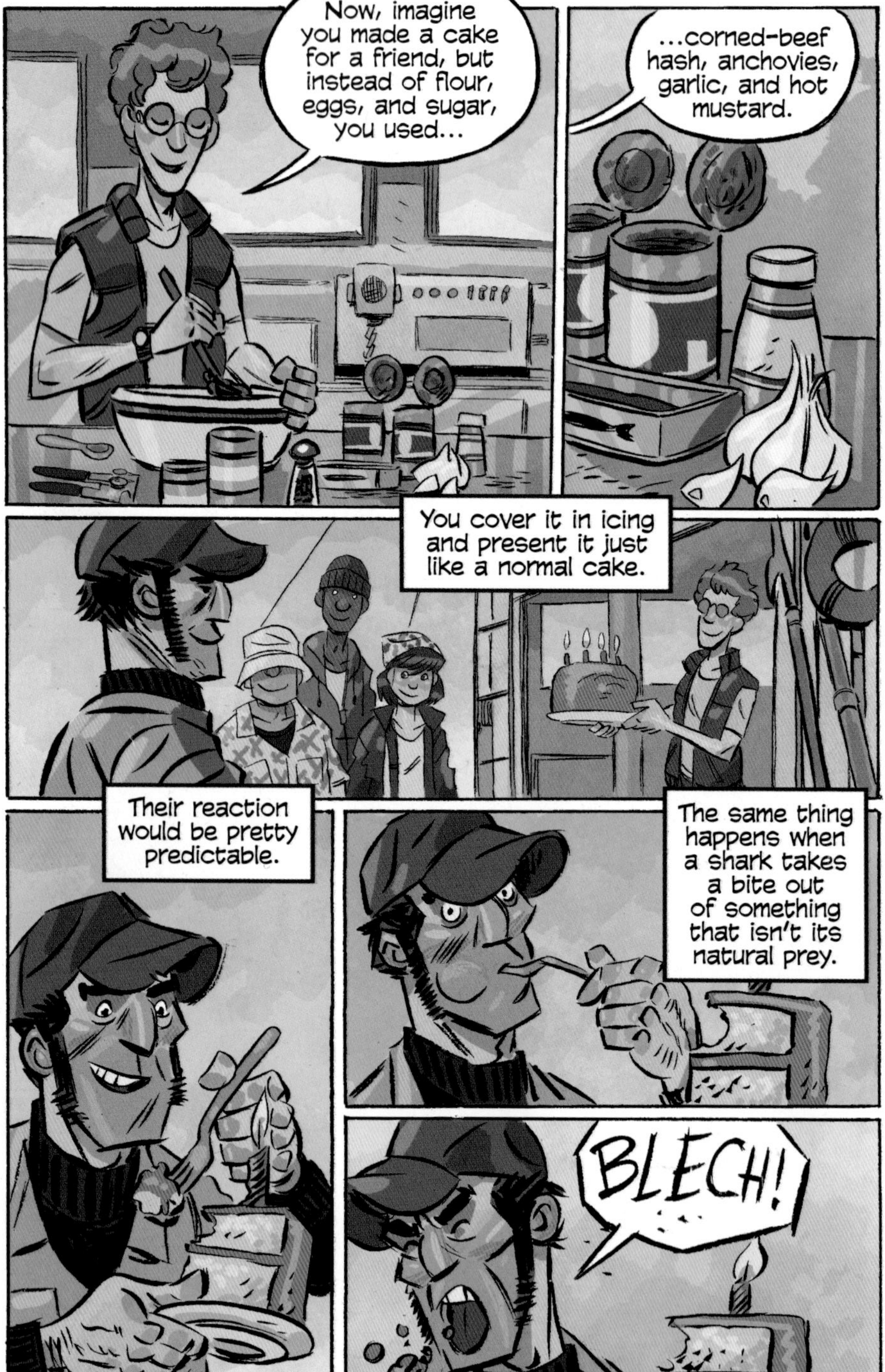
Now, imagine you made a cake for a friend, but instead of flour, eggs, and sugar, you used...
...corned-beef hash, anchovies, garlic, and hot mustard.
You cover it in icing and present it just like a normal cake.
Their reaction would be pretty predictable.
The same thing happens when a shark takes a bite out of something that isn't its natural prey.
BLECH!

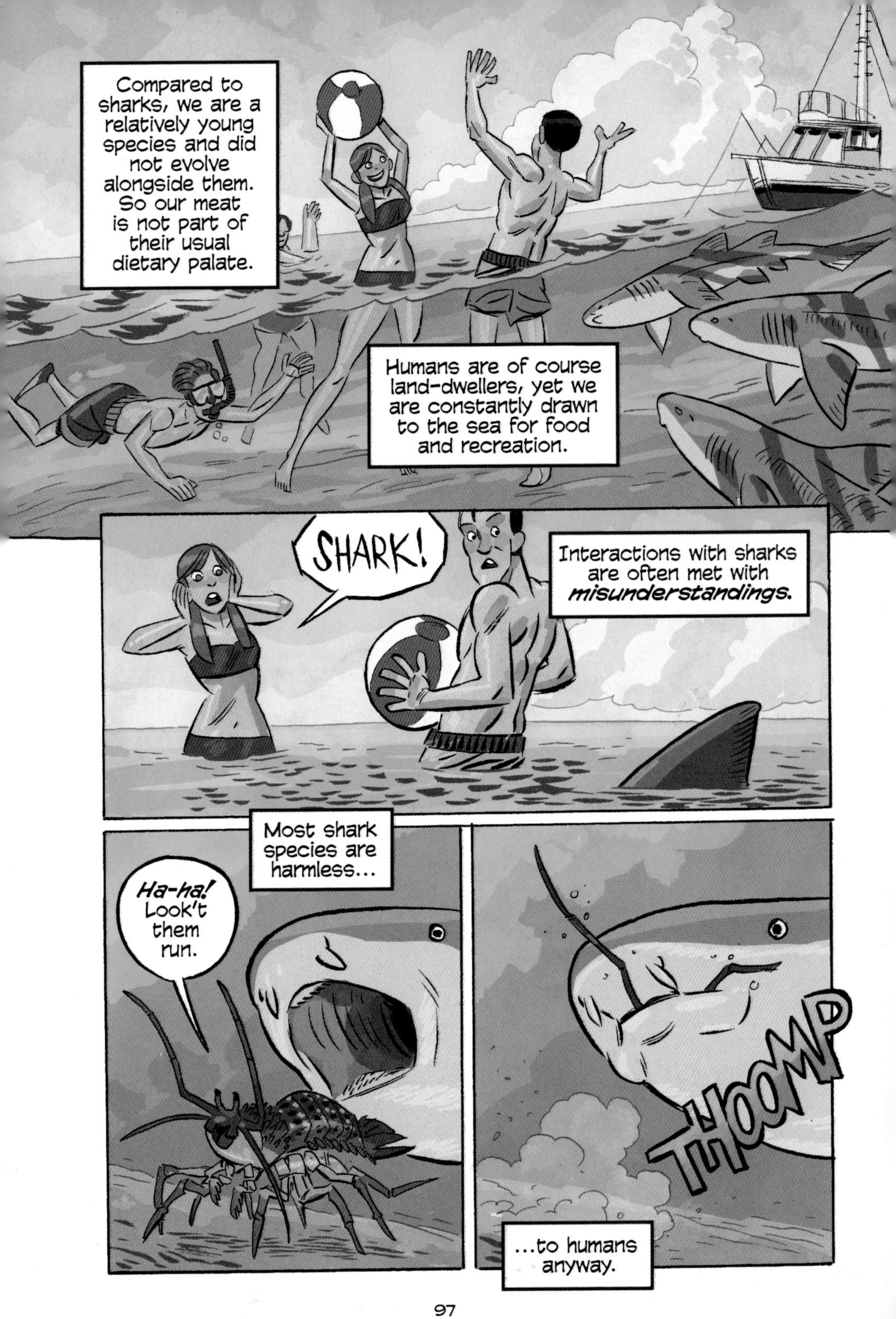
Compared to sharks, we are a relatively young species and did not evolve alongside them. So our meat is not part of their usual dietary palate.
Humans are of course land-dwellers, yet we are constantly drawn to the sea for food and recreation.
SHARK!
Interactions with sharks are often met with *misunderstandings.*
Most shark species are harmless...
Ha-ha! Look't them run.
THOOMP
...to humans anyway.

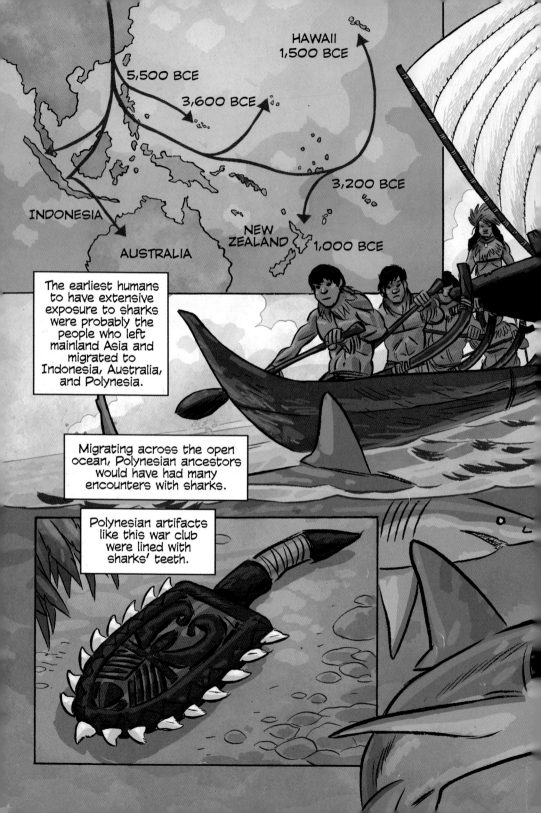

HAWAII
1,500 BCE

5,500 BCE

3,600 BCE

3,200 BCE

INDONESIA

AUSTRALIA

NEW
ZEALAND 1,000 BCE

The earliest humans to have extensive exposure to sharks were probably the people who left mainland Asia and migrated to Indonesia, Australia, and Polynesia.

Migrating across the open ocean, Polynesian ancestors would have had many encounters with sharks.

Polynesian artifacts like this war club were lined with sharks' teeth.

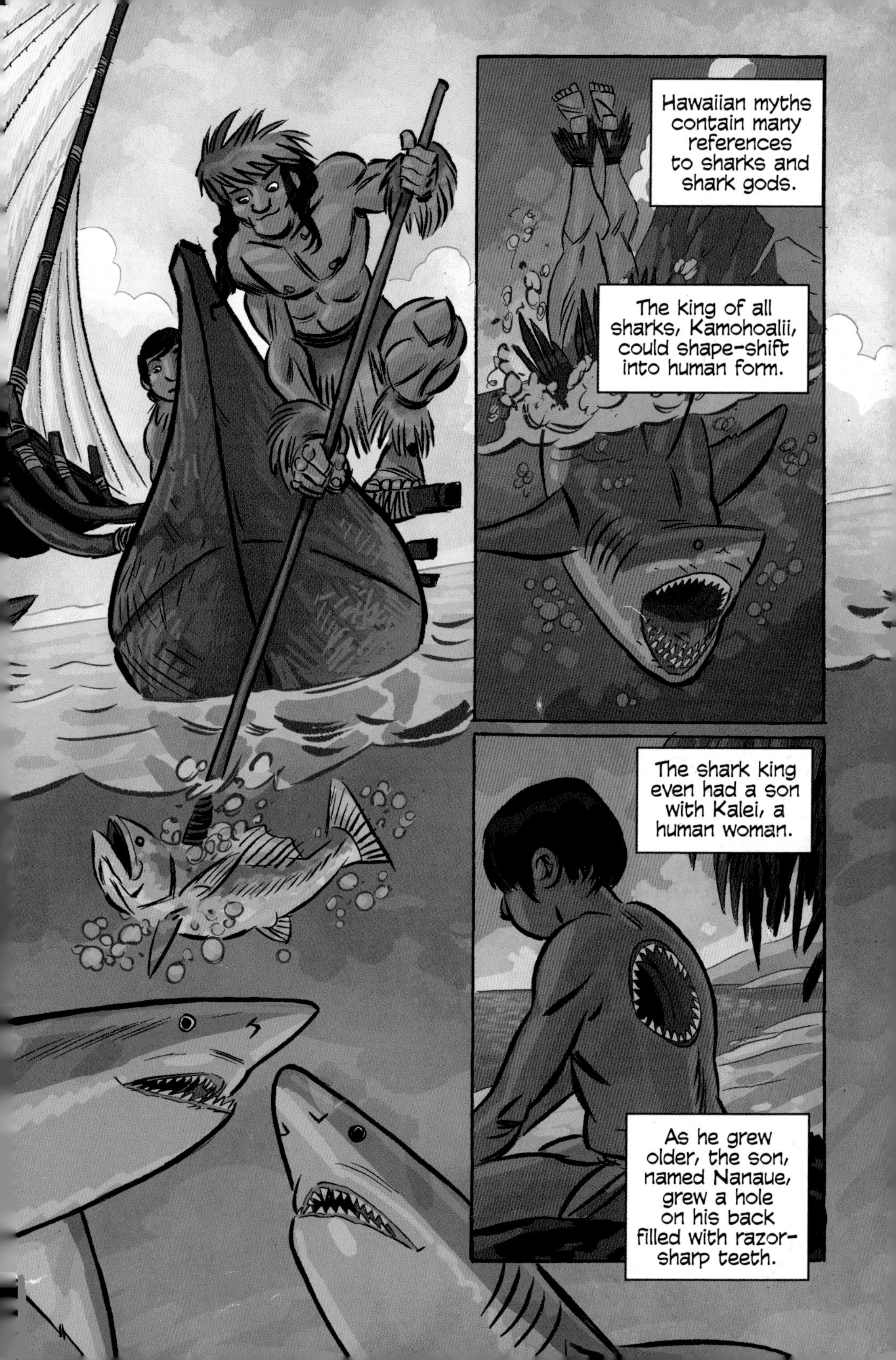
Hawaiian myths contain many references to sharks and shark gods.
The king of all sharks, Kamohoalii, could shape-shift into human form.
The shark king even had a son with Kalei, a human woman.
As he grew older, the son, named Nanaue, grew a hole on his back filled with razor-sharp teeth.

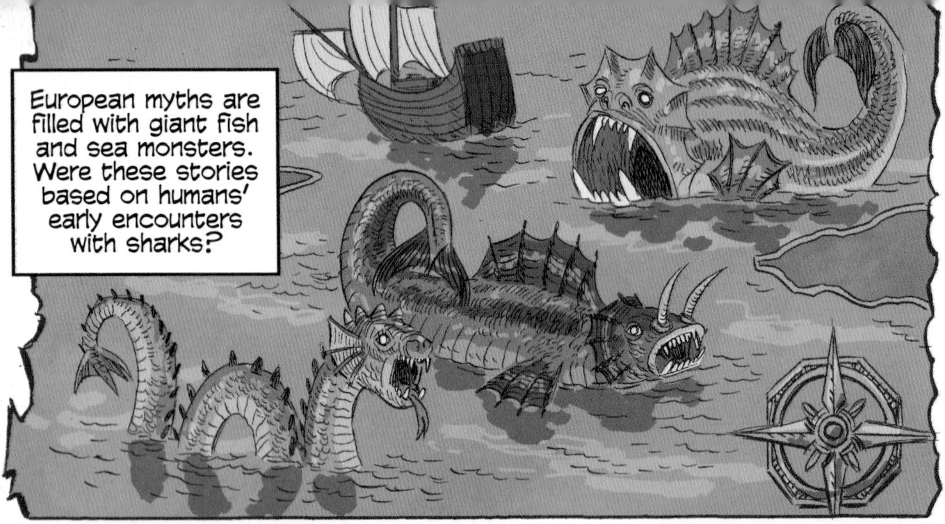
European myths are filled with giant fish and sea monsters. Were these stories based on humans' early encounters with sharks?

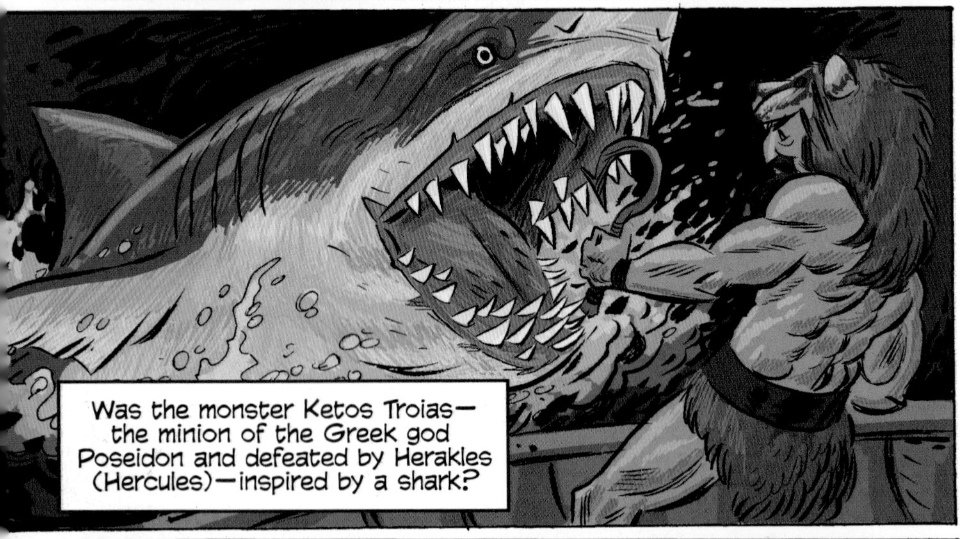
Was the monster Ketos Troias—the minion of the Greek god Poseidon and defeated by Herakles (Hercules)—inspired by a shark?

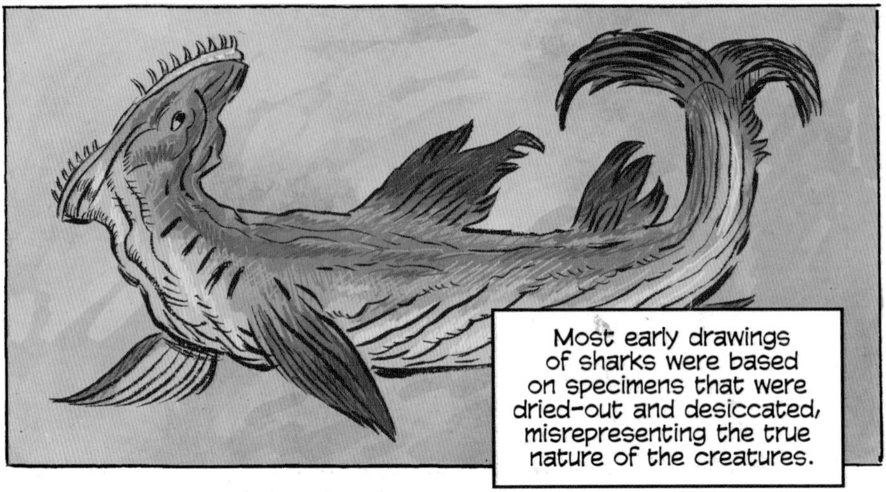
Most early drawings of sharks were based on specimens that were dried-out and desiccated, misrepresenting the true nature of the creatures.

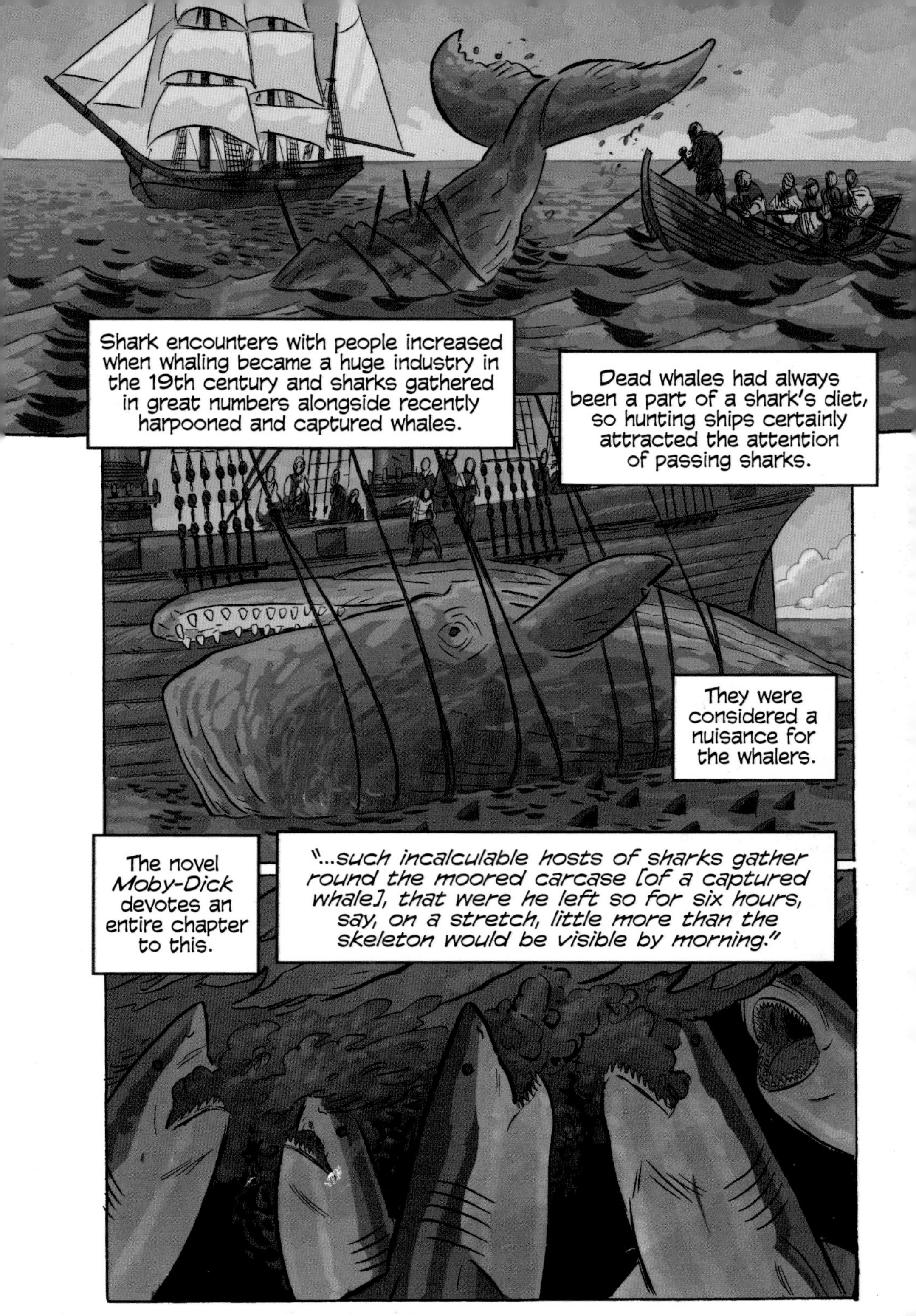
Shark encounters with people increased when whaling became a huge industry in the 19th century and sharks gathered in great numbers alongside recently harpooned and captured whales.
Dead whales had always been a part of a shark's diet, so hunting ships certainly attracted the attention of passing sharks.
They were considered a nuisance for the whalers.
The novel *Moby-Dick* devotes an entire chapter to this.
"...such incalculable hosts of sharks gather round the moored carcase [of a captured whale], that were he left so for six hours, say, on a stretch, little more than the skeleton would be visible by morning."

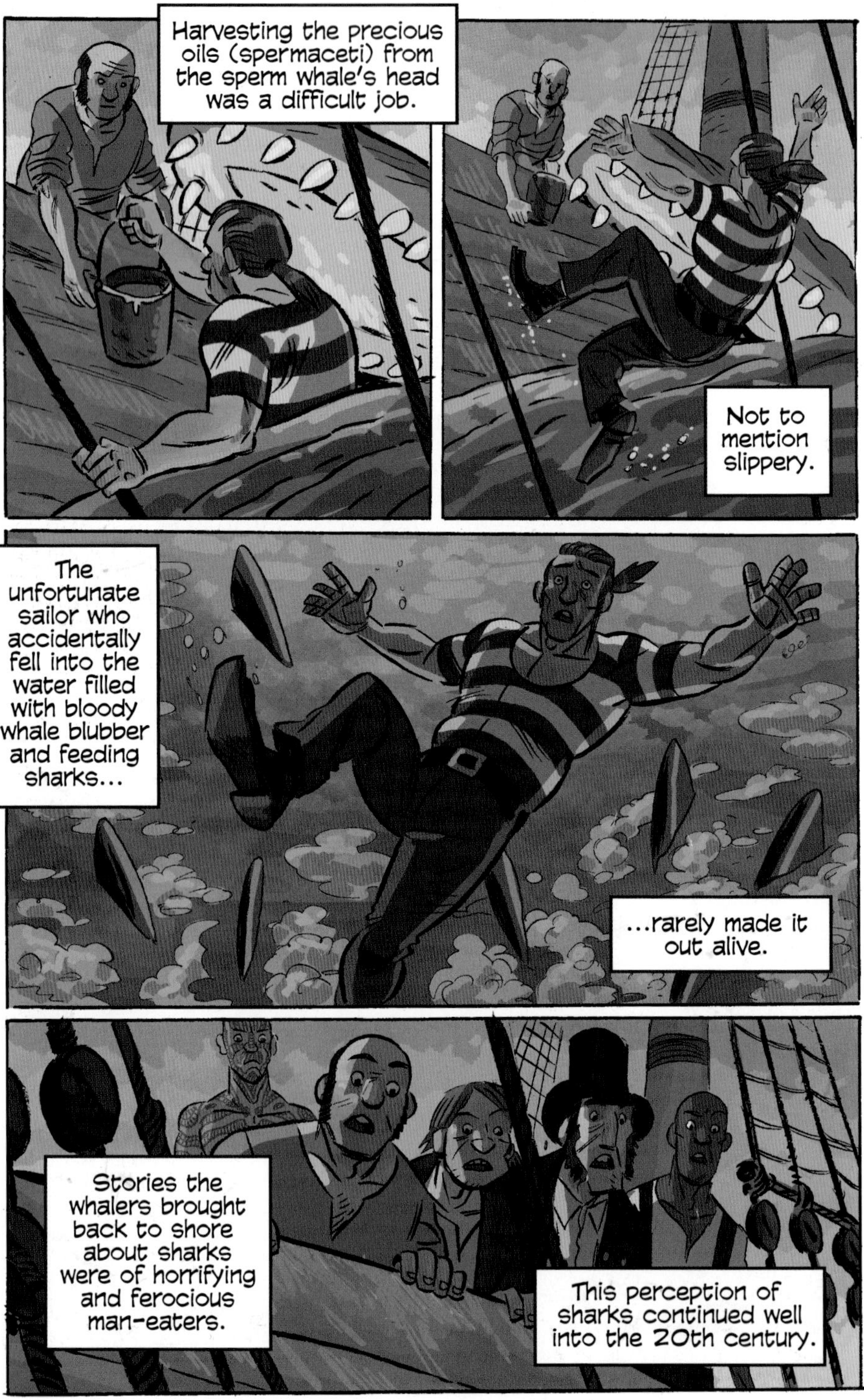
Harvesting the precious oils (spermaceti) from the sperm whale's head was a difficult job.
Not to mention slippery.
The unfortunate sailor who accidentally fell into the water filled with bloody whale blubber and feeding sharks...
...rarely made it out alive.
Stories the whalers brought back to shore about sharks were of horrifying and ferocious man-eaters.
This perception of sharks continued well into the 20th century.

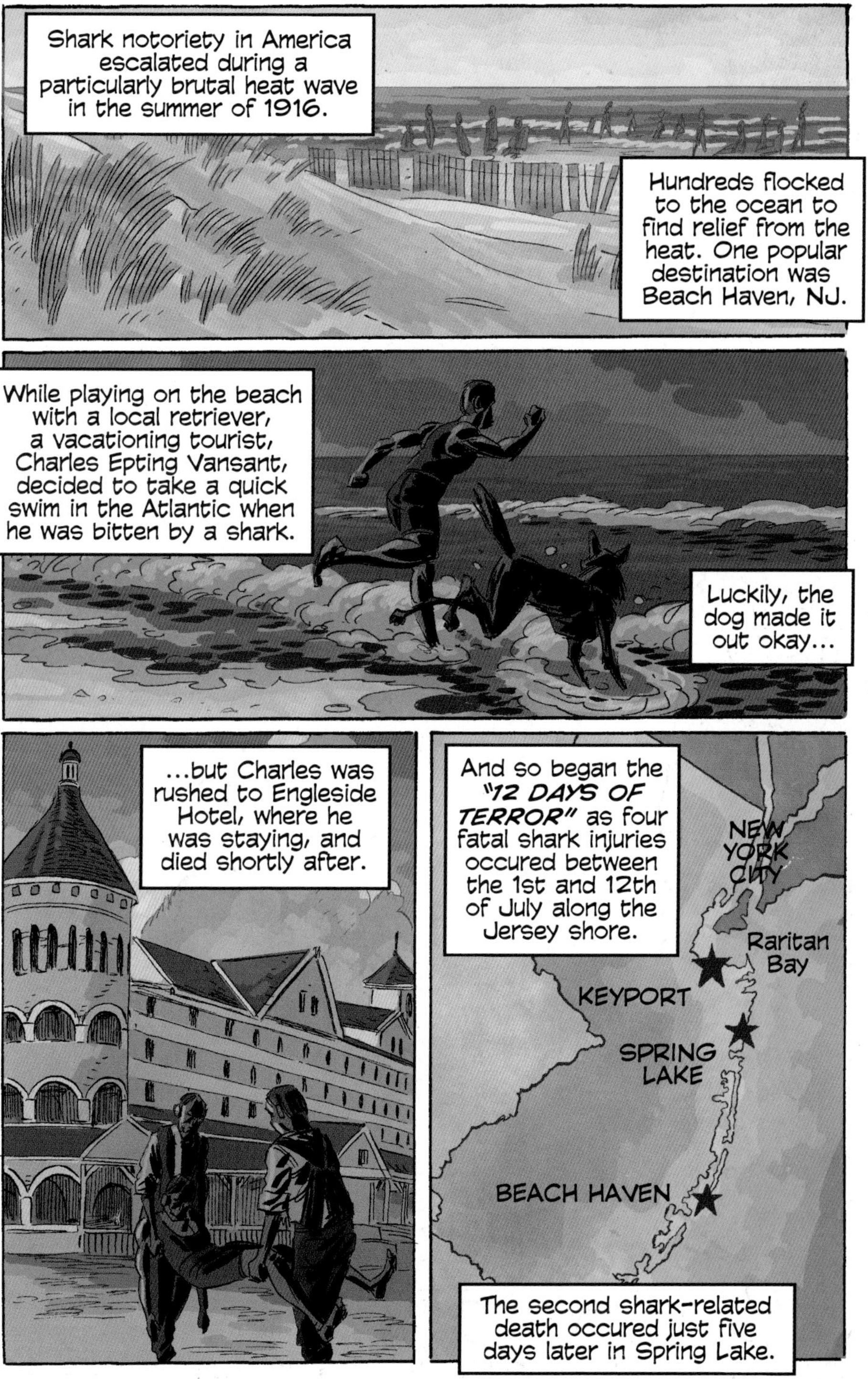
Shark notoriety in America escalated during a particularly brutal heat wave in the summer of 1916.
Hundreds flocked to the ocean to find relief from the heat. One popular destination was Beach Haven, NJ.
While playing on the beach with a local retriever, a vacationing tourist, Charles Epting Vansant, decided to take a quick swim in the Atlantic when he was bitten by a shark.
Luckily, the dog made it out okay...
...but Charles was rushed to Engleside Hotel, where he was staying, and died shortly after.
And so began the *"12 DAYS OF TERROR"* as four fatal shark injuries occured between the 1st and 12th of July along the Jersey shore.
NEW YORK CITY
Raritan Bay
KEYPORT
SPRING LAKE
BEACH HAVEN
The second shark-related death occured just five days later in Spring Lake.

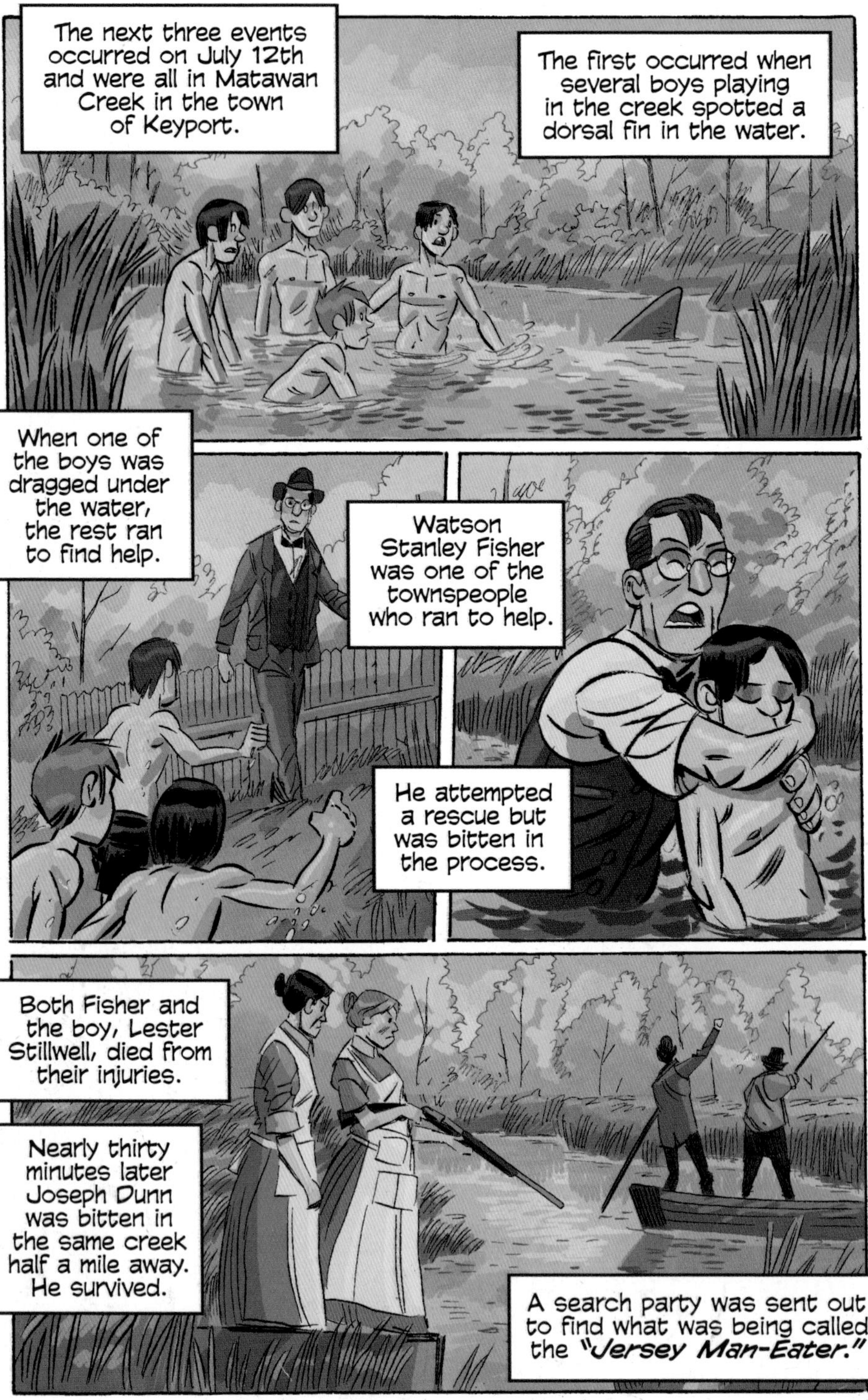
The next three events occurred on July 12th and were all in Matawan Creek in the town of Keyport.
The first occurred when several boys playing in the creek spotted a dorsal fin in the water.
When one of the boys was dragged under the water, the rest ran to find help.
Watson Stanley Fisher was one of the townspeople who ran to help.
He attempted a rescue but was bitten in the process.
Both Fisher and the boy, Lester Stillwell, died from their injuries.
Nearly thirty minutes later Joseph Dunn was bitten in the same creek half a mile away. He survived.
A search party was sent out to find what was being called the *"Jersey Man-Eater."*

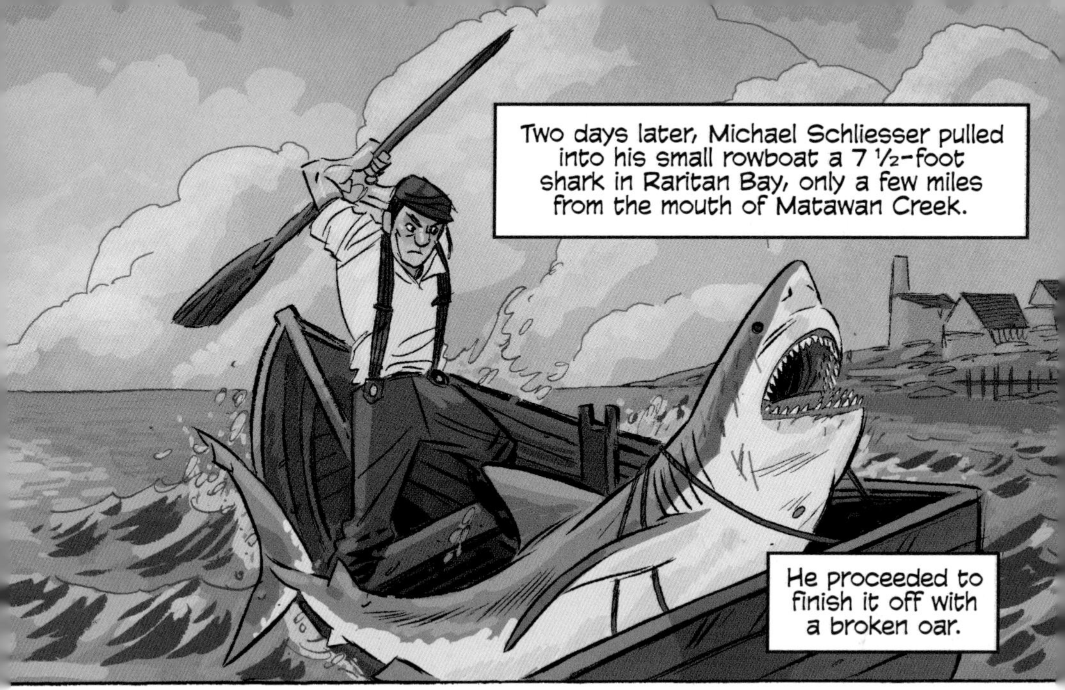
Two days later, Michael Schliesser pulled into his small rowboat a 7 ½-foot shark in Raritan Bay, only a few miles from the mouth of Matawan Creek.
He proceeded to finish it off with a broken oar.

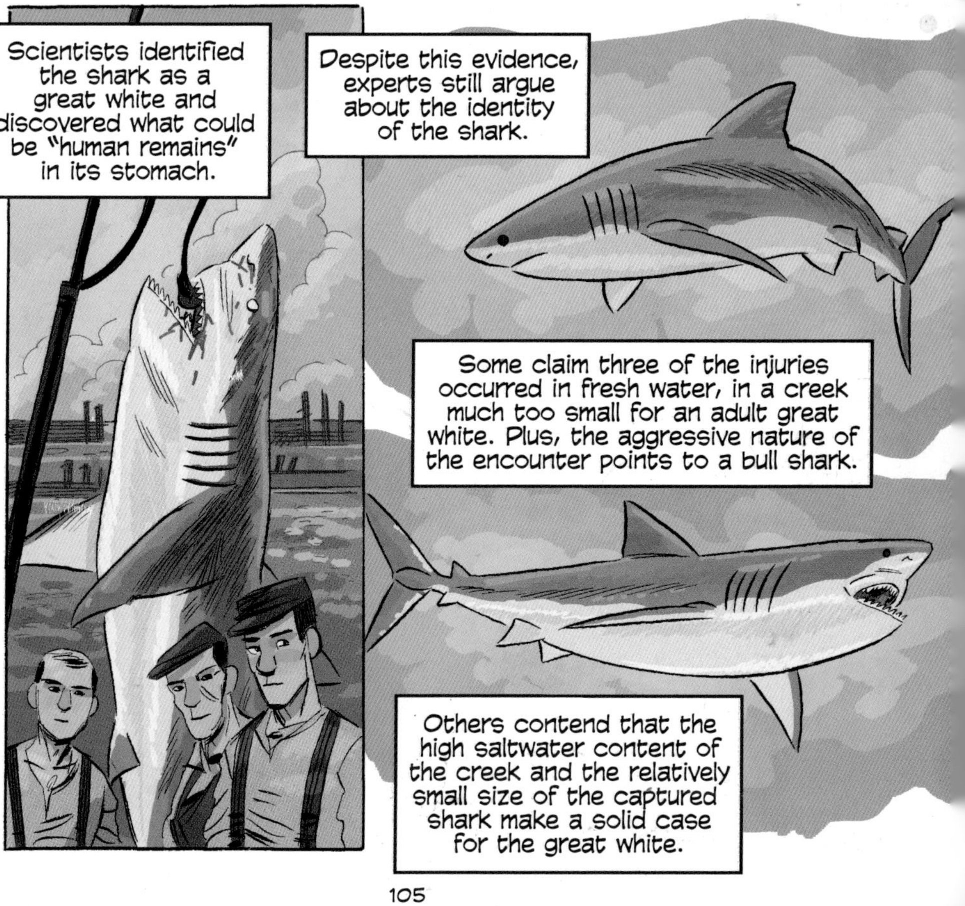
Scientists identified the shark as a great white and discovered what could be "human remains" in its stomach.
Despite this evidence, experts still argue about the identity of the shark.
Some claim three of the injuries occurred in fresh water, in a creek much too small for an adult great white. Plus, the aggressive nature of the encounter points to a bull shark.
Others contend that the high saltwater content of the creek and the relatively small size of the captured shark make a solid case for the great white.

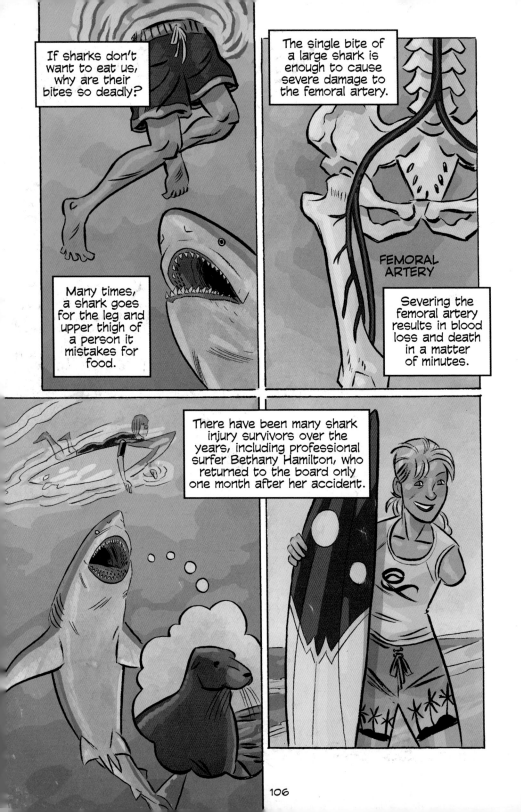

If sharks don't want to eat us, why are their bites so deadly?

The single bite of a large shark is enough to cause severe damage to the femoral artery.

Many times, a shark goes for the leg and upper thigh of a person it mistakes for food.

FEMORAL ARTERY

Severing the femoral artery results in blood loss and death in a matter of minutes.

There have been many shark injury survivors over the years, including professional surfer Bethany Hamilton, who returned to the board only one month after her accident.

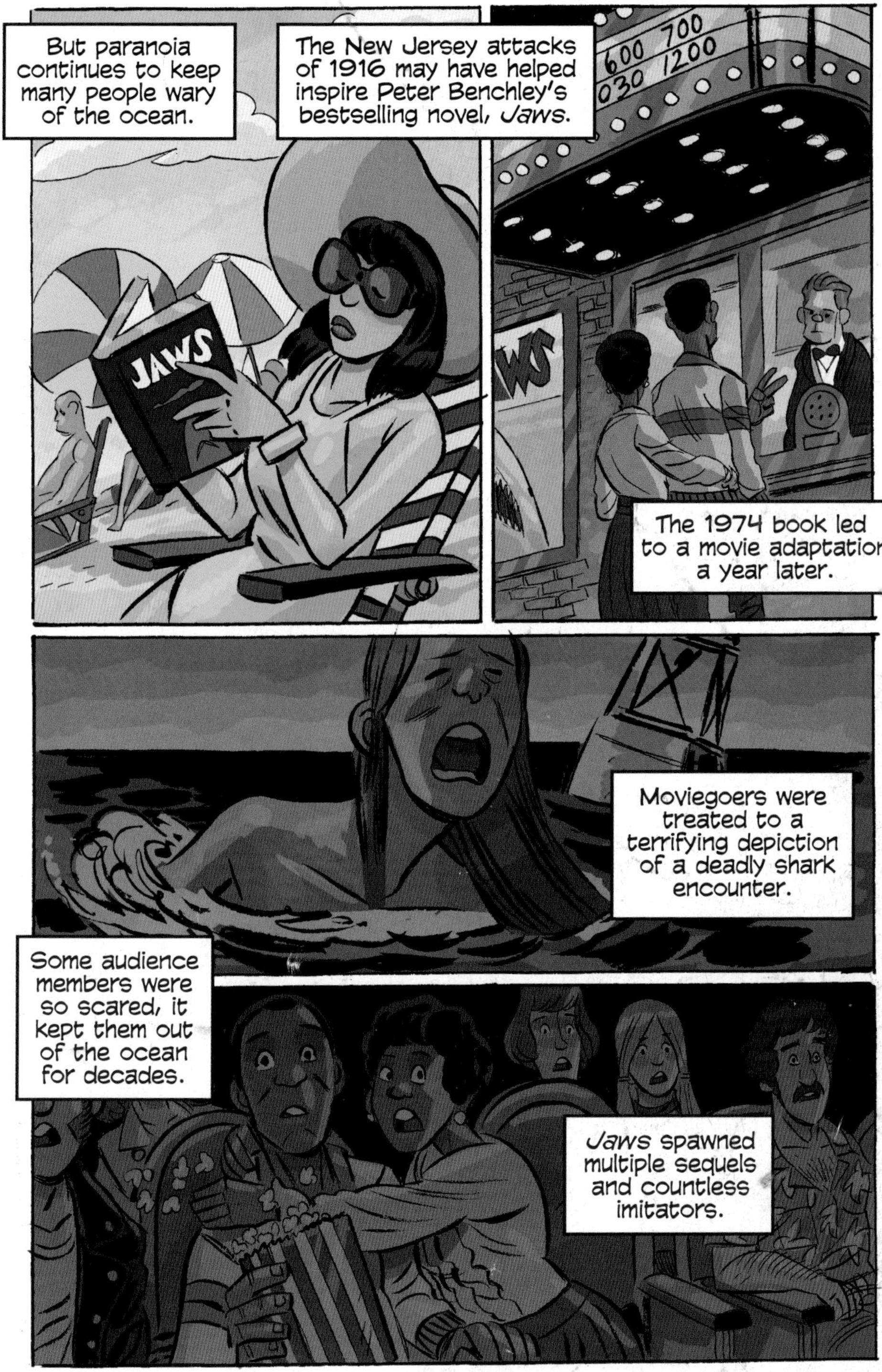
But paranoia continues to keep many people wary of the ocean.
The New Jersey attacks of 1916 may have helped inspire Peter Benchley's bestselling novel, *Jaws*.
600 700
030 1200
JAWS
JAWS
The 1974 book led to a movie adaptation a year later.
Moviegoers were treated to a terrifying depiction of a deadly shark encounter.
Some audience members were so scared, it kept them out of the ocean for decades.
Jaws spawned multiple sequels and countless imitators.

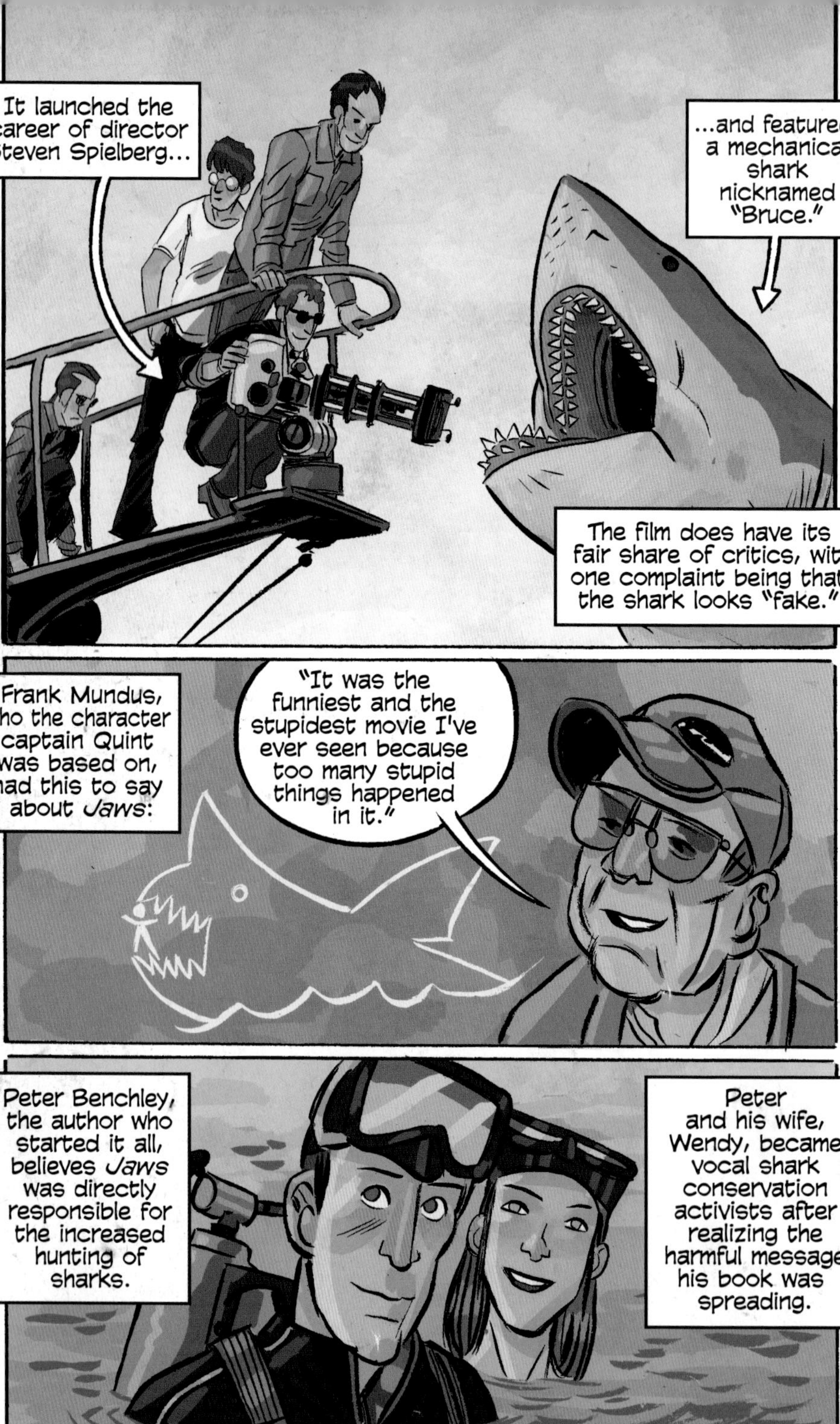
It launched the career of director Steven Spielberg...
...and featured a mechanical shark nicknamed "Bruce."
The film does have its fair share of critics, with one complaint being that the shark looks "fake."
Frank Mundus, who the character captain Quint was based on, had this to say about *Jaws*:
"It was the funniest and the stupidest movie I've ever seen because too many stupid things happened in it."
Peter Benchley, the author who started it all, believes *Jaws* was directly responsible for the increased hunting of sharks.
Peter and his wife, Wendy, became vocal shark conservation activists after realizing the harmful message his book was spreading.

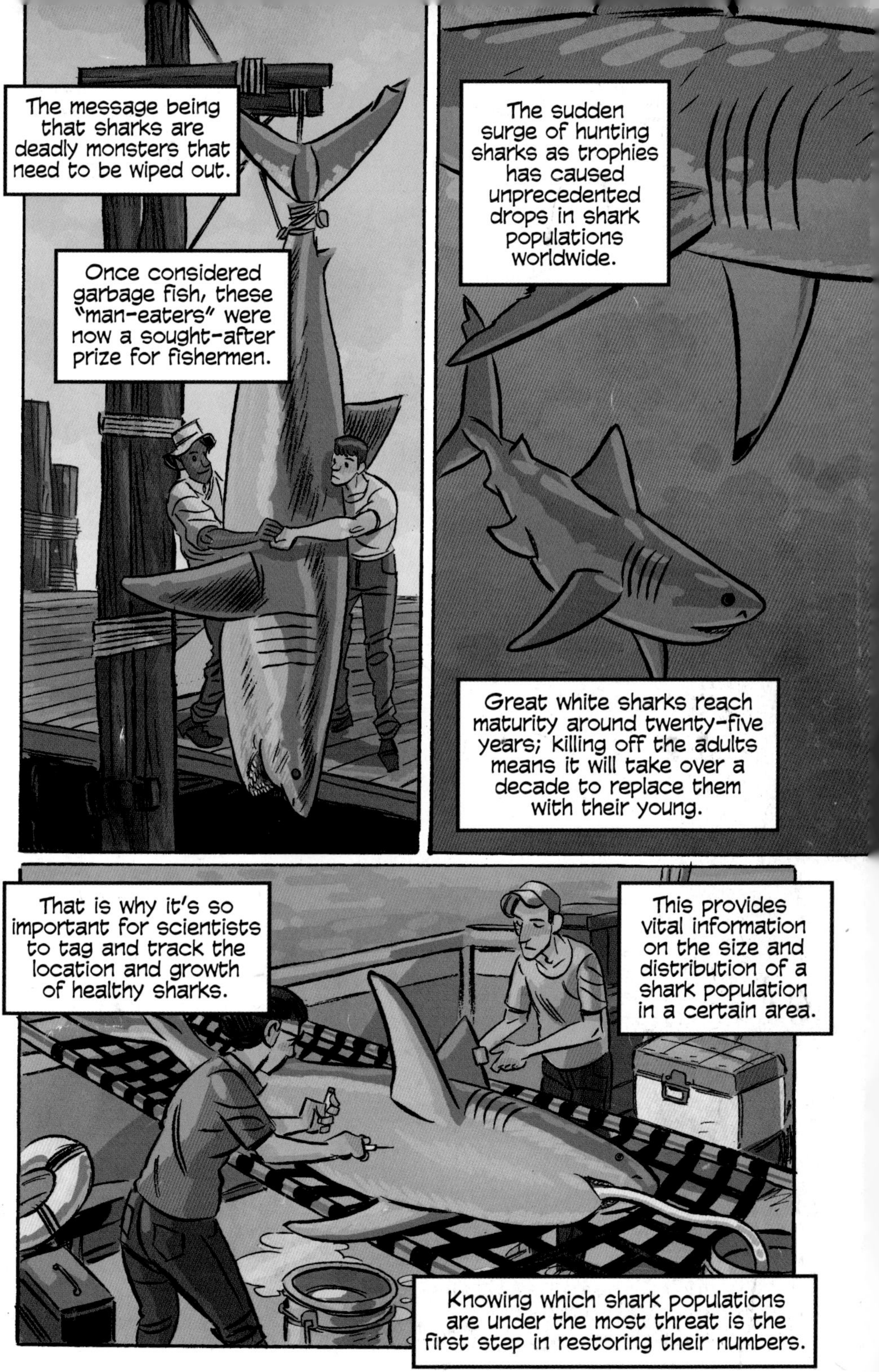
The message being that sharks are deadly monsters that need to be wiped out.
Once considered garbage fish, these "man-eaters" were now a sought-after prize for fishermen.
The sudden surge of hunting sharks as trophies has caused unprecedented drops in shark populations worldwide.
Great white sharks reach maturity around twenty-five years; killing off the adults means it will take over a decade to replace them with their young.
That is why it's so important for scientists to tag and track the location and growth of healthy sharks.
This provides vital information on the size and distribution of a shark population in a certain area.
Knowing which shark populations are under the most threat is the first step in restoring their numbers.

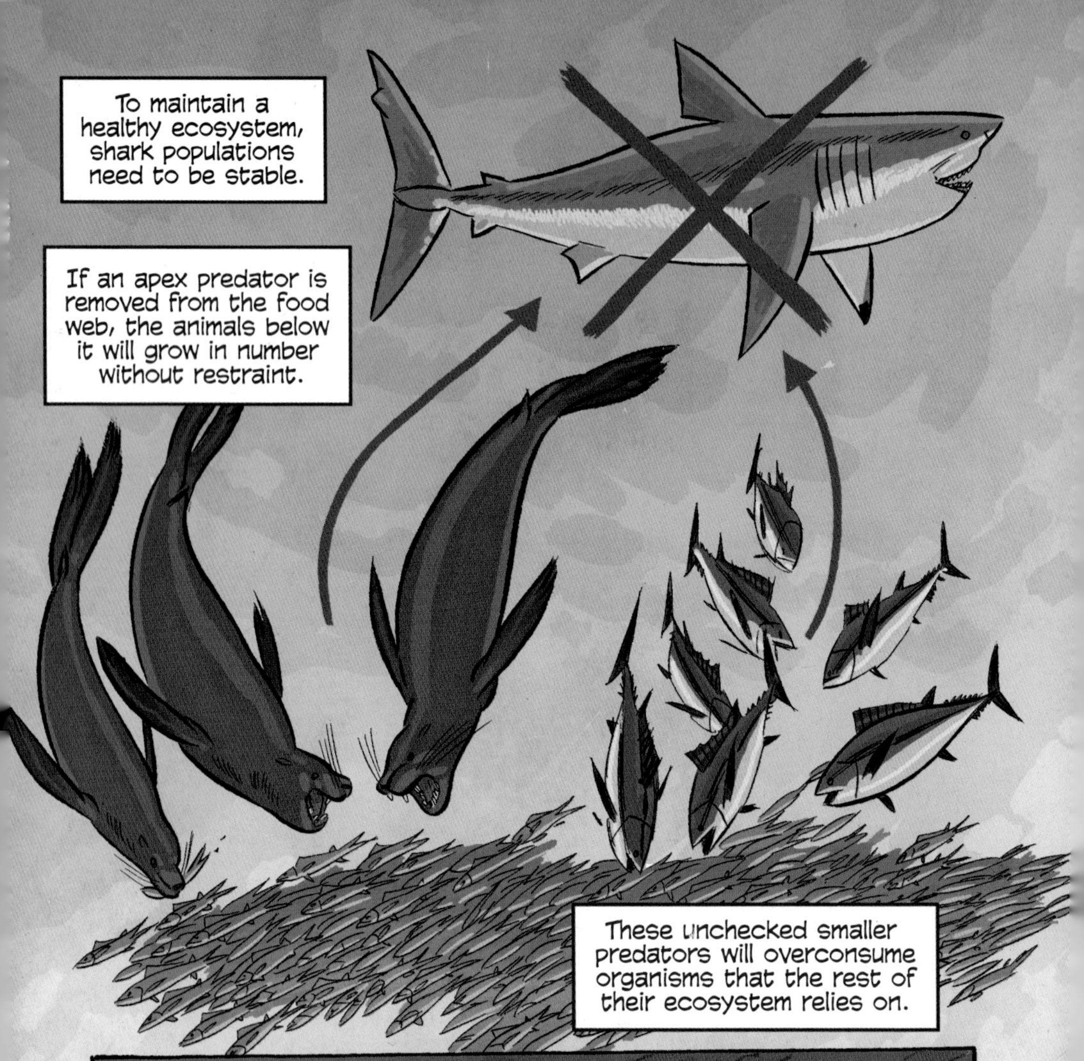
To maintain a healthy ecosystem, shark populations need to be stable.
If an apex predator is removed from the food web, the animals below it will grow in number without restraint.
These unchecked smaller predators will overconsume organisms that the rest of their ecosystem relies on.

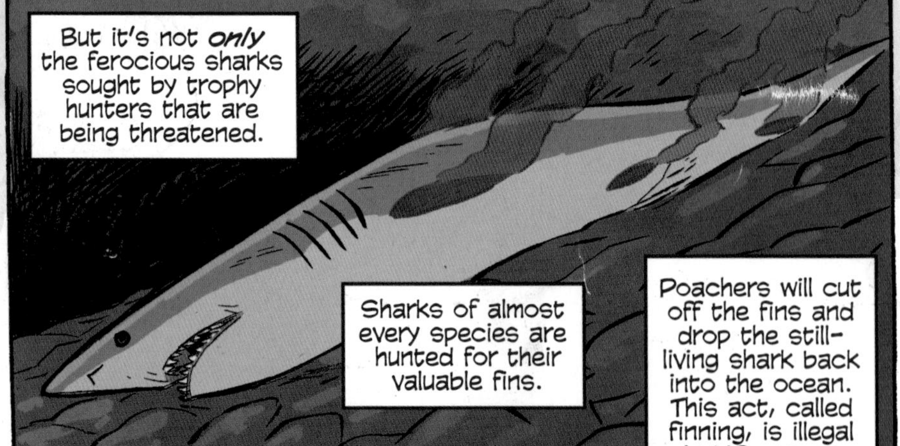
But it's not *only* the ferocious sharks sought by trophy hunters that are being threatened.
Sharks of almost every species are hunted for their valuable fins.
Poachers will cut off the fins and drop the still-living shark back into the ocean. This act, called finning, is illegal in US waters.

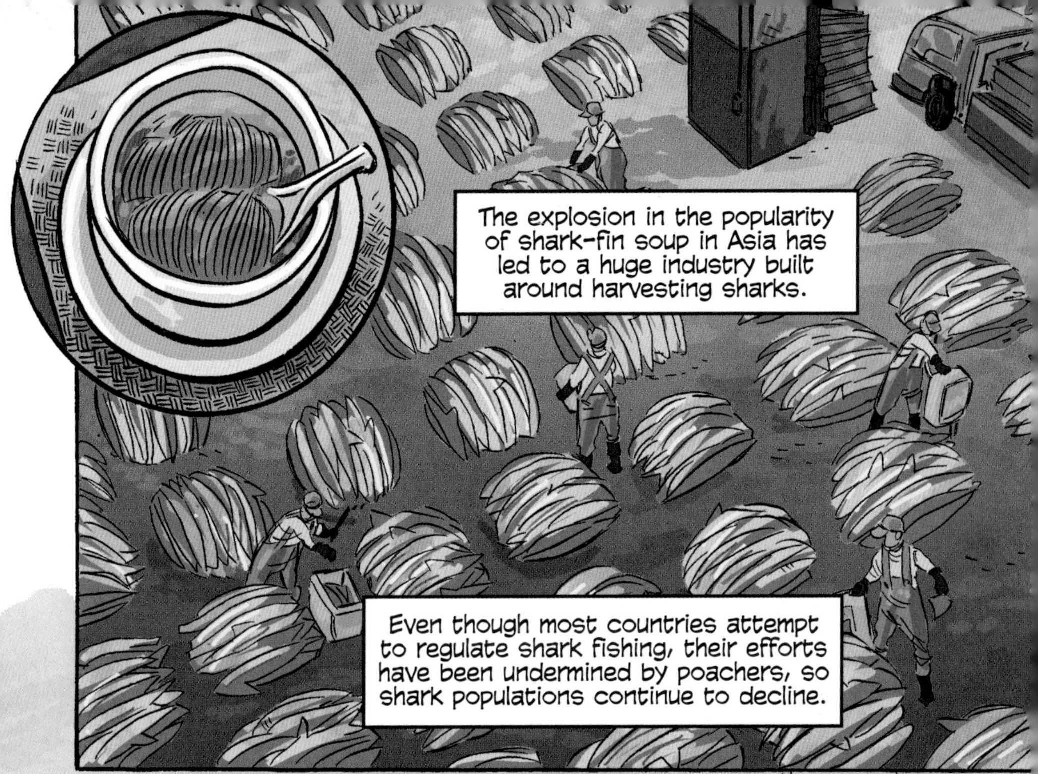
The explosion in the popularity of shark-fin soup in Asia has led to a huge industry built around harvesting sharks.
Even though most countries attempt to regulate shark fishing, their efforts have been undermined by poachers, so shark populations continue to decline.

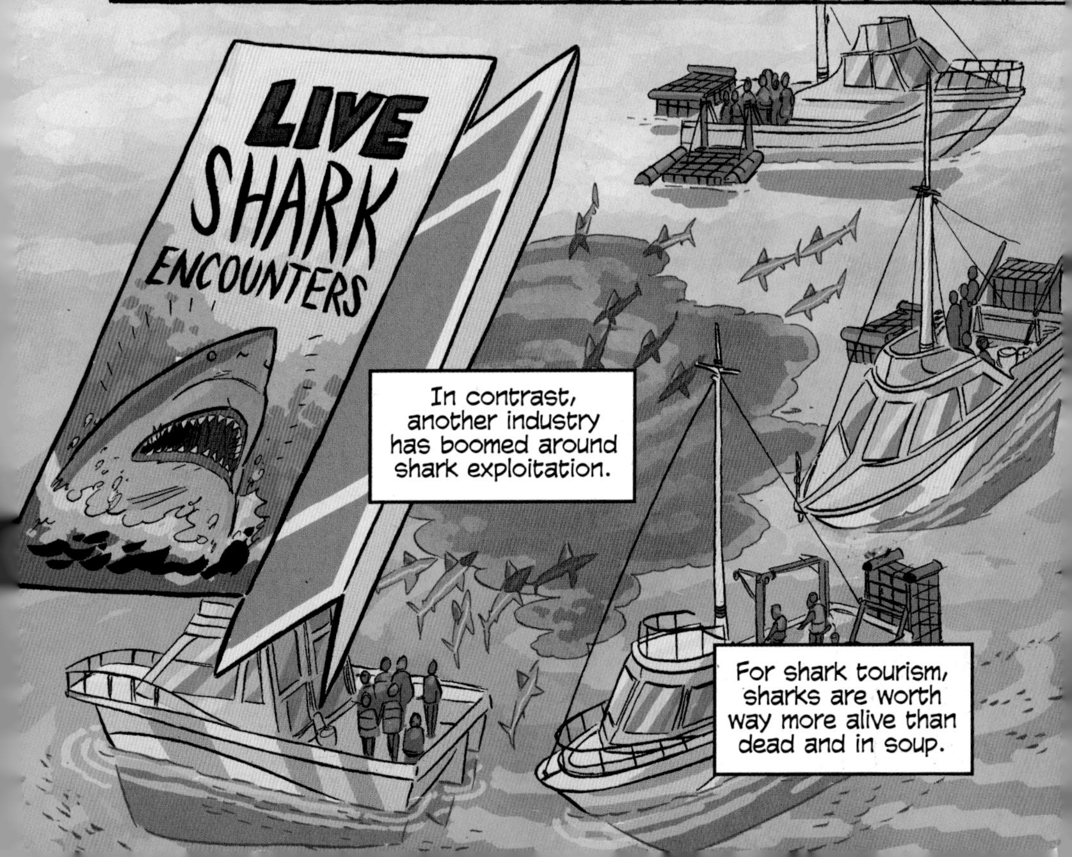
LIVE SHARK ENCOUNTERS
In contrast, another industry has boomed around shark exploitation.
For shark tourism, sharks are worth way more alive than dead and in soup.

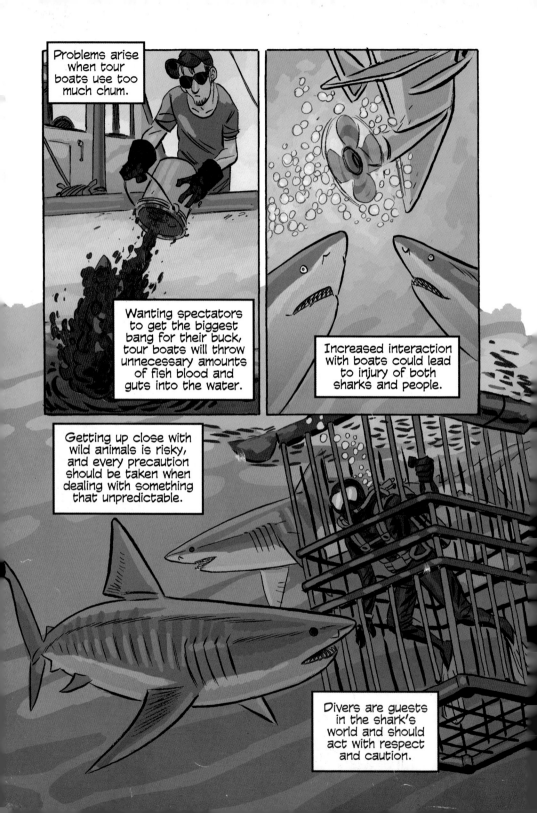

Problems arise when tour boats use too much chum.

Wanting spectators to get the biggest bang for their buck, tour boats will throw unnecessary amounts of fish blood and guts into the water.

Increased interaction with boats could lead to injury of both sharks and people.

Getting up close with wild animals is risky, and every precaution should be taken when dealing with something that unpredictable.

Divers are guests in the shark's world and should act with respect and caution.

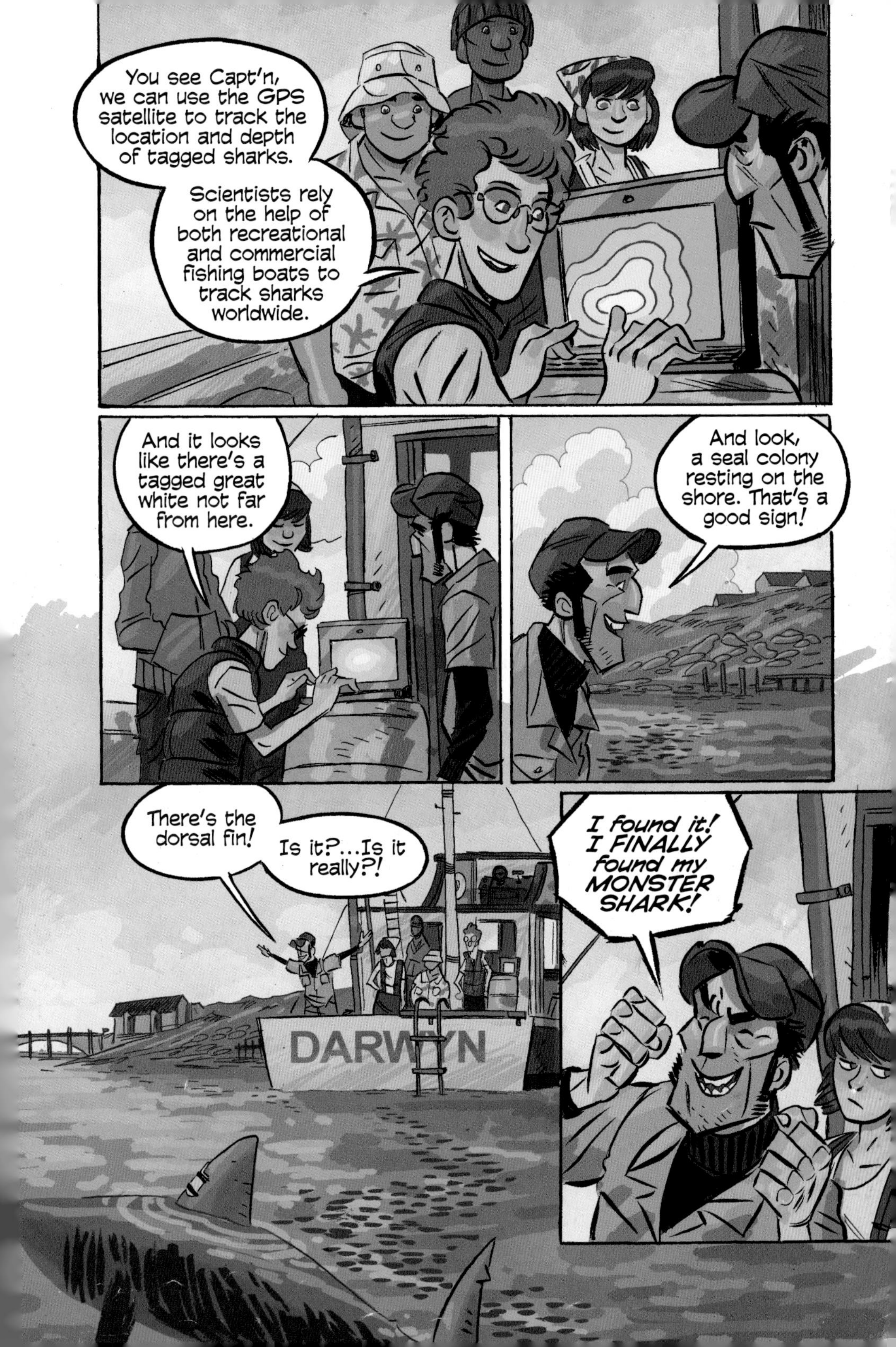

You see Capt'n, we can use the GPS satellite to track the location and depth of tagged sharks.
Scientists rely on the help of both recreational and commercial fishing boats to track sharks worldwide.
And it looks like there's a tagged great white not far from here.
And look, a seal colony resting on the shore. That's a good sign!
There's the dorsal fin!
Is it?...Is it really?!
DARWYN
I found it! I FINALLY found my MONSTER SHARK!

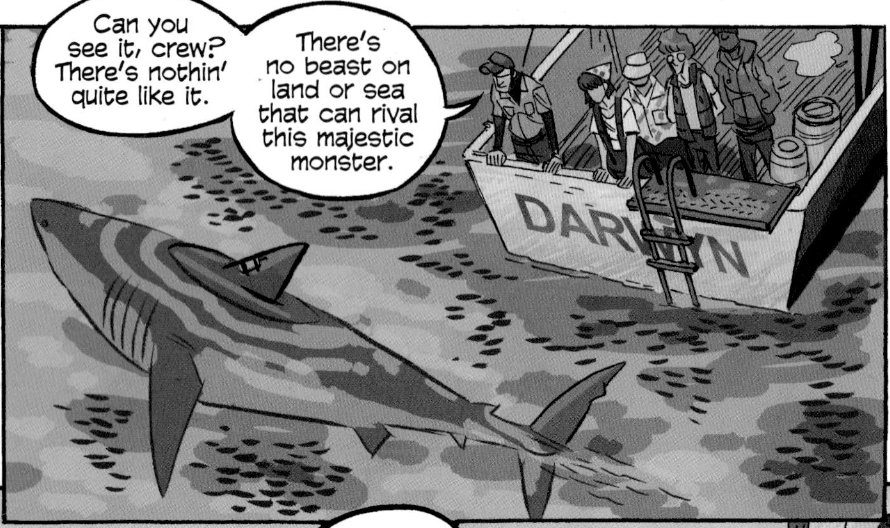
Can you see it, crew? There's nothin' quite like it.
There's no beast on land or sea that can rival this majestic monster.
DARWYN

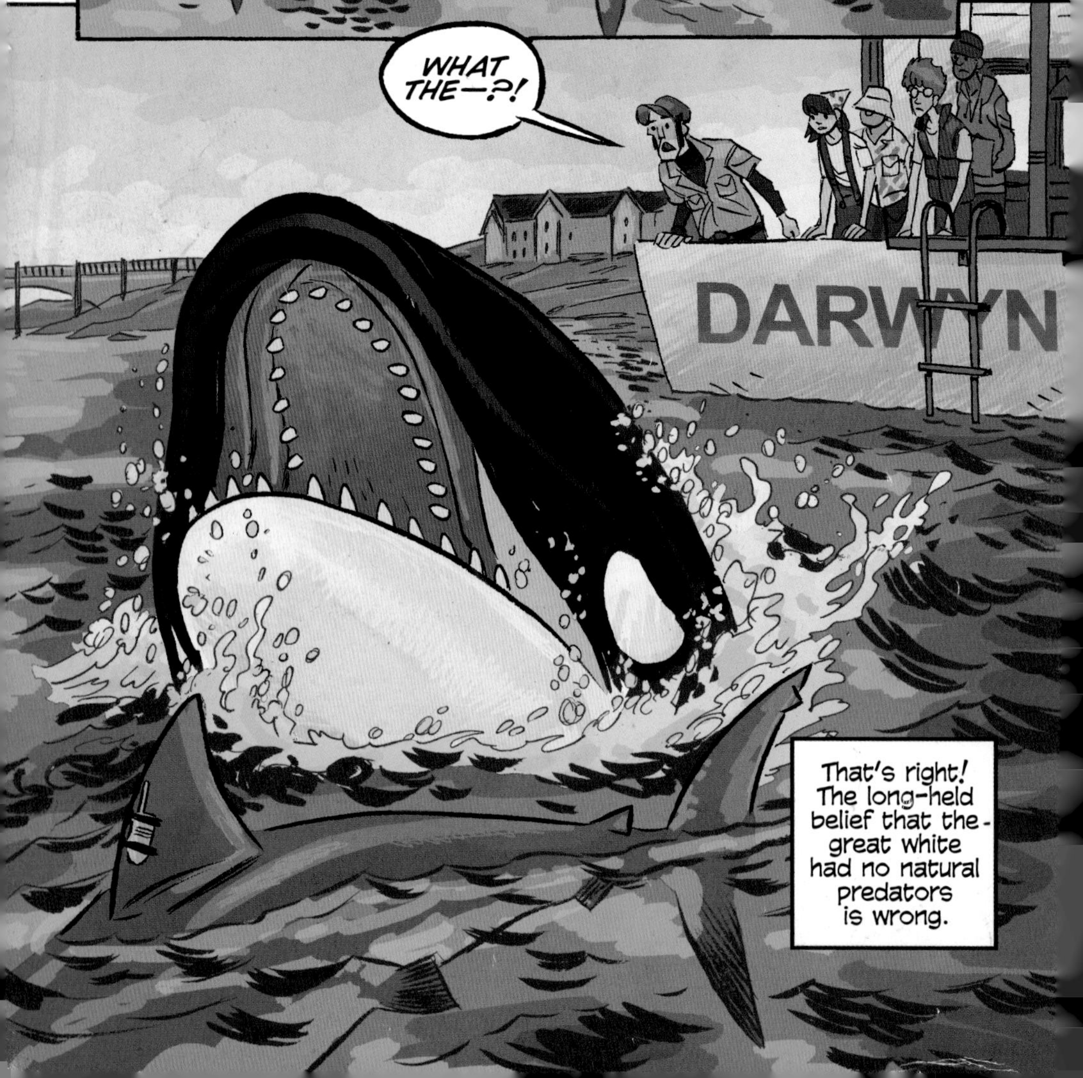
WHAT THE—?!
DARWYN
That's right! The long-held belief that the great white had no natural predators is wrong.

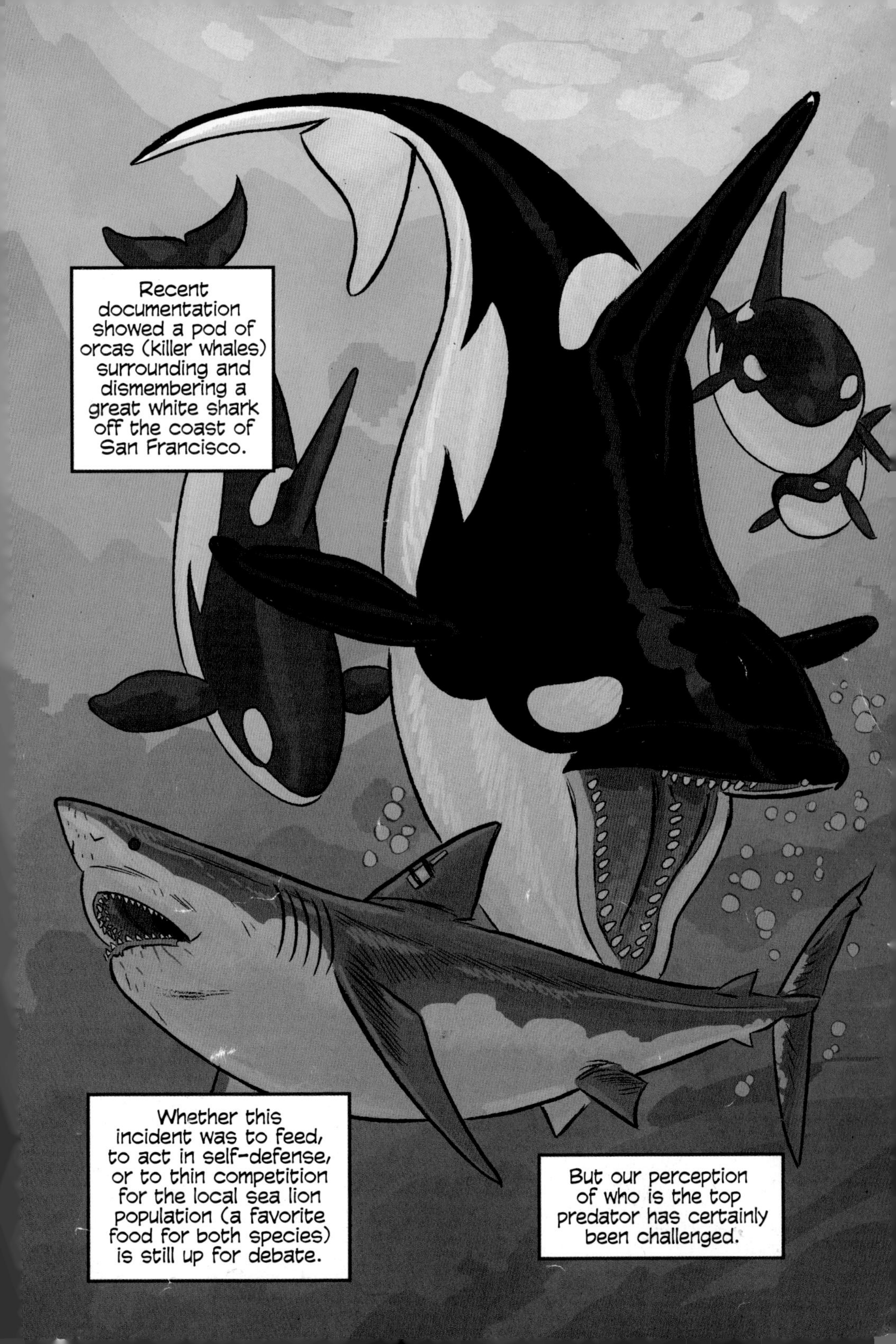
Recent documentation showed a pod of orcas (killer whales) surrounding and dismembering a great white shark off the coast of San Francisco.
Whether this incident was to feed, to act in self-defense, or to thin competition for the local sea lion population (a favorite food for both species) is still up for debate.
But our perception of who is the top predator has certainly been challenged.

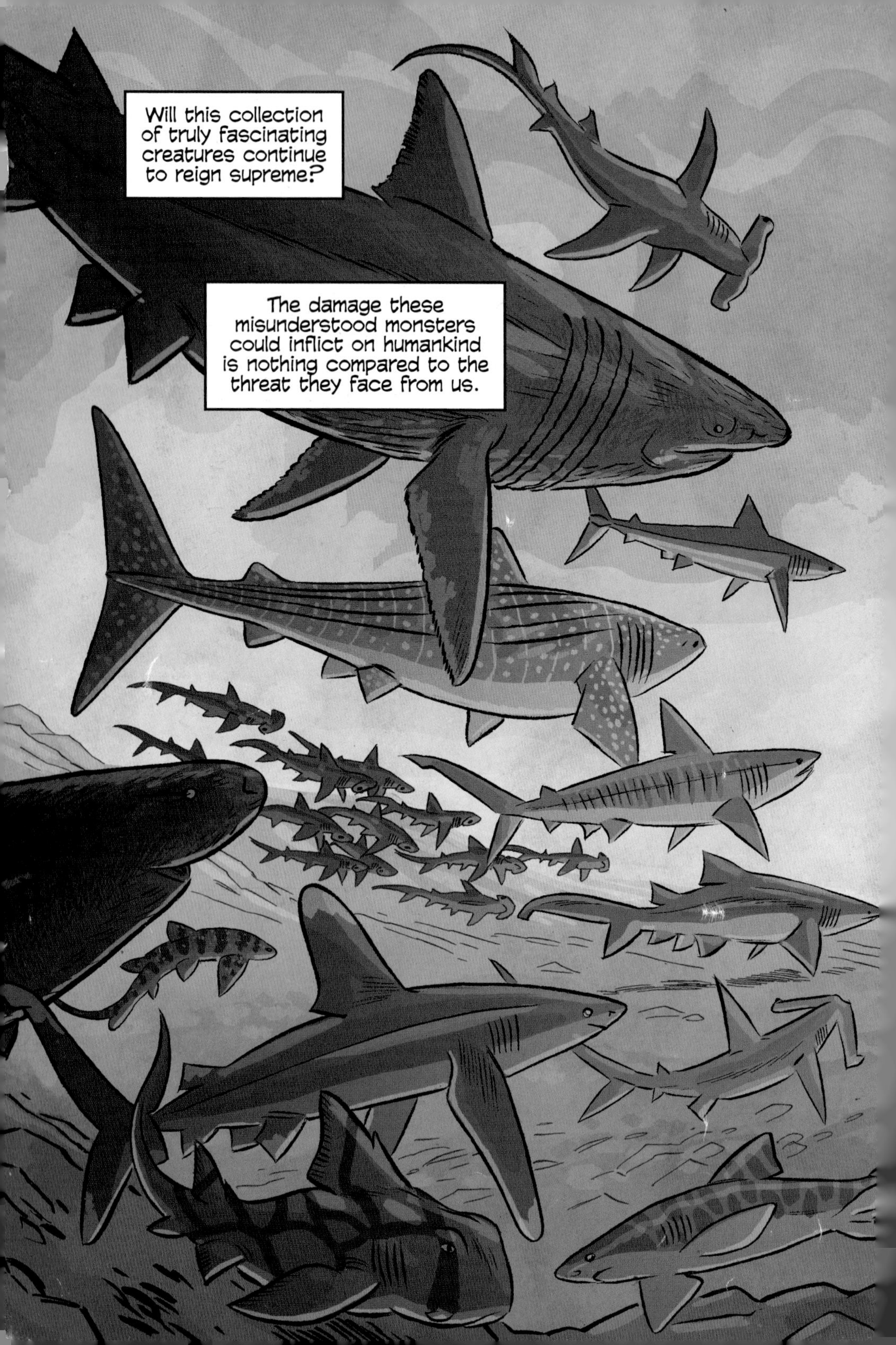
Will this collection of truly fascinating creatures continue to reign supreme?
The damage these misunderstood monsters could inflict on humankind is nothing compared to the threat they face from us.

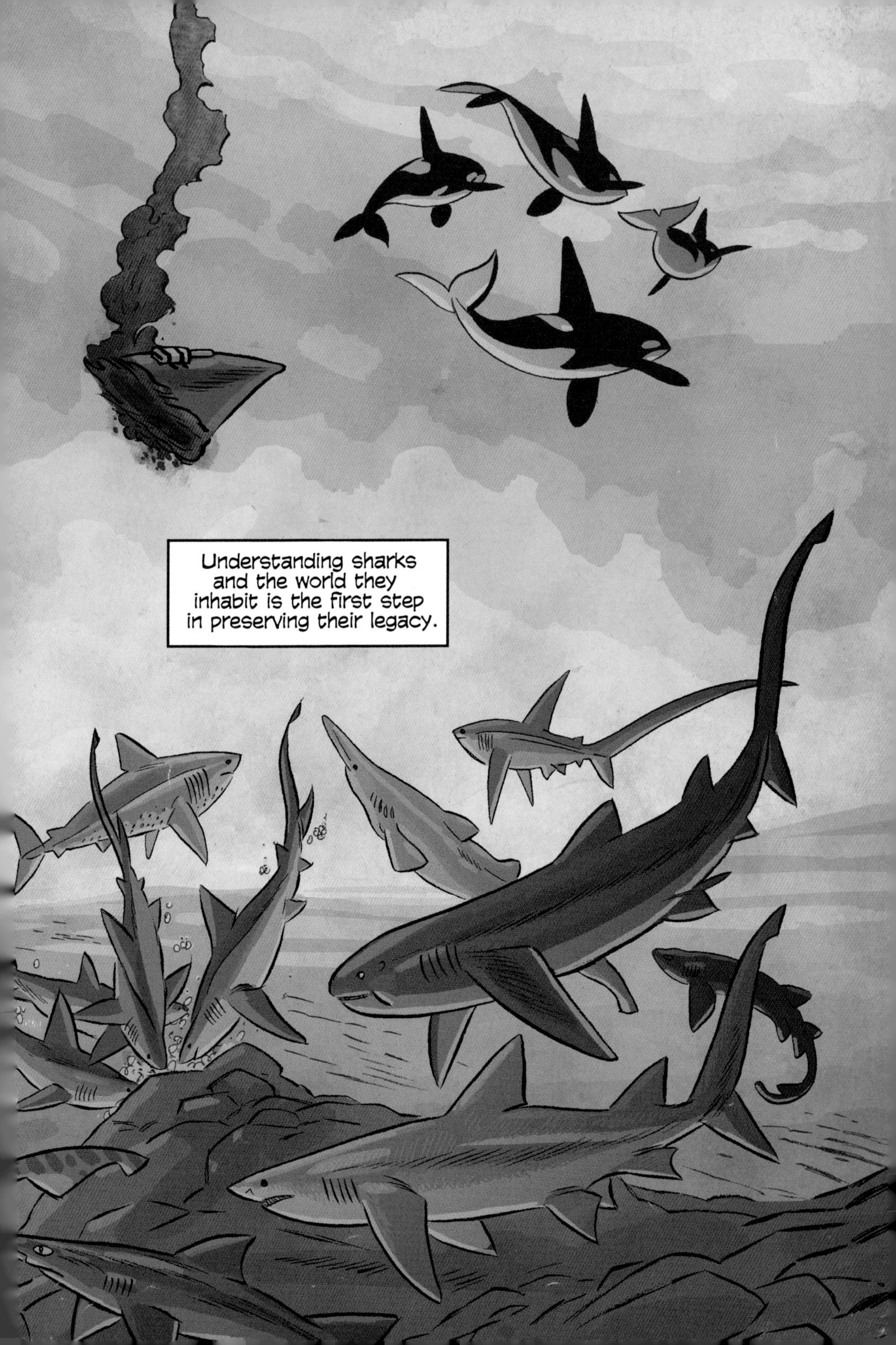
Understanding sharks and the world they inhabit is the first step in preserving their legacy.

—GLOSSARY—

Apex predator
> The top of the food chain. Nothing eats it.

Barbel
> A pair of fleshy filaments growing from the mouth or snout of certain fish. In some cases they house the taste buds and are used to search for food in murky water.

Buccal pumping
> A method of respiratory flow in which the animal moves the floor of its mouth in a rhythmic manner.

Buoyant
> Something capable of staying afloat or rising to the top of a liquid or gas.

Cartilage
> Firm connective tissue that is softer and more flexible than bone.

Chondrichthyes
> A class composed of cartilaginous fishes with paired fins and well-developed jaws. This class includes sharks, skates, rays, chimeras, and related (sometimes extinct) forms.

Cold-blooded
> Having a body temperature varying with that of the environment.

Electroreception
> The biological ability to perceive natural electrical stimuli in other animals.

Estuary
> The tidal mouth of a large river, where the tide meets the stream.

Femoral artery
> A large muscular-walled tube located in the human thigh that is the main blood supply to the lower limb.

Linnaean system
> The system of taxonomic classification originated by Carolus Linnaeus. In the Linnaean system, organisms are grouped according to shared characteristics into a hierarchical series of fixed categories ranging from kingdom at the top to species at the bottom.

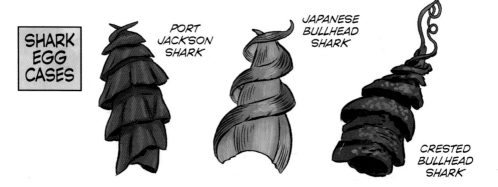

SHARK EGG CASES

PORT JACKSON SHARK

JAPANESE BULLHEAD SHARK

CRESTED BULLHEAD SHARK

Migration

Movement from one region to another, often based on seasonal or environmental changes.

Mangrove

A tree or shrub that grows in chiefly tropical coastal swamps that are flooded at high tide. Mangroves typically have numerous tangled roots aboveground and form dense thickets.

Osteichthyes

Popularly referred to as the bony fish, a diverse taxonomic group of fish that have skeletons primarily composed of bone tissue, as opposed to cartilage.

Ram ventilation

The method of respiratory flow in some fish in which the mouth is opened during swimming, such that water flows through the mouth and across the gills.

Rete mirabile

Latin for "wonderful net." A complex system of arteries and veins lying very close to one another, found in many warm-blooded vertebrates.

Serrated

Having a jagged, sawlike edge.

Symmetrical

Made up of exactly similar parts facing one another or around an axis; showing harmony.

Taxonomy

The science of defining groups of biological organisms based on shared characteristics.

Vertebrate

An animal of a large group distinguished by the possession of a backbone or spinal column, including mammals, birds, reptiles, amphibians, sharks, and fishes.

Warm-blooded

Having a system that maintains a constant body temperature, typically above that of their surroundings, by metabolic means. Most warm-blooded animals are mammals or birds.

HORN SHARK

ZEBRA BULLHEAD SHARK

MEXICAN HORNSHARK

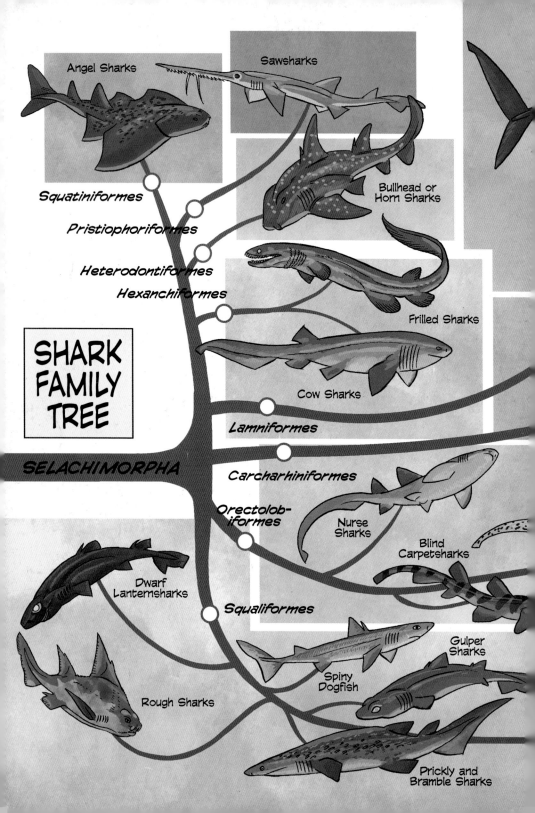

Angel Sharks

Sawsharks

Squatiniformes

Bullhead or
Horn Sharks

Pristiophoriformes

Heterodontiformes

Hexanchiformes

Frilled Sharks

SHARK
FAMILY
TREE

Cow Sharks

Lamniformes

SELACHIMORPHA

Carcharhiniformes

*Orectolob-
iformes*

Nurse
Sharks

Blind
Carpetsharks

Dwarf
Lanternsharks

Squaliformes

Gulper
Sharks

Rough Sharks

Spiny
Dogfish

Prickly and
Bramble Sharks

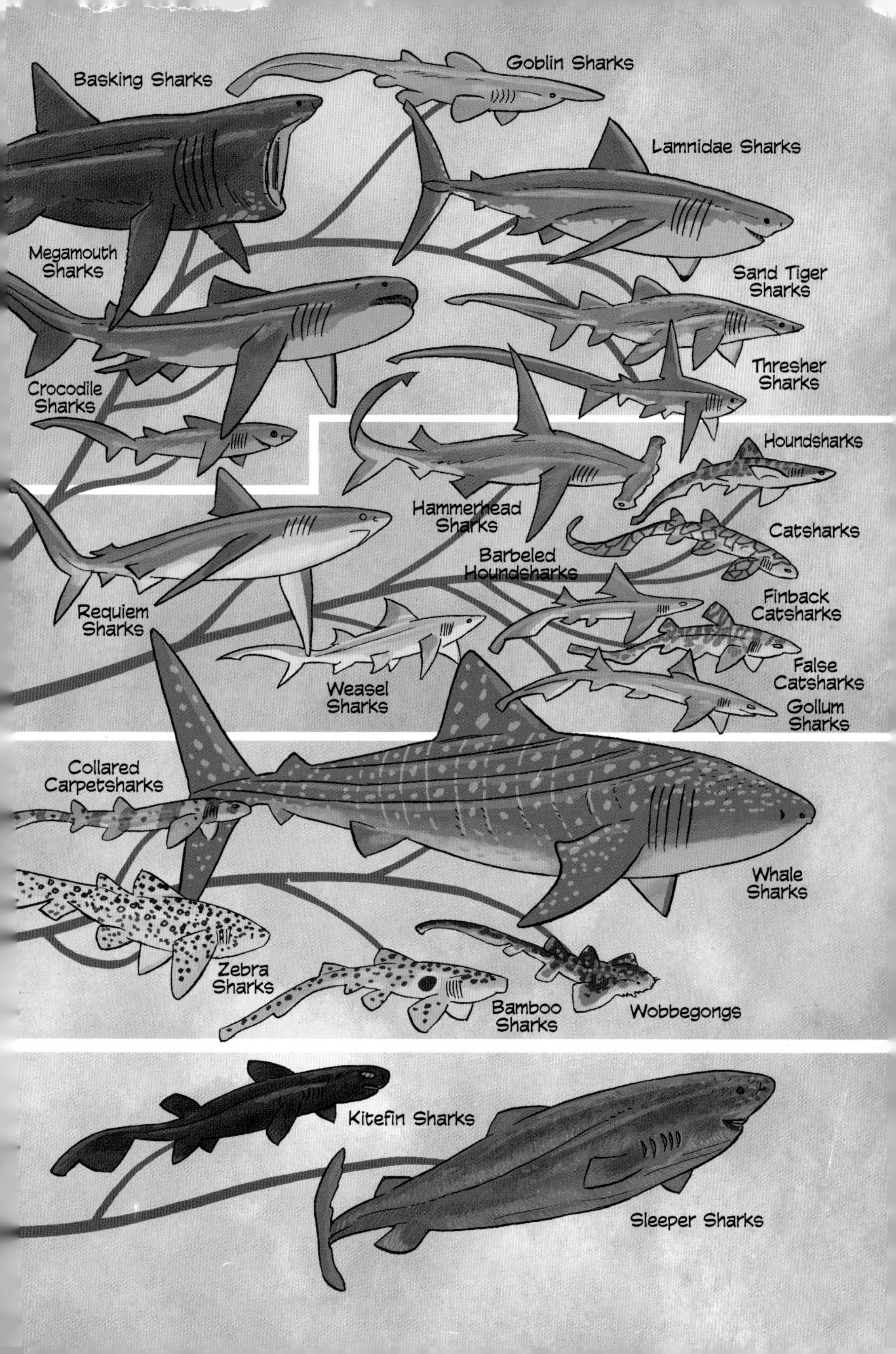

Basking Sharks
Goblin Sharks
Lamnidae Sharks
Megamouth Sharks
Sand Tiger Sharks
Thresher Sharks
Crocodile Sharks
Houndsharks
Hammerhead Sharks
Catsharks
Barbeled Houndsharks
Requiem Sharks
Finback Catsharks
False Catsharks
Weasel Sharks
Gollum Sharks
Collared Carpetsharks
Whale Sharks
Zebra Sharks
Bamboo Sharks
Wobbegongs
Kitefin Sharks
Sleeper Sharks

—DON'T SAY "SHARK ATTACK"—

The American Elasmobranch Society (the world's oldest and largest professional society of shark researchers), based on a scientific paper by Christopher Neff and Robert Hueter, has proposed that journalists avoid using the inflammatory phrase "shark attack." They suggest these more accurate descriptions:

Shark sightings
: Sightings of sharks in the water in proximity to people. No physical human-shark contact takes place.

Shark encounters
: Human-shark interactions in which physical contact occurs between a shark and a person, or an inanimate object holding that person, and no injury takes place. For example, shark bites on surfboards, kayaks, and boats. It might also include a close call like a shark physically "bumping" a swimmer without biting.

Shark bites
: Incidents where sharks bite people resulting in minor to moderate injuries. Small or large sharks might be involved, but typically, a single, nonfatal bite occurs. If more than one bite occurs, injuries might be serious but the term "shark attack" should never be used unless the motivation and intent of the animal—such as predation or defense—are clearly established by qualified experts.

Fatal shark bites
: Human-shark conflicts in which serious injuries take place as a result of one or more bites on a person, causing a significant loss of blood and/or body tissue and a fatal outcome.

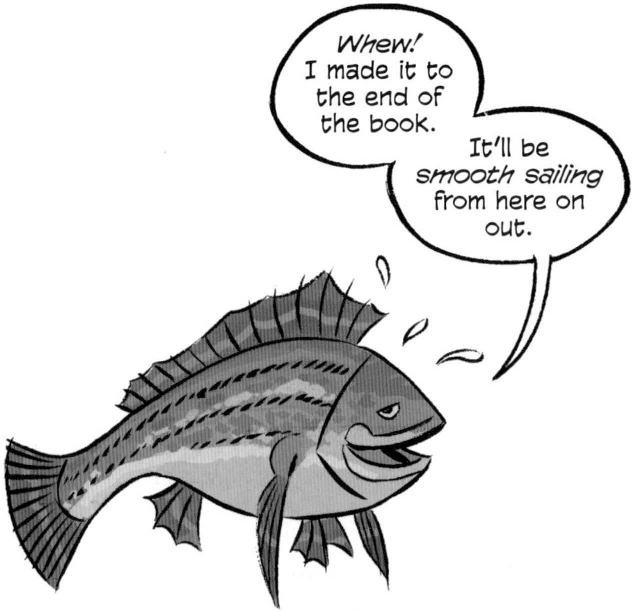
Whew! I made it to the end of the book.
It'll be smooth sailing from here on out.